Forgiveness at Ground Zero

Forgiveness at Ground Zero

A Journey of Service, Loss, and Redemption after 9/11

Lyndon Fitzgerald Harris

BLOOMSBURY ACADEMIC
NEW YORK • LONDON • OXFORD • NEW DELHI • SYDNEY

BLOOMSBURY ACADEMIC
Bloomsbury Publishing Inc, 1359 Broadway, New York, NY 10018, USA
Bloomsbury Publishing Plc, 50 Bedford Square, London, WC1B 3DP, UK
Bloomsbury Publishing Ireland, 29 Earlsfort Terrace, Dublin 2, D02 AY28, Ireland

First published in the United States of America 2026

Cover design: Diana Nuhn
Cover image © Cavan Images / Getty Images

Library of Congress Cataloging-in-Publication Data
Names: Harris, Lyndon Fitzgerald author
Title: Forgiveness at Ground Zero : A Journey of Service, Loss and Redemption after 9/11 / Lyndon Fitzgerald Harris.
Description: New York : Bloomsbury Academic, 2026. | Includes appendix. | Includes bibliographical references. | Summary: "Genuine forgiveness is elusive, arduous, and necessary. Stories can help. From the ashes of Ground Zero, Rev. Lyndon Harris' poignant memoir of how his ministry at St. Paul's Chapel after 9/11 transformed lives-and how, after he lost his faith and left the church, radical forgiveness transformed his own"-- Provided by publisher.
Identifiers: LCCN 2025045917 (print) | LCCN 2025045918 (ebook) | ISBN 9798216279006 HB | ISBN 9798216278979 ePDF | ISBN 9798216278993 eBook
Subjects: LCSH: Harris, Lyndon Fitzgerald | Episcopal Church--New York (State)--Clergy--Biography | Trinity Church (New York, N.Y.). St. Paul's Chapel--History--20th century | Trinity Church (New York, N.Y.). St. Paul's Chapel--History--21st century | September 11 Terrorist Attacks, 2001 | Forgiveness--Religious aspects--Christianity | LCGFT: Autobiographies
Classification: LCC BX5995.H348 A3 2026 (print) | LCC BX5995.H348 (ebook)
LC record available at https://lccn.loc.gov/2025045917
LC ebook record available at https://lccn.loc.gov/2025045918

ISBN: HB: 979-8-2162-7900-6
ePDF: 979-8-2162-7897-9
eBook: 979-8-2162-7899-3

Typeset by Deanta Global Publishing Services, Chennai, India

For product safety related questions contact productsafety@bloomsbury.com.

This book is dedicated in loving memory to the late Reverend Dr. Frederic Burnham, mentor, beloved friend, co-conspirator, and companion in dangerous and joyful endeavors. Eschewing all the official titles and honors you had rightfully earned, you much preferred to be called simply the "Monday Night Guy"—the person who oversaw the 9/11 relief work of Saint Paul's Chapel's mission to Ground Zero on Monday nights, from September 2001 to June 2002. You taught me that the true measure of priesthood is found in loving service to others, especially when it's hard to do and when there's a cost. The radiance of your loving engagement with life will brighten our hearts forever. I have been transformed by your kindness, generosity, courage, and compassion. During the season of our service at Saint Paul's, you gave words to the core meaning of what we all were grateful to have experienced there: "We discovered the emotional magnificence of life." Well said, dear friend.

In loving memory of
The Reverend Dr. Frederic Bradford Burnham, aka the "Monday Night Guy"
July 21, 1938–January 23, 2019
Nulla dies umquam memori vos eximet aevo.
(No day shall erase you from the memory of time.)
Virgil

Fred Burnham *receiving communion from firefighter chaplain.*

Contents

Foreword

Reading this wonderful memoir by Lyndon Harris, I thought of Mary Oliver's famous last lines from her poem "A Summer Day." *Tell me, what is it you plan to do with your one wild and precious life?* Lyndon Harris embraced that question with both hands, and this honest, passionate, riveting, and erudite book is his answer.

Lyndon lived through and greatly contributed to what he calls the sacredness of 9/12. For months following the September 11, 2001, attacks in New York City, where he served as an Episcopal priest at historic Saint Paul's Chapel, Lyndon gave his all for the impossible dream of creating a community of love in response to terror. As trauma turned to PTSD, he suffered for his excesses, struggled to make peace, and ultimately strived to forgive himself and others. His struggle as told in this book is also his contribution, guiding us as we all struggle and make problems for ourselves that we do not realize we are making.

His desire to help on 9/11 and in its aftermath is remarkable and shows both a character and willingness to sacrifice that are admirable. Unfortunately, he did so while employed near the bottom of the power hierarchy in a historic, international church. No matter how noble his intentions, the ministry at Saint Paul's (directly across the street from the former World Trade Center) did not belong to him alone. A priest's mission is a shared one, and in this case, he and the church were sometimes misaligned.

As the headwinds pushing back on him kept on getting stronger and stronger, Lyndon had the impression that he understood God's will to be his continued, persistent resistance as he sought to respond to what he felt were urgent human needs. But discerning God's will is difficult in the best of times, and likely close to impossible under the stress of the aftermath of 9/11. However, sometimes escalating adversity and pushback can be a reminder to check our assumptions, and while it took years for him to do so, that's exactly what Lyndon did.

Remarkably, Lyndon gives us access to both his hero and his shadow throughout this challenging, vulnerable journey. As someone who has been a therapist for 30 years, let me remind you how rare that is. We humans lie to ourselves all the time in order to maintain our comforting illusions, yet here Lyndon is dismantling his illusions and offering them to public scrutiny. The courage that this takes is a powerful example of his evolving humility and growth, which may prove to be Lyndon's enduring teaching and life's message.

After all these years, it is comforting indeed that Harris finds himself still trying to make the world a better place. He still holds onto an impossible dream. Now that dream is to teach others about the healing that can come through forgiveness—lessons we now know that he learned the hard way. This book is part of his legacy, offered to help us all find a path through our difficult circumstances and personal mistakes. In our present time of political polarization and grievances, this welcome message of forgiveness, with its insistence on treating others with dignity and not contempt, is an invitation for all of us to take responsibility for healing our communities.

No matter the question, Lyndon suggests that forgiveness of ourselves and those who hurt us is the answer, and he is a valuable spokesperson for the healing power of this process. Both a cautionary tale about non-forgiveness and an inspiring example of the transformation that forgiveness brings, this book offers the reader access to a wild and precious life indeed.

Dr. Frederic Luskin
Director of the Stanford Forgiveness Project

Author's Note

A long time ago, in a city far, far away, I used to be a priest. I was assigned to a historic and, at the time, fairly moribund church: Saint Paul's Chapel, in the financial district in Lower Manhattan. This was the church where George Washington worshipped on the day he was inaugurated as our country's first president. Imbued with a glorious past, it had nonetheless fallen on hard times. In April 2001, I was hired to start a new congregation, breathing life into this stately old church. In those exhilarating days before 9/11, we had no idea what was in store. And afterward, well . . .

As humans, we share so many common experiences. One is that life has a tragic element. We will all have ups and downs, successes and failures, triumphs and heartbreaks. In some ways, I think this life is an arena for our development, a classroom where we're meant to learn important things. But, as far as we know, our growth can only be accomplished within the brief, finite span of life. This became shockingly clear to me on the terrifying day of September 11, 2001, as I was standing at the foot of the South Tower of the former World Trade Center as the second highjacked airplane exploded into it. And I want to share with you the life skill that helped me navigate my journey after that: forgiveness. I wish I could have learned it earlier.

Before we begin, I want to make sure that you know I'm okay. For all that has happened to me over the past 20+ years, I am happy and healthy and have joy and love and stability in my life. I am strong now, having found a way to make peace with my past. While I will share some of the circumstances precipitating my journey into the Slough of Despond,[1] this is not a "victim's narrative" inviting you to commiserate with me or a revenge plot meant to shame any who challenged my work or ideas. Rather, it is a teaching memoir—a hero's journey recounting my experience as a cautionary tale, relaying the suffering that can happen if you choose to forego the invitation of forgiveness. It's a Gordian knot—a huge tangle of trauma and tragedy, mistakes, heartbreaks and betrayals—that I will endeavor through the course of this memoir to untie. And by the end of my tale, I hope to have offered you the gold that I have found on this journey, a treasure that is most valuable when it is shared.

I also want to be clear that I mean no ill will for anyone I speak of in these chapters—only light and love and joy. The crises and challenges that I have recounted were necessary fodder for the lessons I needed to learn to bring me to my new joy in life. What's more, as you will see if you stay with me on this journey, I have come to the place of desiring the same light and love and joy for myself. This is a journey of self-love and self-discovery, fueled by the wisdom of forgiveness. The great analyst Carl Jung said that very rarely do we fix our problems, but we can outgrow them[2]—a quest which I continuously pursue. With the wisdom of forgiveness and the kindness of fellow companions, I press on. I write this memoir to offer a gift - a gift that I couldn't even give myself until recent years. It's the gift or realizing how absolutely precious life is, and the last thing you want to do with such a precious gift is to squander it in the negative emotions of resentments, anger, and desires for revenge.

The story I tell is, de facto, from my perspective—both limited and biased, as perspectives tend to be. This is not an academic or historical objective rendering of the movements in and around the important historical contribution of Saint Paul's Chapel after 9/11. For that, see my friend Courtney Cowart's inspiring account, *An American Awakening: From Ground Zero to Katrina: The People We Are Free to Be.*[3] Courtney's on-the-ground in-the-moment reflections capture the beautiful spirit of the community behind Saint Paul's Chapel's mission to first responders at Ground Zero in NYC after 9/11.

The narrative that I share in this memoir includes the wider Saint Paul's story but is focused on my own personal internal odyssey during and after that ministry, moving from ecstasy to despair and ultimately, to new beginnings. It's the truth of my experience, while responding to the very real traumas that I faced—both from the 9/11 attacks and the conflicts I had with the folks I reported to at my church—and how I sought resolution to them. I ultimately discovered for myself that the path to healing comes through forgiveness. To that end, I will also introduce you to the research and teachings of my friend, Dr. Frederic Luskin, bestselling author and the director of the Stanford Forgiveness Project.[4]

I first met Fred through our mutual friend Rod Beckstrom in the early 2000s. Rod came to meet me in NYC and suggested that I consider pursuing the work of forgiveness. At the time, I could not have been less interested. But he persisted, and thanks to Rod, and later Fred, forgiveness gained a toehold in my heart. As it grew, this healing modality would not only change my life but also be the heart of my calling and mission. Rod introduced me to Fred Luskin when his bestselling book *Forgive for Good: A PROVEN Prescription for Health and Happiness* was gaining traction. Rod is one of the most incredibly generous humans I ever met, and in but one of his kindnesses, he used to ship boxes of Fred's books for me to give out generously to people I saw in pastoral counseling.

In September 2003, Fred was kind enough to speak at an event my colleagues and I planned for the observance of the International Day of Peace. We became fast friends. I am trained in Fred's forgiveness methods, and I have collaborated with him for almost 20 years in doing forgiveness talks and trainings. Fred's research at Stanford University has been groundbreaking and proven efficacious in a wide variety of interventions for 25 years. Hundreds of thousands of people across the world have benefited from his research and teachings. Fred is the director of the Stanford Forgiveness Project. In March 2025, New Harbinger Press published a workbook on forgiveness for people in recovery that Fred and I co-authored. Fred has been both mentor and friend, and I am beyond grateful for him and for his transformative work. In this memoir you will see how fundamentally important Fred's work has been for my journey.

Like any one of us, I can chart the progress of my life through the pattern of the hero's journey. The call to "adventure" came in the form of an invitation to develop a humanitarian response to the urgent need of 9/11 workers, issued by many heralds, one who also happened to be the star of the television show *ER*,

Julianne Margulies. I was challenged by threshold guardians and shapeshifters, and I was inspired by mentors and allies. I went into the innermost cave to do battle with the demons of my shadow, befriending that same shadow even as I sought to subdue the cunning dragons of deceit that held me back. Like the tale of Arjuna, I engaged the gauntlet within. And I have learned from the yogi who stood up to Alexander the Great: "I am conquering my need to conquer the world."[5] This journey continues—one of self-love, self-discovery. Of empathy for all who have differed from me or disagreed with me, and compassion for myself as I came to terms with those conflicts. I have finally arrived at a place in my heart where I do not need to be defended. I simply see the beauty of spiritual master Ram Dass's teaching that we are all just walking each other home.[6]

And what is home? It is a place of connection and kindness, where all of us are welcome, and everyone is acknowledged and honored. It's the place of longing of tender young Dorothy after facing her greatest challenges in the Land of Oz—the place where she knew she was loved and cared for, seen and celebrated, safe and peaceful. It is a place we all long for, especially during our present time of conflict and crisis, where grievances hand us our coffee in the morning and tuck us into bed at night. I think of this spiritual home in the metaphor that John Knox uses to describe the church: "a fellowship in the love of God that seeks to be an ever-widening sphere of an ever-deepening reconciliation." Ever-widening, ever-deepening, wholly inclusive.[7] For a brief fleeting moment, in the midst of the crisis that was 9/11, a handful of us serving in the relief mission of Saint Paul's Chapel to the rescue workers at Ground Zero caught a glimpse of this experience of home—and it changed our lives forever. I will share about that experience.

And so, here I am, at home in my study, looking out across the mystical fecund salt marshes bordering the historic Ashley River in the fabled port city of Charleston, SC. After living in the large urban areas of New York City and Los Angeles for more than 20 years, I have made my way back home to South Carolina. But wherever I lived, my home state went with me. Anchored in my heart, the state's motto daily inspires me, in words attributed to the ancient Roman orator, Cicero: "Dum Spiro, Spero"—"While I breath, I hope."

I share this home with my beloved wife, Maria Lund, and our feisty aging cocker spaniel, Maggie. We live in Charleston so that we can be close to my cherished daughter Margaret and her loving family.

In my workspace, I am surrounded by talismans, paraphernalia, knickknacks, and gewgaws that I've collected over the years. The one I'll share with you today is an artwork that I often look to for inspiration. It's a beautiful picture by Brian Andreas, from the organization The Story People. A knight with a sword faces a dragon, each bearing a quizzical, mildly perplexing sideways glance toward the other. Beneath it is the text, "Anyone can slay a dragon, he told me but try waking up every morning and loving the world all over again. That's what takes a real hero."[8]

Each day, as I start my work, I do my best to take upon myself the mantle of this kind of heroic love—for myself, my community, and the world. It's this love that has inspired me to finish this book after 23 years. This is the story of all of us—everywoman and everyman—played out against the backdrop of extraordinary, time-stamped circumstances.

It's a love story about Ground Zero in New York City and the spiritual crisis that guided me toward the path of forgiveness. It's a love story about the 9/11 first responder community, full of respect and gratitude for all the men and women who gave so much of themselves in the days, weeks, and months after the attacks. It's a love story about those who died during the traumatic events of 9/11 and those who have since passed on from its aftermath. It's a love story about our volunteers at Saint Paul's Chapel—more than 15,000 people who helped create at SPC an oasis of radical hospitality during our "season of love."[9] And after 23 years, this book exists because I finally love myself enough to tell my story too.

The story is one of life and death. Of tragedy and trauma, of betrayal and mistakes, and of the great privilege of losing almost everything I have held as precious in life. But it is also a story of new beginnings, maturation, healing, and a return of hope. "Dum Spiro, Spero."

And if you look closely, you might see glimpses of your story in mine.

"First the fall, then the recovery from the fall, and both are the mercy of God."

Julian of Norwich, 14th Century English Mystic

Revelations of Divine Love

Prologue

New York City: A Love Story

Whether I knew it or not, I had been trying to get to New York City my whole life. Growing up in the small town of Gaffney, South Carolina, I somehow knew there must be more to the world out there. Not that there's anything wrong with a small town. I just wanted that "more." My childhood hobby, shortwave listening, gave oxygen to my wanderlust. During the day, I was tasked with school, homework, sports, chores, and the usual middle child brotherly mischief. But at night, I listened to the world—the BBC broadcasting from London, Radio France, Radio Moscow, Radio Free Europe, and my favorite Radio Nederland broadcasting from Hilversum, Holland. Tuning across the dial with the accompanying atmospheric squeaks and squeals, the rise and fall of hisses and Morse code was mesmerizing. If I tuned a station "just right," I could pull in the signal out of the background noise that sought to overwhelm it. And there was always the intriguing possibility that I might discover a spy station. The announcers on the airwaves offered me an escape into a more international world of imagination. Working my radio dial, I felt like a wizard overlooking a magical, electronic cauldron of magnetism and physics, conjuring up visions of exotic lands. I would put on my headphones, begin the search, and dream. I had no idea at the time how my life would unfold, but I felt hopeful, ambitious, that I might someday make a difference for good in the world. Even though we struggled financially, especially after my father died when I was twelve, my mother instilled in me an unshakeable confidence that I had a contribution to make. After all, she named me for presidents.

Years later, I made good on those childhood dreams to engage the big wide world when I moved with my wife and daughter to New York City, an epicenter of magic and wonder I had longed to see. We moved there for me to pursue a graduate degree in theology. The first weekend in New York City, before I even began my studies, I walked to Frankie's, the nearby bodega on 9th Avenue and 20th Street, to get coffee. I was awestruck by the energy of the swirling tempests of traffic—taxi cabs, delivery trucks, sports cars, and "beaters" thundering down 9th avenue. Suddenly, there was a miraculous opening in the traffic—like Moses parting the Red Sea—where a large black furry dog was galloping at a breakneck pace, with a tow rope attached to his collar. He was gleefully pulling his owner behind him, riding a skateboard. Over time, I came to see such a sight with the eyes of most New Yorkers—just another crazy magical day in the city. But it always remained more than that to me.

In New York, I felt like the main character in Stephen Schwartz's musical, *Pippin,* looking for my corner of the sky: "Rivers belong where they can ramble, eagles belong where they can fly. I've got to be where spirit can run free—gotta find my corner of the sky!"[1] In New York City, I found it. And I fell in love with this amazing city—its people, its food, its cultures, its energy. And its music.

I was already a jazz lover and found my obsession full blown at the Village Vanguard, the Blue Note, Smalls, and a million other tiny no-name clubs. Then I discovered opera! From my first opera at the Met, I was enthralled. The comedic operas like *Le Figaro* were entertaining, but the operas I liked best were full of pathos: the foreboding prelude to Wagner's *The Flying Dutchman* forever condemned to sail the treacherous seas; the scream of Donizetti's *Lucia di Lammermoor* going mad; Verdi's *Rigoletto*, with his fateful cry when he discovers that his paid assassin has killed the wrong person. The sheer power of the music in these scenes is like an emotional bomb exploding into catharsis.

I could write a whole book about all the things I love about New York City—the theaters on and off Broadway, Central Park—especially the skate dancers—the museums, the crazy characters—but that's not what this book is about. My story begins with starting work on a doctoral degree at General Theological Seminary, the Episcopal seminary in the Chelsea neighborhood that, I hoped, would land me a faculty position teaching at a theological seminary somewhere. From the first, I loved my classes and enjoyed my 4 years working with students as a tutor in theology (the Oxford model). I supplemented my work at General by cross-registering for courses uptown at Union Seminary in Harlem. It was a supreme delight to study at Union—the institution where so many of the theological giants of the twentieth century taught: Paul Tillich, Dietrich Bonhoeffer, Reinhold Niebuhr, Phyllis Trible, James Cone, and a host of others. The pinnacle of my academic career was taking three brilliant classes from Cone.

In my doctoral studies I worked hard. I applied myself. I felt that my research and writing were not just an "academic exercise"—I wanted my work to count for something in the real world. My passion and work were rewarded by the Episcopal Church Foundation (ECF). I was selected from a national pool to be an ECF Fellow for 4 years. With a sense of urgency in my studies, I sought greater clarity on an issue that had occupied my thoughts for years. It was, in fact, the central theological concern that had brought me to New York in the first place: What was God calling the church to do and/or be as we approached the beginning of a new millennium? There were so many ideas floating in the ether about how the world was going to change in the new century/millennium. I was driven by a desire to stake out a position for the church as an agent of transformation, healing, and community. The vision that inspired me was a definition of the church offered by theologian John Knox (not the sixteenth-century reformer, but a professor at the above-mentioned Union Seminary in the sixties). Knox wrote a short essay on the church entitled "The Identifiability of the Church," solicited for a volume of essays commissioned by the Presiding Bishop of the Episcopal Church, John Hines. It was intended to address the crises of poverty and inequality being identified by leaders in the Civil Rights Movement. In it, Knox penned a definition of the church that has haunted me ever since: "a fellowship in the love of God that seeks to be an ever-widening sphere of an ever-deepening reconciliation." Ever-widening. Ever-deepening. Reconciliation. *Brilliant!* Even my dreams were haunted by this positive constructive vision of the church's mission. I committed a decade of my life trying to articulate such a vision for the church, in which no one was left out, where all—regardless of race, gender, sexual preference, or financial status—were included in the loving embrace of God's love and the church's community. Essential to this vision was an important Greek word, *kenosis*, which means "self emptying." In the New Testament book of Philippians 2:5–7a

> *"You should have the same attitude toward one another that Christ Jesus had, who though he existed in the form of God did not regard equality with God as something to be grasped but emptied himself. . . ."*

In my work I envisioned a church that emptied itself—choosing not to settle for bringing "sinners" into the fold of our cozy sacred places of control, but instead, with courage going forth into the world to discover what kinds of exciting divine things were already happening and to learn from them.[2] A church that emptied itself of pretense and guilt, dogmatism and demagoguery, from asking people to be something other than human. I wanted a church that might be willing to empty itself and go out to the edge of culture and explore. It was about this time I saw a quip that I would come to adopt as a personal mantra: "If you're not living on the edge, you're taking up too much space." I wanted to go out to the edge and see how the church might thrive there.[3] One small way I practiced this was in sermon writing. Instead of secluding myself in whatever sacred cloistered space was available to me to write, I chose to go out, with laptop in hand, to a coffee shop to feel the pulsing, sometimes frenetic energy of the community I wanted to address.

In the mid to late nineties, in addition to being a student, I had several different side hustles to help pay the bills. I offered myself to cover Sunday services when clergy were out of town, and I got trained in interim ministry and worked with churches in conflict and transition. I had the opportunity to be trained in the community organizing methodology of the Industrial Areas Foundation, which allowed me to integrate a community organizational method into theology and church work. I was also part-time chaplain for Saint Hilda's and Saint Hugh's Episcopal School across the street from Columbia University. Virginia Connor, slight in stature but mighty in authority, the head of school, was and is a great friend. I was happy to continue the tradition of bribery to recruit acolytes for chapel services: doughnuts! I also served at

Grace Church in Greenwich Village, a stunningly beautiful church on the bend of 10th Street and Broadway. Its beauty, with its transcendent tower and its exquisite Tiffany stained-glass windows, was surpassed only by the beauty of its thriving, loving congregation. I helped lead Sunday night worship services that were more accommodating for a younger crowd, inspired by a variety of contemporary musical influences.

Over those exciting and often exhilarating 5 years as I pursued my doctorate, my various activities must have been noticed by the Episcopal hierarchy in New York. Early in 2000, I got a call from my friend and fellow priest, Stuart Hoke. On a hot day late that summer, I took the subway down to Trinity Church on Wall Street to meet Stuart for one of our regular lunches. Tall, rangy, with a straightforward pastoral manner, Stuart was the assistant to the rector of Trinity Church, Dan Matthews. Trinity is the parish of the Wall Street financial district, and Dr. Matthews was an influential figure in the religious life of the city, as well as the global Anglican Communion. Stuart surprised me that day by suggesting that we eat at the prestigious India House, not one of our usual haunts. This exclusive private restaurant, with its soothing, cream-colored walls, large floral displays, and ship models enclosed in glass cases, is a place that speaks of deals proposed, contracts negotiated, and futures assured or destroyed. The tables are spaced far apart, where businesspeople speak in murmurs. As a small-town guy from South Carolina who had lived and worked in New York City for some years, I knew about places like this, but I certainly didn't frequent them.

The second surprise was that John Howard, Trinity's vicar, was coming to lunch with us. The Reverend Howard, the second most powerful man in Trinity parish, oversaw the daily operation of Trinity Church and Saint Paul's Chapel, Trinity's up-the-street subsidiary. I knew something was up.

John Howard was a stocky man with a round, almost quarrelsome face that without a doubt gave weight to his role as a federal prosecutor before he became a priest. I suspected he managed Trinity with a heavy hand, running interference for the Rector, just as he had when he was a lineman on his high school football team. As a former football player myself, I had a strong bodily respect for that kind of style.

After perusing the menu, I ordered a spicy fish curry and waded through the small talk in anticipation of whatever it was Stuart and John wanted to discuss with me. Finally, it came. Trinity wanted to revive Saint Paul's Chapel on Broadway across from the World Trade Center, seeking to attract the "Gen X" crowd. A rich mixture of artists and musicians, workers in the financial district, families, and singles of all sorts were filling the area's rezoned apartments, constructed in repurposed factories and offices. Trinity rightly anticipated what the 2000 census would later demonstrate: that Lower Manhattan had the highest concentration of twenty- and thirty-somethings anywhere in the city.

John and Stuart wondered what I thought of their idea to create at Saint Paul's a different kind of congregation, gathered in a new and more contemporary style of worship. Although cautious, they seemed prepared to invest a lot of effort into this experimental project, which they referred to as the "Saint Paul's Initiative." Though they admitted they had no idea exactly what it would entail, they wanted to transform what was now just a handful of parishioners gathering for worship on Sunday mornings into a congregation that would be lively and youthful. It seemed like a great idea, given the influx of people downtown, the positive public relations generated by Trinity's prestigious noon concert series, and the number of people who regularly lunched on the comfortable benches in Saint Paul's shaded cemetery. For people working downtown, especially those working at the World Trade Center, Saint Paul's Chapel and its beautiful cemetery offered an urban oasis of green space and peacefulness in the middle of the hustle and bustle of Lower Manhattan.

As Stuart and John outlined their ideas, I felt I knew exactly what they meant, even how it might work, and how to prepare the ground for this new initiative. We would find and hire the best musicians, the best singers, the best sound and lighting, the best technical resources. The ecclesiastical mad scientist in me started fantasizing as I forked down my curry and drank iced tea. I could see us putting together a world-class jazz ensemble and running images and video during the services, cutting ourselves loose from the prayer books, hymnals, and other liturgical playbooks. My mind whirled even as I remained calm on the outside. This would be a commitment at the level I had always hoped for from the church. If Trinity Church wanted to get hip with Saint Paul's Chapel, I would be thrilled to help make it happen.

This exciting invitation echoed my mantra, "If you're not living on the edge, you're taking up too much space." Now I'd have a chance to try it out; this assignment would be way out on the edge. If I succeeded, it would be big. If I didn't, well, I didn't want to think about that. By all counts, this was a dream job. I dreamed of how I might incorporate my love of New York City into the experience of worship—to explore what it means to say that God loves the city, and to see the city itself as a theological text.

I felt something else, too. I'd been wandering around for a few years, having moved to New York 5 years before to work on a doctoral degree, concentrating on the theology of the church, pondering the nature of the institution and how it ought to exist in this age and in this city. In the meantime, I'd been supporting my family by part-time work in various churches in and around the city. A job with Trinity would take care of my need to find side gigs to make ends meet. My wife Kirsten worked as a registered nurse, which helped significantly, but I felt I needed to earn more. Our daughter Margaret was in seventh grade. Not only would it help to make ends meet, but a position with Trinity would also give comfort and financial security to my family.

I yearned to explore something new, another kind of church, a church willing to roam the vanguard of the cultural and religious revolution emerging right before our eyes, to explore a new ministry that resonated with the urban beats and rhythms of the city, as we explored what it might mean to be "a fellowship in the love of God seeking to be an ever-widening sphere of an ever-deepening reconciliation." I am a devout Episcopalian in love with our liturgy, but I have often thought that, as a denomination, we needed to become more user-friendly to newcomers. There are more people in this country who believe that they have been abducted by aliens than who belong to the Episcopal Church![4] Having felt for a long time a sense of urgency about the widening gap between church and culture, the Saint Paul's initiative was for me the opportunity of a lifetime; it was more than I could have hoped for.

At lunch, I knew better than to express the fullness of my enthusiasm. After we finished lunch and ordered coffee, they asked if I might be interested in this new ministry. I said that I was, very much, and thanked them for asking me. They said it would take some time for the decision to be made but were glad to hear I might be interested. Great, I thought, I just won't breathe until I hear from you.

After lunch the three of us walked along the curve of William Street over to Wall Street. In this part of Manhattan, the layout is older and less orderly than the grid pattern of upper Manhattan. Streets start, stop, get renamed, and pick up again. Through all of it, Broadway serves as a kind of spine, linking the island together. As we turned right from Wall Street onto Broadway, the bulk of Trinity Church itself was facing us, surrounded by its somber graveyard. John took leave of us at this point, but Stuart took me up to Saint Paul's for a look.

I had not been in Saint Paul's Chapel for close to 20 years—the year right after college I decided to go on a road trip from South Carolina to visit friends up the coast and "find myself." Ironically, when I first visited Saint Paul's Chapel I wasn't even an Episcopalian. I was enthralled with the place. I had taken lots of pictures.

Saint Paul's Chapel had always been beautiful but austere, something of a colonial museum, best known for being the church where George Washington prayed after his inauguration. Built in 1766 of fieldstone with brownstone quoins at the corners, classic in architectural style, with columns and a pediment containing a statue of Saint Paul. It didn't have a significant congregation or full-time clergy. Maybe, I thought, its beauty was off-putting rather than inviting, communicating a message of lovely but irrelevant antiquity. It would be an astonishing feat to transform this quiet, slumbering space into a vibrant place with a lively congregation. If the proposal to revive it was passed by Trinity's vestry and I was chosen to lead the project, I would be Saint Paul's first full-time pastor in 25 years.

As Stuart and I stood inside Saint Paul's, I couldn't help but think about how we could transform its serene pink and blue rectangular space into a place which would accommodate audiovisual projections and other lively liturgical experiments. Could we, I wondered, replace the orderly, forward-facing white painted pews and create a more intimate feeling for the space? Put down a labyrinth? Offer yoga classes? Create space for sacred dance? I loved the historical significance of the pulpit that soars up to the level of the galleries that circle the church, the two box pews where our country's first president and New York's first governor had once sat (and where, above Washington's box pew hung an oil painting of one of the earliest versions of the Great Seal of the United States). I couldn't help but speculate about what it would be like to do the *newest* thing in Manhattan's *oldest* continuing church.

After a thorough interview process, I was offered the position. In my heart, I could hear Etta James warming up to sing, "At last!" I felt I had been given the opportunity of a lifetime, a very demanding job. But that's exactly the kind of job I've always wanted: a powerful opportunity to make a difference. I felt as if my whole life had been in preparation for a moment like this. It was more than a job; it was an opportunity for me to rise to my calling.

And so, 6 years after moving to New York, in April 2001 I began work to develop and lead the "Saint Paul's Initiative." Little did we know at the time what kind of church Saint Paul's Chapel would become after the planes hit the World Trade Center Towers, only six months later, on 9/11/2001, and life as we had known it was forever changed. But that is the story I want to tell.

Before I began writing this book, I imagined a documentary about what happened at Saint Paul's after 9/11. Before that, I thought I would be starting an ongoing jazz mass at Saint Paul's Chapel instead of a ministry to first responders. Before that, I imagined being mentored by clergy leaders overseeing a thriving global ministry. But none of that happened. With each successive change, with each disappointment, I have learned an important lesson: each one of us has been or will be given a "no" by life. Actually, many of them. Equally important, I learned that forgiveness is the most important, in fact the only effective, response when you get a "no." And I came to see that forgiveness as a set of practical tools was the beginning of growing that ever-widening, ever-deepening sphere of God's love that John Knox wrote about. Fundamentally, forgiveness is about making peace with the word "no": you wanted "A," but life gave you "B," "C," or sometimes "Z." We struggle to make peace in this gap, between what we wanted and what we got. Our (questionable) strategies for dealing with them—as I well know and will share—include resentments, blaming, drama, self-sabotage, and for many, addictions. The one thing I have discovered that can surely help us cope is forgiveness. But forgiveness is often misunderstood. The forgiveness methodology I will share is that of Dr. Frederic Luskin, director of the Stanford Forgiveness Project. Fred's pioneering research into forgiveness has been proven successful in a wide variety of applications for over 20 years.

Forgiveness empowers us to acknowledge that either we didn't get what we wanted or we got something we didn't want. Acknowledging this disparity helps us to grieve. Only by acknowledging life's "no" and the new reality it brings forth are we able to work through our grief to get unstuck. As Joseph Campbell put it, "We must be willing to let go of the life we planned so as to have the life that is waiting for us."[5]

The story I will share is the story of my journey to forgiveness after the planes hit the World Trade Center, and after all that followed. The question I seek to address is the question that all of us will, at one point or another, need to ask: *what do I do when my life falls apart?* Ultimately, I had to say goodbye to the priesthood, and I had to say goodbye to New York City. I had to let go of the golden ring of continuing to sustain a community I helped build. I lost my identity, my calling, many friends, and my sense of purpose. In frequent panic attacks late in the nights that followed, I even questioned whether I had stepped outside of or had been cast outside of the ever-widening sphere of God's ever-deepening reconciliation. During my long dark night of the soul, I experienced firsthand the searing pain of exile, and an agonizing dose of existential loneliness that might make even Kierkegaard shudder. In many parts of my journey, the heartbreak is almost unbearable, unspeakable.

But I have found joy and love again. Somehow, I have made it through to the other side. And so can you. Everything has changed, to be sure, and there is no going back. The working definition I use for the word "tragedy" is "something that is broken that can't be fixed." In my life I have experienced tragedy, and my tragic experiences and mistakes can't be fixed. But what I have discovered, and most importantly, what I want to share with you, dear reader, is that even though a tragedy can't be fixed, through the mercy of God, the encouragement of kind and dear friends, and the power of forgiveness, a tragedy can be healed.

Losing my calling as a priest was beyond devastating for me; I loved being a priest. But now I have a newfound call to ministry that gives me meaning and fulfillment: doing the humble work of a forgiveness teacher. Perhaps it was my deepest calling all along. I've often heard it said that we teach what we most need to learn, and that's certainly true for me. If I can spare you, on your own journey, precious time wasted in grievances and resentments, I will be grateful. Sharing the healing work of forgiveness gives my life meaning and purpose. Let me tell you about that.

1

My Dream Job

I was exhilarated by the invitation to join the staff at Trinity Episcopal Church on Wall Street to develop and lead the new ministries at Saint Paul's Chapel. It answered all the key questions for me: "What do you love?" "What are you good at?" "What does the world need from you?" and "What can you get paid to do?" If I had drawn a Venn diagram of those four questions in April 2001, they would all have met in one large circle: the "Saint Paul's Initiative." It was almost like God might have been saying, "OK, Lyndon, show me what you got." I felt like I had been given an ecclesiastical laboratory to explore the cutting edge of what the church might do and be as we sought to build community in Lower Manhattan in the new millennium.

After a long winter of interviews and meetings with various people from Trinity, I was offered the position. But that was just the beginning. I also had to convince the Trinity vestry[1] that the Saint Paul's Initiative was worth the investment. These tough-minded men and women, drawn from the business, academic, and cultural life of New York City, were not an easy crowd to convince of anything. So, I prepared and overprepared for the meeting that was set for June 6, 2001, just three days after my fortieth birthday. I taught myself how to use PowerPoint and gathered a set of visuals that I hoped (along with my preaching abilities) would help the vestry envision just what I hoped to do at Saint Paul's.

The night of the meeting I started my presentation with the famous image from Georgia O'Keeffe's painting of the back of "Ranchos Church," an adobe church in Taos, New Mexico. The painting is elegant, but it looks at the church from the rear—no windows or doors. I told the vestry, "Saint Paul's is much like this church—beautiful, but it gives the impression of being a place that's hard to enter. I want to open the doors of Saint Paul's wide enough to welcome the world." The presentation ended with a video I had taken from the NASA website of the familiar view of our blue planet from outer space. As the vestry watched, the image cleverly turned into a video and slowly zoomed in ever closer, centering at first on the United States, then the Northeast, then New York, then Manhattan, then the lower part of the island, and finally settling on the tops of the two World Trade Center Towers about a quarter of a mile from where we were sitting, all set to the theme song from the TV show "Star Trek." I got even cornier when I changed the slide to an image of Saint Paul's Chapel, saying that the Saint Paul's Initiative had as its mission "to boldly go where no church had ever gone before." I couldn't quite read the room. Were the few nervous smiles an indication they were wondering, "What in the world have we gotten ourselves into?"

I had already moved into my office on the third floor of our office building, 74 Trinity Place. As I unpacked boxes that had been looking for a home for years, I discovered a trove of photographs I had held on to from my twenties. I was surprised to find some of the photographs were of Saint Paul's Chapel, evidence of the road trip—actually, a sort of pilgrimage—I had taken up the East Coast after college graduation.

On that journey, when I visited New York City, one stop was to Saint Paul's Chapel. At the time, I wasn't a priest. I wasn't even an Episcopalian yet. But something about that church resonated deeply within me. It left an indelible impression of beauty and peace, of quiet and possibility that only came into clarity more than a decade later.[2]

At the end of June 2001, I gathered a team, and we began our first pilot program of contemporary worship at Saint Paul's, set to run for six weeks through the middle of August. It was a stiff challenge figuring out just what we were going to do each Monday night. We had scheduled the service for Monday nights, knowing that many young people escape New York City on summer weekends, going to the beaches of Long Island and the Jersey Shore. I had to master PowerPoint and Apple's iMovie, shooting and editing video with the help of colleagues from Trinity's TV department, while collecting images and ideas from friends.

If you had happened to be strolling down Broadway one of those Monday nights in the summer of 2001, you would have heard music blasting from the wide-open windows and doors of that old stone church behind its high wrought iron fence. One visitor commented, "This is music like you'd never heard coming from a church before!" Creative ads adorned sandwich boards on the sidewalk proclaiming our welcome for all who came. The music was not the soft sounds of an organ playing a Bach prelude, but high-energy jazz pouring out of amplified instruments, most notably music from my favorite jazz musicians, like John Coltrane and Miles Davis. This experience was truly "a love supreme." Flashing on a large screen were images from the city, images from great paintings, photos of all kinds of people living their lives in this urban collective. Behind all we did were the questions: What does it mean to see the city as a theological text? A liturgical text? What does it mean to say, "God loves the city"?

I was very fortunate starting out at Saint Paul's to have the help of some of the young people who had been involved in previous ministries, such as Jessica Stammen (Ives), an art student from Cooper Union College, Isaac Everett, a jazz pianist and composition major at New York University, and Amy Boldosser (Boldosser-Boesch), who worked for the Rockefeller Foundation. Amy brought to Saint Paul's her gifts as an organizer and her knowledge of PowerPoint. It became clear that I could lead the effort, generate ideas, and fiddle with the technology, but I needed Amy's steady, competent help organizing such a massive undertaking.

We had a great band we called Urban Blend (the name of my favorite coffee at Au Bon Pain, the pastry shop across the street), led by Everett and Peter Moffitt. They were a talented, eclectic, and professional group of successful local musicians who could do anything—classical, jazz, rock, gospel—and do it well. Besides the massive Steinway that was already in the church, the band used electric keyboards, guitars, sax, harmonica, an Australian didgeridoo, and all kinds of percussion. We had vocalists accomplished in everything from opera to gospel. One night, with the help of a young trombonist from the Walter Thompson Orchestra, we even experimented with a style of jazz music known as "sound painting"—creating pure sound without melody or rhythm. Accompanying a poem I wrote entitled "The Spirit Broods over Creation," the sparse squeaks and tones moved the congregation to a quiet, meditative moment.

In fact, we envisioned church as a jazz ensemble: a community of people who enjoyed making music together guided by melody, rhythm, and beat, with everyone having an opportunity to offer their gifts by participating and soloing. It was so exciting! The band was elated. In the summer of 2001 in the Financial District of New York, the music also took down barriers that separated us and built a beautiful loving community.

On those summer nights, as the high-energy jazz sounds wafted out onto the sidewalks, people wandered in to see what was going on. We had been told by Trinity's leadership that if we could attract fifty people by the end of the summer, we'd be doing well. Two hundred showed up for the first night, and one hundred to one hundred and fifty almost every night after that.

At our last Monday night service in August, we featured as our theme, "The Spirit and the City." We contrasted images of Giacometti's sculpture, *Walking Man* (1960), an angular, emaciated depiction of a man walking through a square, his thick feet symbolizing the heaviness and anxiety of human existence (especially in the aftermath of the Holocaust and the bombings of Hiroshima and Nagasaki), with video of the skate dancers who appear every weekend in Central Park, robed in cheerful costumes and shiny adornments, jubilantly skating while DJs spin disco and house music.

At the end of that last service of our pilot program, after I shared a blessing with the congregation, I told them we were taking some weeks off but would gather again on September 17. I said I hoped they would all come back. Spontaneously, Urban Blend burst into vigorous embellishments on jazz riffs as I announced the dismissal. But I soon discovered the service was far from over. With shock and amazement, I watched as people quickly and rhythmically stepped out from their pews, forming a conga line that stretched around the church. With great joy, they were dancing down the aisle, laughing and celebrating this bliss-filled moment. I was ecstatic. This surprising moment of pure joy was more than I could have hoped for.

After the pilot program at Saint Paul's ended, I was exhausted and happy and ready for a couple of weeks off. My wife Kirsten, our daughter Margaret, and I made our yearly pilgrimage south to Edisto Island, off the coast of South Carolina, where our extended families would join us. As a family, we had been going to Edisto for more than a decade, through the generosity of dear friends who have been kind enough to share their vacation home with us. Edisto is a quiet little place south of Charleston and is about as different from New York City as you can get. There's only one stoplight, and most of the time it's blinking.

These fleeting two weeks were some of the most precious times we had spent with our families. It was joyful, yes, but also bittersweet. We knew we would miss them and they us, but they could see how joyful I was in my work, feeling and knowing that I was where I needed to be. That made our goodbyes more manageable.

Refreshed, tanned, and five pounds heavier, we returned to New York so I could begin work on shaping the Monday night services that would resume on September 17. Although I felt inspired and encouraged by what we'd done over the summer, I wanted the fall services to be even livelier and more innovative. One might say I'm an overachiever in some things.

I set a rehearsal for Urban Blend and the rest of the group for Monday evening, September 10, 2001. Even though the kind of high-energy services we'd been doing appear spontaneous, they require a great deal of advance planning and rehearsal to make them work. As the rehearsal group gathered at Saint Paul's, a ferocious wind began to whip torrents of rain down on us. I had trouble getting the key to open the lock on the fence at Saint Paul's, so we (and the pizzas I'd brought for dinner) were all soaked and cold by the time we got inside. But our spirits were high.

A few of us walked to the rear of the church and out onto the covered porch that overlooks the small, well-tended graveyard that is bordered by Church Street. We were captivated by the dramatic storm as it hurled leaves and debris about and pounded the deserted streets with rain. We gazed across the broad avenue to the many buildings of the World Trade Center, watching flashes of lightning dance around them.

Beginning the rehearsal, I immediately noticed that the expensive (and indispensable) sound system that I'd asked to be set up for the rehearsal was missing. I was mortified, worried it might have been stolen. After making several telephone calls I found out that it had been reclaimed by Trinity Concerts and returned to its "rightful place": sitting in a storage closet. Fuming, I wondered who'd given the order to return it to Trinity Church and why. As I tried to figure out how to hold this rehearsal without the sound system, I wondered whether I'd stepped on someone's toes, or whether some unnamed someone thought that our experiment had gathered just a little too much attention and success. In the intense corporate life of Trinity, I discovered that the human tendency toward jealousy and envy was just as evident as anywhere else.

I curbed my anger in front of my crew, but inside I was seething. How could I be expected to run this project if I couldn't be sure that what I'd asked for, what we needed, wasn't available? Saint Paul's was my responsibility, and I had to have some authority over how things were handled. I decided I'd take that up with the Vicar the next day.

No one on our crew, however, was daunted by the missing sound system. They were good at improvising. A liturgical dance troupe from New York University set to make their Saint Paul's Chapel debut began to practice their routine. As they moved their lithe athletic bodies, their improv routine was sensual; I had a flash of caution. I figuratively looked over my shoulder. How would this play with church leadership? Should I ask the dancers to tone it down? I decided to sleep on it. There would be ample time to decide before next Monday.

The rest of the rehearsal went ahead as the storm continued outside. We finished on a high note, confident that we were ready for whatever lay ahead. As we ate the remaining cold pizza on the back porch of Saint Paul's, we watched the lightning and listened to the thunder rumbling through these man-made canyons. Someone remarked that the storm that evening would probably mean the next day would be beautiful. As we were leaving, the sky began to clear.

We had no idea what was in store for us.

2

Ash Tuesday

The next morning was indeed beautiful, as predicted. The sun was bright, the skies a gorgeous shade of blue, with a few puffy white clouds floating on the horizon. The air was crisp with the promise of autumn. It was one of the most beautiful days I can remember. On that bright Tuesday morning, I was excited to participate in a discussion, planned by Trinity television, with one of my heroes, the Archbishop of Wales, Rowan Williams (who would later be elevated to become the Archbishop of Canterbury). Archbishop Williams was in town to explore with us the "Shape of a Holy Life," the kind of presentations that Trinity often sponsored. I was one of a group of spiritual practitioners who had been asked to be present for his talk. And since we didn't want to overload the video with clerical collars, I came dressed that day in coat and tie. But my mind was a mixed bag—inside I was still seething over the sound system debacle from the night before.

I took the subway to work early, getting off at the Cortland Street station in the World Trade Center, making my way through the crowded underground mall and down the street to my office at 74 Trinity Place. Before the taping, I was determined to deal with the mysterious disappearance of the sound system the night before. Preoccupied with this predicament, I didn't register the magnitude of the loud blast at 8:46 a.m. that sent everyone else in the office to the windows to see what had happened. At a colleague's insistence, I reluctantly abandoned my inquest and got up to look out the window. The email I started was never finished.

There have been many vivid and moving descriptions of that terrible day of September 11, 2001, of how first one plane, then another, slammed into the World Trade Center Towers. Stories of the people trapped inside and their last desperate messages to loved ones; the heroism of firefighters and other rescue workers; those who escaped by running blindly, madly away from the towering plumes of acrid smoke and the rain of debris. Most are undoubtedly more eloquent than what I can tell, but here is what I experienced.

Outside the third-floor office window, the sky on that clear, crisp September morning was full of smoke and paper, thousands and thousands of pieces of paper floating, twisting, and turning. It looked like a ticker-tape parade for the Yankees after a World Series win, except the edges of the papers were all burned. Behind me, I heard chatter reporting that a small plane had crashed into the World Trade Center.

I called Kirsten to report that there'd been an accident, but that I was OK. She was at work, so I left a message on our answering machine, knowing she would check it periodically throughout the day. I told her I was going to the site to see if I could help. I wasn't thinking much at that point, only that I was a priest, this was my parish, and that I would undoubtedly be needed. Hearkening back to an accident earlier in the summer when I helped a woman who fell going down the escalator in the World Trade Center, I knew a caring pastoral presence could be helpful.

Changing quickly into a clerical shirt and a white "dog collar," I ran down from my third-floor office, incidentally meeting John Allen, director of Communications at Trinity, in the lobby. Being of like mind, we headed up Church Street toward the World Trade Center. The North Tower was billowing with smoke, a scene nearly everyone in this country has now watched countless times, but one that my mind could hardly take in, much less make sense of.

It turned out that the few minutes delay I took to call home and change my shirt probably saved my life. When we stepped out from our building we saw a sky on fire. The air was thick and burning, a gray and black sludge seared my eyes and began stirring panic. Fire and debris were spraying out of the North Tower right in front of us. As John and I ran north, multitudes were running south—a parade of seeming zombies in suits covered in ashes, white shirts covered in soot and blood. The sounds of screaming, explosions, destruction, sirens, helicopters overloaded our senses. Then the ground-convulsing explosion of the second plane colliding with the South Tower created an apocalyptic fireball that put us in a state of shock.

Although the South Tower was the second building to be struck, it would be the first building to collapse less than an hour later. John and I felt the intense heat of the fire that 24,000 gallons of jet fuel had ignited. There were constant bangs and crashes as computer monitors, office furniture, airplane parts, shattered glass, and other objects rained down from the sky. It was 9:02 a.m.[1]

In shock, John and I ducked into the lobby of the American Stock Exchange. When we felt it was safe enough, we dashed back to Trinity's office building a few doors down. Outside, thousands of people continued fleeing down Church Street in front of us at Trinity Place, away from the World Trade Center and toward Battery Park and the Staten Island Ferry. The incessant stream of debris continued to float down, with window blinds undulating through the air mocking the idea of a celebratory ticker tape parade.

Trinity's rector, Dan Matthews, was in his elegant dark-paneled twenty-fifth story office when the Towers were hit; he was a horrified observer of both plane crashes. Dignified, benign appearing, even grandfatherly, Matthews, who looks every bit the CEO he is, was profoundly shaken. At 69 years old, he'd been planning for an orderly retirement in a few years. Now, I imagine, he was wondering whether the calm progress that had marked his years at Trinity would be sent careening off in another direction. He sent his executive assistant, Stuart Hoke, to lead a prayer service in Trinity Church. None of us—not Dan, not Stuart, none of the Trinity staff—had any idea of the magnitude of what had just happened.

My first thought once I was back at the Trinity offices was the preschool, where the staff was evacuating the sixty children from their third-floor classroom to the basement. The attacks had happened just as the children were being dropped off, so many of the parents were still there, along with the teachers and the school director, who held her own baby in her arms. When everyone was safely in the basement, the teachers began to lead the children (and the adults) in "Itsy Bitsy Spider." As I listened to the quavering voices,

I crouched among them, trying to sing along, wondering if I needed to be elsewhere and what I should do. There was no way to know.

At 10:05 a.m. the South Tower came down with a tremendous roar. We could feel the ground shaking as floors pancaked down, one by one—BOOM BOOM BOOM. Only a few blocks away huge girders stabbed through the air penetrating six floors into the tower's basement, bringing a hundred and ten stories of concrete, metal, and human beings down with it. The whole sky went dark, thick with black smoke. Stuart Hoke was at that moment in Trinity Church, leading a congregation of about fifteen in singing, "O God Our Help in Ages Past." The power of the blast sent people ducking under the pews. Stuart managed to finish the hymn and then dashed back to the office building over the bridge that connects it to the church. They dismissed the gathered congregation at the suggestion of organist-choirmaster Owen Burdick, who said, "Stuart, we've done enough praising the Lord. Now it's time to get the hell out of here!" Most of the congregation dispersed. A thick cloud of debris and smoke consisting of jet fuel, burning insulation, and hot ashes blew swiftly down the street, forcing Stuart to hold on to the railings to keep his footing. For this, I am told he would later receive the "Man of the Year" award in his home state of Arkansas. I'd vote for that.

After quickly assessing the situation with the children, I went back upstairs. I switched places nervously, not knowing what to do or what might happen next. As people from the street poured into the lobby of the Trinity building for shelter, at Dan's request, I kept watch in front of the door leading to the basement room where the children were. We sought to shield the children from the ash-covered, panicked adults who were seeking refuge. Instead, we directed the people seeking protection into the building's lobby.

I went back downstairs to the room where the children had been evacuated just as thick black smoke from the Towers began filling the room, infiltrating from outside. I joined a few others who were already in a bathroom tearing paper towels from the dispenser to wet them down and use them to cover the children's mouths. They wouldn't come out fast enough, so I ripped the dispenser from the wall. As we soaked the towels in water and held them over the children's noses and mouths, they were unusually quiet and cooperative.

The adults helping covered their anxiety with a veneer of quiet determination. I still am struck by how remarkably calm we all remained in the face of the terror that was going on above us.

After conferring with Jim Doran, director of property management, I agreed with a doctor from a nearby clinic and Mike Borrero, Trinity's building manager, that we should make a run for it. Mike shouted, "Let's get out of here. The North Tower might be coming down soon, and if it does, it could fall right on top of us." So, we all—children in tow—ran out of the back of our building and headed south away from the towers, in the direction of the Staten Island Ferry Terminal. One mother with two children insisted on carrying both herself. Our colleague GayAnne Silver, despite her recent recovery from a broken ankle, took a child and carried him as far as she could, hobbling with every ounce of strength she could muster. What a beautiful, courageous heart.

For those of us who were able, we each were tasked with carrying a child. I carried a 4-year-old girl named Jasmine, who clung bravely to me, inspiring me with her trust. I remember feeling close to her and thinking that if I had to die, I would at least die connected to a precious child. Somehow, during the fear, chaos, and danger, we all managed to keep moving and to focus on the evacuation, on getting the children to a safer place.

Out the back doors of the Trinity office building we ran, heading down Greenwich Street to Battery Park and the Staten Island Ferry building. As we ran, the North Tower fell behind us, once again with floors pancaking down on each other producing those same earth-shaking and horrifying sounds. A powerful shock wave ripped the ground, and the noise of tons of steel and concrete falling became a cacophony of terror, mixed with the shrieking of sirens and the screams of escapees, as thick dark clouds engulfed us.

My eyes were stinging, and it was hard to see. I could practically chew the dark, thick air smothering us. Debris and paper covered the street, making it impossible to see where the street ended and the curb began. In places, it was six inches deep. I ran blindly along, with Jasmine clinging to me, until I spotted the corner of a building about 15 feet away and dashed into the alley for cover.

We stopped for a second. I caught a breath. Jasmine lifted her face from where she'd pressed it into my shoulder. I asked her if she was alright. "I'm OK," she said. But her eyes said, "Keep running!" Holding her helped me keep my sanity. Clearly, she was taking care of me every bit as much as I was taking care of her.[2]

Jasmine and I were part of a huge wave of running, stumbling, fleeing people that included Rowan Williams, Fred Burnham, head of Trinity Institute, and Courtney Cowart, who worked in Trinity's grants program. Fred was a hero of mine, and Courtney a dear friend; from them I have more details of what happened that day.[3] Courtney, Fred, and Archbishop Williams had been waiting with others in a windowless studio at Trinity, thinking it was the safest place after the first plane crashed. Until the power went out when the South Tower came down, they had been watching the whole thing on television. As they watched the disaster unfold, Elisabeth Koenig, the much beloved professor of ascetical theology at General Seminary, remarked that, if it came to it, she could hardly think of a better, more loving group with whom to die.

Fred and Courtney later told me that their group ended up in a construction trailer, beckoned in by a kind-hearted worker who had just become a Christian. Shortly after their entrance, the worker announced that he would like to lead them in prayer, and did so, unknowingly, with the future Archbishop of Canterbury holding hands on one side, and the Prior of the Episcopal Order of the Holy Cross, Brother Douglas Brown, on the other. He was surrounded by more distinguished ecclesiastics and scholars than he could have imagined. But prayer comes from the heart of the believer, and this man's heart was full of love and compassion for the people under assault that day.

Archbishop Williams, in his writing and speaking about the experience of 9/11, contends that confrontation with death might lead one to a deeper, more radical compassion for people. Though the archbishop never got the opportunity to speak on the panel as planned, we learned that day a profound truth: that the shape of a holy life (the panel's topic) is cruciform, the shape of a cross (Figure 2.1). Contrary to the fears of many—that God had abandoned Lower Manhattan—I felt that God was very present. I am convinced that the first heart to break on 9/11 was the heart of God. Playing through my mind was a verse of scripture I learned as a child in the Baptist church that brought

Figure 2.1 *The Cross at GZ became an everpresent reminder of the tragedy of 9/11.*

me comfort—that nothing can separate us from the love of God (Rom. 8:38). Not even terrorists.

Somewhere in the maelstrom of Lower Manhattan were Dan Matthews, the rector, and his assistant, Stuart Hoke, both shaken to the core. Because he suffers from a condition in which his eyes do not readily produce tears, I suspect that the rector was in terrible pain from the debris and smoke. He and Stuart eventually made it to a Staten Island Ferry, escaping across the harbor. Stuart later told me that, adding to the general panic, the ferry was so crowded they were afraid—ferry personnel included—that it might actually sink.

When Jasmine and I got to the Staten Island Ferry building, everyone from the preschool was congregating in one spot. I turned Jasmine over to her teacher and went immediately to every pay telephone in the terminal just in case one was working, so I could call home to let my family know I was OK. I was worried because I had left a message on the machine that was naïve given the enormity of the evil visited upon us. It was a very different world now. It would be several hours before my family would hear from me again.

I paced back and forth in the terminal, speaking to every identifiable Trinity leader I could find, trying to figure out what had happened and what to do next. It was really hot in the ferry terminal—I felt like an orchid in a hothouse. The power was down and so the air conditioners were disabled. But we stayed inside because the air outside was billowing with acrid thick black smoke.

Eventually, city officials began evacuating us on buses to uptown. Many people took the ferry over to Staten Island. I didn't. I figured that if I did, I'd be stuck in Staten Island for days. I wanted desperately to get home to see my family.

About 11.30, I got on an east side bus headed uptown and got off at 34th Street, walking down to Gramercy Park on Twentieth Street. It was such a beautiful afternoon. In that magnificently coiffed park, I felt out of place. I was like a zombie, covered head-to-toe in ashes, with red eyes. Sitting there, I tried to clear out my mouth and throat; I picked up some water at a pizza joint along the way. I was distressed by how much my hands were shaking as I paid.

Finally, covered with ashes and still trembling from the experience, I began to walk my weary path to our apartment, eventually passing Grace Church on the way. Parishioners I knew were handing out water and hugs to all on the sidewalk. Some burst into tears when they saw me. I had never been happier to see these familiar faces. After experiencing near-death and destruction, it was refreshing to affirm the goodness of life through loving friends. They told me that Kirsten had been by to pick up Margaret from Grace Church School and to pray. They had taken her into the church to say special prayers with her for my safety. How grateful I am now and will always be for their kindness and love.

When I got home, my tearful family was happily relieved to see me. I bathed, changed clothes, and lay down on the couch to watch the news, but I was restless, the adrenaline from the day's experiences still pumping through my body. I kept thinking about my Trinity colleagues, wondering how they were doing, where they were. I started making phone calls. John Allen had made it to his home in New Jersey and was busy trying to reconnect the Trinity staff. Jamie Calloway, head of Trinity's grants program and the preschool, called to tell me that the children and all their parents were OK. "You won't believe it, Lyndon," Jamie said. "Remember that the head of school handed her baby to one of the teachers as the Trinity building was being evacuated? She didn't know until about an hour ago that her baby was with a group that ended up in Brooklyn. When she got there to pick her up, baby Julie was eating pizza and singing songs with everybody else, happy as a little lark. Isn't that something?" I agreed that it was, indeed, one of the many small miracles on that day of enormous tragedy.

That night I took great pleasure in an ordinary task I did every day—walking our two dogs, one a Cavalier King Charles Spaniel named Charlie, and the other a Rat terrier named Grammar. As usual, they were generally oblivious to all but their own doggy lives, except that for months after the attacks, Grammar would not eat his dinner at night until I got home safely, even if it was midnight. Kirsten and Margaret were equally traumatized and worried about my safety every day I traveled down to the Ground Zero site. Living in Lower Manhattan, you couldn't escape the anxious reality of the devastation; the toxic smell infiltrating our apartment was a constant reminder.

As the dogs sniffed the usual fire hydrants and lamp posts, I looked pensively downtown to the empty gaping hole in the skyline where the Towers had stood, now filled with flickering lights from the fires and emergency lamps. I thought to myself of the countless times I had looked in that same direction at the gleaming Towers and said to myself with joy, beaming with pride, "That's my parish." That night my heart was broken. The city that I love had suffered a devastating loss. The cover of the newspaper, the *Village Voice*, expressed the desolation we all felt. Against the backdrop of the blighted NYC skyline, someone held up a touristy postcard of the Twin Towers, in the place where they should have been. The headline read, "Wish you were here."[4]

I spent the night sleepless and in shock, but I kept thinking that I had to get to Saint Paul's. I needed to see what happened to my church. I decided I'd wait for daylight. I worried about victims who might be trapped under the wreckage, wondering what we might do to help. How could we support the first responders doing this dangerous and urgent work of finding desperate and wounded survivors? At the same time, my mind raced, worrying about Saint Paul's. I didn't see how Saint Paul's could have survived the Trade Center blasts. How could an eighteenth-century church remain standing when late twentieth-century modern buildings across the street had been completely destroyed?

3

We Showed Up

On the morning of September 12, 2001, I got out of bed after a long and anxious night. I had been watching the news almost continuously, overwhelmed by the nature and enormity of the attacks on the World Trade Center. Besides my sorrow over the loss of life and the devastation, I was worried about Saint Paul's Chapel, watching endless clips of the attacks and hoping, longing, to see any sign, any evidence that Saint Paul's had survived. Seeing none, my assumption was that Saint Paul's Chapel had been demolished.

I had to go see, no matter what. So instead of my usual black wingtips, I pulled on my work boots—boots I used for heavy chores in our yard back home in South Carolina—and jeans with a black clergy shirt and collar. As I left, Kirsten and Margaret pleaded with me to be careful, and I vowed that I would. We were on edge—our tearful reunion when I got home the night before had been an emotional catharsis. After hearing rumors of possible anthrax being spread in the dust of the attacks, we didn't know, even away from the site, if we were safe or not. The vulnerability and sacredness of life, in the face of all this destruction and danger, was palpable.

I was frightened by thoughts of what I might encounter at the devastation but somehow managed to put on my "game face." I set out from the high-rise apartment we shared on 8th Street and Broadway. As I left our building and walked down Broadway, the streets were noisy and congested, but not with people—sirens keened, echoing through the urban canyons, helicopters buzzed overhead, earth-moving machinery lumbered and clunked toward the site.

Few people were out, and the ones who were out were somber and silent. Businesses I had relied on for breakfast or coffee in the past were closed. I carried the archaic skeleton keys to open the doors of my eighteenth-century church and a bag full of five or six bottles of water, all that I had, intending to share them with whoever needed them. I had never used those keys before and had no idea even how. Being on the staff at Trinity, Wall Street, meant that I had a whole team of staff members to open and close gates and doors. That wasn't going to happen today.

Given Saint Paul's Chapel's proximity to the World Trade Center, I pictured it in ruins, covered in debris. As I walked down Broadway toward Houston and then Canal Street, I could see that barricades had been erected to serve as checkpoints to, I assumed, keep people from getting near to what we would come to call Ground Zero. Armed Humvees and soldiers, police cars, fire trucks and firefighters, as well as other security personnel were standing by, probably nervous and certainly on high alert for anything or anyone who might be threatening or suspicious. No one knew if more terrorist attacks were coming.

All Lower Manhattan was a smoky mess of ash and soot. The air was thick with the black and gray smoke of asbestos clouds and pulverized concrete. The smell of smoke from still-burning fires was choking, with reflections of the smoldering flames glimmering off buildings. I felt like I was in a dangerous war zone and braced myself to keep going. At each checkpoint, suspicious-eyed military cradling AR-15s asked for identification and waved me forward after they examined my Trinity Church ID. I felt the crisis, the fear, the uncertainty as I continued through streets that felt like a descent into Dante's Inferno. As I moved closer to the site, the spreading smoke and the stench became more and more intense. My eyes watering, I coughed but kept going, thinking about Dante's description of hell, especially the lowest level that he describes as a layered, funnel-shaped pit deep in the Earth. That's where I was headed, I thought grimly, to the lowest level of hell.

As I walked through the mostly deserted, chaotic streets to the center of the devastation at Ground Zero, the atmosphere felt more and more menacing. But I was driven to find out what had happened to my church.

When I reached the mayor's office at Chambers Street and Broadway, I was stunned. Against the backdrop of the fires and the smoke, helicopters, and all the horrors of Ground Zero, I glimpsed the gleaming white spire of Saint Paul's Chapel, standing strong. I stood there, staring, in shock. How could it have survived? How could an eighteenth-century building still be standing when modern twentieth-century buildings all around it were utterly destroyed? In every step of my descent down Broadway that morning I had braced myself for the sight of Saint Paul's Chapel in ruins. But by some miracle it survived. I fell to my knees on the sidewalk and wept. It was all I could do besides looking up again and again to confirm that what I was seeing wasn't a mirage. It didn't feel as though Saint Paul's Chapel was standing in defiance—its history as a colonial and revolutionary classic church made it too dignified for that. Saint Paul's Chapel had been a witness to many significant events and had stood the test of time. I felt deep inside that it was raising its spire in a spirit of courage and steadfastness. I breathed in a breath of that courage and pressed on. I was especially relieved to think that the painting of one of the earliest renditions of the United States Seal inside Saint Paul's might be unharmed. I would soon discover that it was fine; the blast had left it hanging only slightly askew.

Inside the eerie quiet of the chapel, soot and ashes covered the floor, the pews, and the elevated pulpit where so many famous sermons had been preached. The chapel was surprisingly intact—not even a broken window. There were ashes inside because, since Saint Paul's was not air conditioned, members of our men's shelter sleeping there rightly left the windows open for ventilation. As I walked through the nave, taking in the sights, smells, and sounds, I felt the spirit of this noble church gathering its energy, coming to life. It felt like a refuge, a sanctuary, but also exuded a kind of electricity; it felt as if sparks were flying off my boots as I walked. The serenity of this sacred space, in such proximity to the disaster site, was surreal.

A few minutes after I arrived, a firefighter still in his dusty, bulky gear showed up at the Broadway side entrance. His face was haggard, and I could tell he was exhausted beyond measure. He told me he had been at the site since right after the attacks and had been working non-stop ever since, at least 24 hours. He asked me in a husky voice if he could possibly take a nap in the pews. I hesitated, wanting more than anything to say yes to him, but I didn't know if the blast might have done structural damage to Saint Paul's. I shook my head, "I'm sorry, but no. I just don't know if this building is safe yet." He nodded as though he understood and turned away, but his pleading face, now crestfallen, began to haunt me. I knew I must get a structural engineer in immediately to inspect the building. In the back of my mind, I began to think about what might be possible if the building were safe. What could we do to help?

Not long after that, another firefighter caught me out in the cemetery next to the church. Like the first man, he was bone-tired and covered in ashes and soot. He seemed desperate to show me something and asked me to follow him to the fence across Broadway. There, he pointed at a section of fence on which many kinds of shoes were hanging—boots, dress shoes, sneakers. He wept as he told me that they belonged to another ladder company that didn't have the time to get fully dressed before they got to the disaster site, like his company did. "Father," he said with tears welling up, "they won't be coming back for their shoes. Please pray for them." I could only stand there, embrace him, and weep.(Figure 3.1)

Thursday morning, still reeling from that encounter, I decided to walk over to survey the devastated former World Trade Center site. I don't know why exactly, except maybe I thought I could help somehow. As I wandered around, I met a Roman Catholic priest, Father James, and a deacon, both slender and rangy, with somber countenances as if they had been in situations like this before. They had been serving since the morning in the first temporary mortuary located in the atrium of the World Financial Center where the initial wave of recovered bodies of victims had been taken.

They were carrying a big plastic bottle with a cross drawn in red magic marker on it, a humble vessel carrying holy oil. They invited me to come with them to anoint and pray for those who had died. "OK," I said, warily shaking my head. "But I must warn you, this is not my thing. Even the fake violence and carnage on TV and in the movies makes me sick. If someone near me were dying and needed first aid, sure, I'd be there in a second. But really, I don't know if I can handle this."

Figure 3.1 *SPC cemetery following 9/11.*

I wasn't just being squeamish; I really thought I'd be useless in that gruesome scene. But Father James, who I later found out was a Vietnam vet, wouldn't take no for an answer. "Look, man, you don't have to be a hero down here. If you got to retch, go retch. Then come back. That's all right." How could I refuse? Facing my fears, I steeled myself to go with them.

Wading through the foul standing water in the once beautiful Atrium, and taking in the disturbing sights and smells, was overwhelming. The atrium had been one of the most beautiful public spaces in the whole World Trade Center site before 9/11. It was a place where I had enjoyed concerts or had met someone for lunch in its elegant light-filled courtyard. The beautiful palm-tree lined, sun-lit space was now a broken, ashen wreck filled with water, smoke, detritus, and the pervasive stench of death and burning. The two clergy had been performing last rites on the body bags brought in by the firefighters and police officers and other site workers since early morning. I could see how body bags were handled, with a kind of tender reverence, that each one was treated with the utmost dignity and respect for the ultimate value of each human being inside them. It was a profound privilege to offer spiritual care in such an urgent context. Doing this sacred work, I was shivering, both from fear and from the cold rain that was beginning to fall. But I was so relieved to find the company of other clergy in this seemingly God-forsaken place, in the lower rings of Hell.(Figure 3.2)

I had no prayer book with me, so I relied on God and memory. I joined forces with the other two, taking turns kneeling beside the bags as they were placed tenderly on the floor. I put my hands over them, asked God to help me, and prayed something like this: "Go forth, dear soul, on your journey from this world. The blessing of the God who created you be with you. May you rest in peace and in the presence of God forever." I anointed each bag with oil, a custom that is common practice for people of faith, a sign of love and caring.

This simple ritual was all we could do for those who had died, so we did it. At first my hands were shaking, and I was riven with the horror that had befallen us. But soon I began to calm down and become more myself. I was eventually able to concentrate on the broken humanity in front of me and less on my small, scared self. I relied on the habits of years in the priesthood—the habit of prayer and respect for the precious humanity of every person.

As I made my way home after hours in the temporary morgue, I was bone weary but also full of conviction that I—we, Saint Paul's—needed to do something. The haggard face of that firefighter asking for refuge haunted me. Something had to happen. And soon.

Friday morning, I walked down Fulton Street to Seamen's Church Institute, where I'd been asked to preside at their communion service. Volunteers from General Seminary and Grace Church were gathering, along with neighbors, friends, and the staff of Seamen's Church Institute to put the food service together, but were stymied by being so far away, a good six blocks from the site.

As I walked back to Saint Paul's, still pondering what we might do, I met Trinity's Building Manager Mike Borrero, and Director of Property Management Jim Doran. Both were busily talking on their cell phones, as usual. Mike had been a heroic leader on Tuesday morning, and Jim was an enormously practical and organized guy, a former Air Force major. At that moment, Trinity's rector, Dan Matthews, was calling Mike from North Carolina, telling him to ring the bell at Saint Paul's at noon in accordance with

Figure 3.2 *Image of the GZ "pile" two days after 9/11.*

President George W. Bush's request for houses of worship across the land. I figured we had more important things to think about than that, but I wanted to be with them when they went over to the church. Characteristically, Mike was the "can-do" guy. If you ask him to get something done, he cheerfully throws himself into it. Jim, older and more cautious, was, I could tell, mulling over the risks. No one had been up in that bell tower for years, and I still had worries about the structural integrity of the building.

We got ourselves through the police lines, past the debris still in the streets, and walked into the stillness of the church. As we stood for a moment looking around, we heard a crashing noise and a slamming of doors. We froze, our hearts pumping, only to see a New York City policewoman coming out of the bathroom buttoning up her trousers. It was clear that no matter what I said, the building was going to serve urgent needs.

Jim, Mike, and I climbed up the tower stairway, beginning with a dusty flight of steps that led to a decent-sized room like an old attic. Since the electricity was still out, there were no lights, though some sunlight filtered through the smoke and a dirty window or two. As we ascended the next flight of old dark wooden steps, we could hardly see each other. The steeple reeked with what came to be a special Ground Zero smell: burned wiring insulation, wood, wallboard, and God knows what else. I didn't want to think about it.

The tower narrowed around us as we got higher. I began to regret that I'd volunteered to make the climb. When we finally reached the bell, Mike straddled it and checked his watch. When noon came, he pounded on the bell with a piece of metal he'd picked up. I stiffened, waiting for the vibrations to move through the wooden tower, worrying that the whole thing might come down. But thank God, it didn't.

Later, we learned from a Trinity staff member who was in the graveyard that the workers on our side of Ground Zero stopped at the sound of the bell, took off their hard hats, put them over their hearts, and paused for a minute. It clearly meant something to them. That alone made the dusty climb and my fears seem inconsequential; I was deeply moved when I heard of their response. That day in the belfry of Saint Paul's Chapel, our collective mission began to emerge in my mind. I knew we were not going to be able to stand on the sidelines. Nor did I want to.

When I got down from the steeple, I found Bishop Frank Griswold, the presiding bishop of the Episcopal Church, in the sacristy writing a note in the service record book. Bishop Griswold was grateful that I was on the job, very encouraging, and gently hopeful that the church could play a serious role in the response to the disaster. I was very touched that the ecclesiastical leader of the whole Episcopal Church found it important to be present and offer his support.

A little while after Jim, Mike, and I descended from the bell tower, the Trinity Church Vicar,[1] John Howard, appeared in front of Saint Paul's on his bicycle. I was relieved to see him, to have someone in leadership to talk to about how we might use the chapel. As we walked together through the cemetery, he commented that he thought we could open Saint Paul's as a center for prayer and meditation—not for the public, but for the police and firefighters. However, as a former lawyer and prosecutor, I wondered if John's caution might rightly have to do with potential issues of liability and safety. Surely a deep-pockets institution like Trinity must always be aware of potential litigation. This is a legitimate concern under normal conditions. But I felt the conditions after 9/11 were far from normal. It was certainly important to protect this historic shrine of a church and to figure out a way to offer it as a place of rest and meditation. Beyond that, neither John nor I had any inkling of what else we might do, or what other pressures might change whatever plans we might make.

Not long after the vicar left, some of the staff from Seamen's Church Institute came over to suggest that we open Saint Paul's as a feeding station. They wanted to cook food at Seamen's Church Institute and truck it over to the church to be served. I said no, pointing out that we had not yet had the building checked out by a structural engineer and therefore couldn't be sure that it was safe. Even as I warned them of potential unseen structural damage, though, I knew I was avoiding the question. I didn't want to commit Trinity Church to a feeding program at Saint Paul's without consultation and approval. I delayed responding to others in this way, but I was beginning to feel like a fraud. Our job was to meet urgent human need, so why weren't we doing it? (Figure 3.3)

That evening the pressure mounted. Members of the neighborhood volunteers or perhaps the Seamen's Church Institute sent Julianna Margulies, the star of the hit television show "ER," to try to persuade me. The thinking

Figure 3.3 *Gathering supplies at Seaman's Church Institute.*

was, I guess, that her celebrity and beauty would somehow be more convincing than their earnest arguments. But while she was passionate and persistent, I held firm. Besides, I didn't watch "ER" and I didn't have a clue as to who she was. I remember saying, "Look, I, more than anybody, want to see something happen at Saint Paul's. But until I'm sure the building is safe, until we have a plan or an idea of what we can do and do well, until we are certain that what we begin can be safely managed and sustained, I can't allow it." I took very seriously my responsibility to protect not only people, but Saint Paul's itself. I couldn't imagine a greater cascading tragedy than to have the first responders' sanctuary collapse on top of them.

Seeing in her no sign of retreat, I proposed an alternative. Assuming more authority than I had,[2] I suggested that we set up a feeding station right on the sidewalk in front of Saint Paul's with cold drinks and sandwiches. This solution seemed to make everyone happy, including myself. So, we set up tables and distributed peanut butter and jelly sandwiches sent to us by New York City school children and gave out cold sodas donated by local restaurants.

As other supplies—eye drops, masks, bottled water, etc.—began to arrive at Seamen's Church Institute, they brought them over to Saint Paul's and set them up on tables on Broadway and Fulton, where they also handed out snacks and first aid supplies. Amy Boldosser arrived and helped with the distribution. As we worked, we started to talk about future possibilities. Amy was one of the first of the former Saint Paul's community to envision a new role for us, offering food, supplies, and services.

By the first weekend, around September 16, deliveries from Seamen's Church Institute (SCI) came by way of a red truck with a huge yellow duct tape cross on its hood, driven by Roger Bentley, who lived around the corner from SCI. Roger and the truck's owner, a friend whom we knew only as Peter X (so-called because no one could pronounce his ten-syllable Greek surname), were a constant presence at Ground Zero and Saint Paul's. Roger, usually an elegantly clad advertising executive, had been transformed into a supply line cowboy with an American flag flying from his hard hat and a cigar dangling from his mouth. He and Peter X tirelessly shuttled all manner of supplies, especially cigars, ice, and food back and forth between SCI and

Saint Paul's. They went to the icehouse at the Fulton Fish Market every morning to collect hundreds of pounds of ice to be distributed to different stations around Ground Zero.

At the same time, there were other spigots of generosity flowing into Saint Paul's. Carter Booth and Dennis Fisin, a team that I nicknamed "The Velvet Fog," came by several times per day and throughout the night with supplies. They would somehow find out just what we needed and then mysteriously appear with it. After a while, they gave us our very own Nextel walkie-talkie that connected directly to them. I learned not to ask where anything had come from; they had their ways. Carter and Dennis were so invaluable and knowledgeable that they later became members of the full-time staff at Saint Paul's. Their good hearts and generosity are among my fondest memories during that chaotic time.

The police set up a command center on Fulton Street. Captain Ron Shindell was in charge, and Officer Gail Douglas was assigned to the Vesey Street side of Saint Paul's. Ron was a careful, quietly powerful man who understood the intricacies of police bureaucracy and could foresee problems with prescient accuracy. He seemed to know instinctively where to draw the line between openness and security. The big pistol he wore on his belt was more a symbol of the burden of the responsibility he carried than a threat. I'll never forget the day he took me into the site to see a place that became known as "God's House"—a section in the North Tower where the collapse twisted steel into an area with seven crosses.

Officer Douglas, who was "on the beat" in front of Saint Paul's, was a warmly personable woman who could at one moment hug a little girl who'd brought a pillow for the workers, and in the next, freeze an obstreperous construction worker with a look. She took care to make sure that the Roger and Peter X Express, and other trucks like them, could get through with our deliveries.

Captain Shindell and Officer Douglas saw and approved of what we were doing. Both were indispensable to us, especially in moving around in the cordoned-off area, getting deliveries, controlling access to the building, helping us convince phonies and disruptive people to leave, and warning us about legalities. They were a key part of our ability to create that slice of heaven. I marveled then and now at how well Gail Douglas balanced the needs of the workers with her responsibility for security at Saint Paul's and elsewhere.

As the days wore on, we were finally able to plan for cleaning Saint Paul's and the Trinity buildings, and to begin using the Trinity Church truck to transport materials. Our insurance company provided a "gator," a small four-wheel vehicle that allowed Mike and Jim to move around quickly.

During those long days after the attacks as we did what we could for the workers at Ground Zero, I was constantly stopped by volunteers and people working in the Pit with requests to use the church. We began allowing people to go in to use the bathrooms. I took the small altar we'd used during the summer and put it by the door. As they moved in and out of the Pit to rest, workers began to leave memorials and keepsakes on it. One of them, John Misha, a retired firefighter who worked at the site every day, left a cross he'd fused together from a chain he'd found at Ground Zero. As others added photos and mementos, it became a shrine that remained for years afterward.

Three days after the attacks, as we cleaned the Chapel, a seminarian at the time, Jennifer Redall asked if she could play the piano. We were so tired, so dirty, and so wrung out that I couldn't say no to such a beautiful offer. She pecked out "O God, Our Help in Ages Past," one of the hymns that Stuart and Owen had led the congregation in singing on the morning of 9/11. We gathered around and, as best we could through our tears, began to sing that old hymn in that historic place, aware that we were surrounded by such a new reality. That hymn, based on the ever-hopeful Psalm 46, gave me a renewed sense of energy and mission.

4

Radical Hospitality

Officer Douglas described Saint Paul's as being "Heaven in the midst of Hell." The brutal context of Ground Zero needed to be offset by a safe haven, circle of support, kindness, hospitality, and compassion. When asked about this, a phrase came to my mind that captured our attention: "radical hospitality." Any example of kindness, any act of compassion, any sharing of hospitality in Hell is a radical act.

This became our driving force and vision.

This was evident when the humble feeding station we had set up early on began to change, becoming what came to be known as the "BBQ on Broadway." Following the distribution of sandwiches and sodas, we needed more. So, we fired up the only grill we had—that of the Saint Paul's Men's Shelter. At the insistence of one of the shelter's residents—and with his help—he and I began grilling the hamburgers and hot dogs that the city had provided for the men of the shelter. It's important to note that this work of radical hospitality was initiated by one of the men living at the Saint Paul's shelter who himself didn't have a home. And we were sharing their food. What little he did have, he offered freely. This has always stood out in my mind as the epitome of radical hospitality and altruistic love. Since we were so close to the disaster site, almost all the workers smelled the comforting aroma of food every time they walked by. (Figure 4.1)

It soon became clear that one grill was not enough. So, Steve Jaskiewicz, a metal worker and neighbor of Seaman's Church Institute, rallied his fellow metal workers from the site. During their lunch hours, they fabricated eight

Figure 4.1 *The BBQ on Broadway.*

or nine beautiful, huge stainless-steel grills—made of refrigerator shelves converted into grill surfaces. Strange as it may sound, those days were some of the happiest I had had in a long time, flipping burgers for the workers at Ground Zero and making even a small difference offering comfort food. Volunteers from the Seaman's Church Institute started bringing us a steady supply of sides and foods to cook burgers and hot dogs: coleslaw, macaroni and cheese, along with fried chicken, potato wedges, fresh fruits, and salads. We created a place of great joy and fellowship—a healing balm for workers as they departed the World Trade Center site.

It all seemed to be going well, but secretly I began to worry, looking over my shoulder. Was I making commitments that Trinity leadership wouldn't support? How much should I—should we—worry about such things when people were hurt, hungry, in need not only of food but also of loving support and encouragement?

I had reason to worry. Trinity Church senior staff met for the first time Monday, September 17, convened by the rector, Dan Matthews, at the midtown offices of the law firm of Davis Polk & Wardwell. Sitting in the elegant conference room of the law firm, I thought the Trinity staff were clearly disoriented. They were out of their usual haunts, unable to get into their office building, torn from their accustomed routines and responsibilities. Like everyone else, they were in a state of shock. But by that time, I had already been working at the site for six days, and during the meeting I tried my best to communicate the indescribable experiences I had—feeding first responders, performing last rites on body bags, seeing body parts at the site. I tried my best to communicate this with urgency, asking for help.

The rector was very straightforward and honest in the meeting. He confessed that he felt he hadn't provided a lot of leadership on September 11 and praised Mike Borrero for the way he'd reacted to the emergency by taking charge and getting people to safety. He spoke of how Mike and Jim had climbed up into the bell tower at Saint Paul's Chapel on the Friday after the attacks, as he requested, and "beat the hell out of that bell." I wondered why he had excluded me.

At the meeting, I made my urgent appeal to the senior staff to set up some sort of pastoral and managerial rotation to take responsibility for what was happening at Saint Paul's. Whether we wanted it or not, the world was going to come into Saint Paul's. Closing the church was not an option. I was already exhausted, at my wit's end, feeling responsible for something that was growing way beyond my capacity to manage. I got the impression that the work I was spearheading at Saint Paul's came as a surprise to the rector and many of the staff. It seemed as if I had caught him flat-footed. I left that meeting wondering what would happen next. It felt like my sense of urgency was met only with incredulity.

At the end of our meeting, everyone present signed up for tasks and responsibilities, but initially only a few actually came to help. That changed only when Trinity staffer Linda Hannick, who was close to the rector, assumed the task of creating a longer-term roster of supervisory volunteers. Ultimately, over the next eight months, we had seventy volunteers from Trinity serving a shift and helping in various ways at Saint Paul's.

The next day (Tuesday), a week after 9/11, church leadership—rector, vicar, and entourage—paid a visit to Saint Paul's for the first time since the attacks. They entered Saint Paul's as the journalist Lee Cowan (then with CBS News) was doing interviews inside the church. Upon their arrival, the Trinity entourage ended the interview, and Cowan was asked to leave. I was given a lecture about media access only being permitted by John Allen, our director of communications. It was clear the senior staff didn't want the media to have the kind of access I had been granting. I was out of my element; I had a lot to learn. To be fair, what was going on at Saint Paul's Chapel was so far outside anything any of us could have imagined. When you first walked in, it was surreal and shocking to see first responders sleeping in pews, food being shared, Kevlar vests, gun belts, and turnout gear scattered on the floor. It's not surprising that church leadership would be shocked.[1]

The next evening Courtney and Fred came to Saint Paul's. They had signed up to take a shift overseeing the chapel, but they hadn't heard back about it, so they came in person to investigate. I was so happy to see them. Fred insisted that he take the shift that night. We worked it out with his schedule that long term he would be the "Monday night guy," a title he cherished for the rest of his life. Courtney became even more active as the days went by—organizing supplies, recruiting specialists that we needed for the developing ministries, and helping strategize next steps. I can't begin to describe how it felt for me when Fred and Courtney showed up. I felt so much support in their partnership and presence.

That same week, Mike Borrero and Jim Doran arranged for the interior of Saint Paul's to be thoroughly cleaned by Maxon Cleaners, the company that takes care of all of Trinity's buildings. It was now possible to go in and find a reasonably clean and comfortable place to relax for a while. We still had no electricity, so volunteers procured and lit votive candles all around, creating a friendlier atmosphere than the glare of the one halogen light that a generator powered, a gift from our friends at Verizon. The chapel began to feel truly like an oasis of peace amid chaos. The more time I spent there, the more I wanted to make sure we kept it that way. More than I realized, I was becoming deeply invested in the 9/11 mission of Saint Paul's.

Happily, the BBQ on Broadway continued, and it was gathering momentum. But we had one huge problem: we came under the scrutiny of the NYC Health

Department. The inspectors told us that what we were doing—even in such an extraordinary context—was illegal. Maybe they thought it was dangerous, a potential risk for food poisoning or worse. Or maybe they were asserting their bureaucratic privilege and enforcing the rules. They told us that the BBQ on Broadway was a problem; we were cooking in the still noxious air at the site and didn't always know where our food came from. It became their mission to shut us down. They visited almost every day and made us stop. But when they left, we'd restart the coals.

Finally, one day after being shut down by the Health Department, I had had enough. I went looking for the police captain who was now in command of our area. A strapping fifty-ish veteran of the NYPD, he was very much in charge, navigating the chaos around him. When I found him, standing next to one of the nearby checkpoints, I yelled in frustration, "The Health Department keeps shutting us down! We are trying to support your guys and all the others in this gruesome mission! Is there *anything* you can *do*?" Cocking his head to one side, he smiled and replied, "Yes, I can. Faddah, you let me know when they come back, and I'll *handle* it."

The next evening, Fred Burnham was in charge at Saint Paul's when the Health Department inspectors came back with the same orders to close. When they showed up with their demands, Fred sent word to the police captain, who then gathered ten or twelve of his biggest, burliest guys and brought them to Saint Paul's. Without saying a word, they encircled the Health Department entourage of five or six people, locked arms, and marched the astonished bureaucrats off the premises. Next morning, when I came in, one of the officers laughingly told me the last time he checked, Health Department officials didn't carry guns. But cops do. Of course, he would never have pulled a trigger in such a conflict. This was merely gallows humor that helped us navigate the anxiety of the time. We both laughed, and I hoped their maneuver had put an end to the meddling.[2]

But it didn't. Eventually, citing orders from Mayor Rudolph Giuliani, the Health Department succeeded in shutting down the BBQ on Broadway, about two weeks after 9/11. But by this time, I had gotten a report from a structural engineer that the Saint Paul's building was sound. Courtney's cousin, Martin

Cowart, a chef with his own restaurant in Tribeca, was helping us. With Martin's expert help, we moved the food service inside the fence of Saint Paul's, and onto the beautiful, covered portico facing Broadway. We declared it an ongoing parish "potluck supper," and were back in business for the next eight months. As a southerner whose mother always taught me to help others if you can—and feed them—I was prouder than ever of what we were doing. I'll never forget a Sunday evening meal of fried chicken, mac and cheese, green beans, served with biscuits and sweet tea. I could feel my mother in South Carolina beaming with pride!

What started out as simple BBQ meals quickly began to evolve into a much greater range of services as we discovered what the workers needed and as more volunteers with all kinds of skills came to help. Our staff grew in extraordinary ways. Courtney came on board as our next chief of staff, following Amy Boldosser, bringing her own enormous creativity and connections to the task. Courtney's tender-hearted courage, combined with the can-do attitude and tenacity of an Olympic athlete, gave us the inspiration we needed. Courtney assessed that "God is certainly present in this, but it goes way beyond the usual contours of institutional religion. There is no blueprint we know for a post-catastrophic, ecclesial rebirth such as this."[3]

As these ministries were developing, I soon learned from another staff member that church leadership had concerns about the historic building and the impact from the demanding scope of our ministry. Exhausted workers and first responders who were pulling double and triple shifts sleeping in the pews brought in dirt and scuffed the pews. How, the leaders asked, did I know whether everyone who was visiting Saint Paul's was really a worker and not someone with shady motives? Were we liable if someone was injured or claimed to be? The tape holding up the children's letters could damage the walls. And so on. We were asked point blank: "Who are all these weird people in our chapel?[4] And why were we taking volunteers and dignitaries into the Ground Zero site to offer supplies, say prayers with the workers, and witness the catastrophe firsthand? Was that really my—or Saint Paul's—proper role?" It felt like I was engaged in a delicate chess game that required great skill and finesse, played out against an emotional and anxious backdrop of the 9/11 crisis.

But we pressed on.

In addition to her cousin Martin, Courtney brought us Bethany Putnam, who ran a non-profit organization called Labor of Love, and her co-worker Katherine Avery. Bethany was kind, organized, and efficient; she had spent a lot of time planning for a response such as this. I was shocked to see Katherine Avery—she had been in my youth group in Spartanburg, South Carolina! I was close to Katherine's family, and I had no idea she was coming to help us. It was quite a surprising reunion. As an accomplished southern woman with a soothing drawl, her beautiful presence belied her tenacity and her ability to kick ass when things needed to get done. Katherine was a steel magnolia and made things happen. Bethany and Katherine began immediately to organize the countless boxes of donated food, clothing, and other items so they could be easily accessed. The chapel was so full of boxes and supplies at this point that they had to work through the night, with the help of volunteers, to organize it all.

Martin was also a game-changer. In addition to catering scrumptious foods, he was later able to get contributions of meals at cost from some of the finest restaurants in New York—Zabar's, Le Zie, the Waldorf Astoria, and many others. Martin's experience as a restaurateur came with solid connections in the Health Department and his oversight of our food service resolved the legitimate issues the Health Department had. And so, we continued serving hot meals—four times a day—plus coffee on demand, offered to us free from our nearby Starbucks. By the end of our food service operation, in eight and a half months, we served over half a million meals to weary first responders and rescue workers. We also provided supplies like boots and parkas, shirts and minor medical incidentals. We offered massage for aching muscles, chiropractic treatments for overtaxed backs, podiatry care for their burned and bruised feet, and pastoral counseling for grieving hearts and souls.

Music also became integral to Saint Paul's ministry. In addition to the quiet ambient music that played much of the time, we had three and four concerts each day, all lovingly performed by some of New York City's finest musicians. Opera singers, rock groups like Dishwalla, and famous string bands like Ethel (whose member Ralph Ferris later assumed oversight of scheduling musicians for us) offered concerts. We even had an inquiry from someone connected to rock star Bon Jovi, but we couldn't work out the details for that. Many New York musicians came and played piano quietly. My personal favorite was on Thursdays when Brenda Landrum always played my favorite Erik Satie piece "Gymnopedia No. 1." Its minimalist, hauntingly beautiful melody never ceased to touch me deeply. When she played, I would take a few minutes to myself and go up into the gallery at Saint Paul's to pray and breathe and, sometimes, weep. All kinds of music mattered, not just to our guests but to all of us who were serving there. From quiet beautiful music to rousing anthems, operatic explosions, and a whole lot of firefighters playing "Danny Boy"—we had it all.

It wasn't long before the media noticed what we were doing. More than once, we were listed as "New Yorkers of the Week" by the local news outlet NY1. *TimeOutNY* magazine declared that landing a gig as a volunteer at Saint Paul's, if one could do so, would be the highest achievement for the Christmas season in 2001. And the volunteers—from Grace Church where I had also served, and schools and civic organizations—came in greater and greater numbers, working in two shifts of twenty people, twelve hours a day. The first team of organized volunteers came from Saint Hilda's and Saint Hugh's Episcopal School, under the leadership of my friend Virginia Connor, the head of school. She organized teams of parents, equipped them with hats signifying their status as helpers, and brought them down from 114th Street and Broadway. And our volunteer pool was wide and deep in its diversity: Christians, Jews, Muslims, Hindus—people of all faiths and no faith served the community we were creating together. What was so beautiful for me is that Saint Paul's volunteers came to embody a humble approach to serving. It was an upside-down world in which corporate CEOs were thrilled to serve coffee to cops, federal judges were honored to make sandwiches for firefighters, and bishops of the church mopped the floors. It was for me a glimpse of the kingdom of God. The reciprocity of love was exhilarating. We discovered what radical hospitality was all about.

As word of Saint Paul's ministry spread, people—not just in New York but across the nation—began sending us all kinds of support: banners reading "HOPE" and "LOVE" and "Never Again" that we hung from the balcony inside and fence railings outside. My favorite banner was created by Jessica Stammen, an art student at Cooper Union College: on a deep red background she inscribed the word COURAGE in a beautiful blue. At the bottom of the banner was a favorite quotation from Anne Lamott: "Courage is fear that has said its prayers."[5] If ever there was a saying that embodied the energy we all felt at Ground Zero, this was it. We received boxes and boxes of peace cranes strung together with twine from school children in Japan, enough to stretch around the entire perimeter of Saint Paul's—a whole city block! We got boxes full of cards and letters, hundreds from school children telling us how much they loved us and how concerned they were for the first responders. When a volunteer first taped some of those letters on the wall inside Saint Paul's, I was peeved, knowing we had just spent a small fortune repainting the interior. But when I saw how it gladdened the workers, I changed my mind. We plastered them everywhere. (Figure 4.2) One letter from Claudia Fischer, an eleven-year-old girl in Scarsdale, NY, was especially precious. I'll quote it here:

> Dear Firefighter:
>
> There are many deaths that I can die. Cancer, heart attack, AIDS, hepatitis, leukemia, natural causes, choking, being strangled, shot, or hanged. I could get the death penilty [note spelling], rabies, or a snake bite, or a wild animal could attack me. I could get run over by a car, be in a car crash, fall, slip, get a concussion, get smallpox, or be stabbed, cracking my skull, get poisoned, heart disease, get stung by too many bees, and many more.
>
> BUT I know that I will never ever die in a fire because people like you, great people, would go into flames to save an ordinary person like me, and that's what makes you so great, courageous, brave, terrific, wonderful, special people.
>
> Yours truly,
> Claudia

Figure 4.2 *SPC photo taken from the gallery.*

We also received donations of money, food, water, and whatever else our good-hearted donors thought we might use. I'll always remember the day a semitruck from my hometown of Gaffney, SC, pulled up outside our gate with a huge load of supplies—much-needed food and water. I was deeply moved by their support. Clearly what we were doing touched the hearts and minds of a city and a nation still trying to recover from this horrible tragedy. From the moment the doors of Saint Paul's Chapel opened, the hearts of volunteers and Ground Zero workers opened as well.

One surprising contribution (there were many!) was from a community in Maine. They sent us boxes and boxes of teddy bears. What the hell were we supposed to do with teddy bears? I asked the volunteers to distribute them to the pews, not sure how they might be received. They were a hit! I was shocked. One night I watched a tall strapping firefighter come in, select two teddy bears, and take them with him to nap on one of the cots we had set up. On any given night, we could have up to one hundred workers sleeping in Saint Paul's, either in pews or in cots. Many with teddy bears.

Meanwhile, my leadership role at Saint Paul's evolved from scrambling to get services up and running to overseeing a robust and growing operation. Courtney, Bethany, and Katherine created for us a command structure to keep the operation organized, and they convinced the leadership at Trinity to endorse it. With support monies rolling in, Trinity approved it, allocating monies for a paid staff of six full-time managers under my direction to handle supplies, services, and volunteers. In addition to these six, at the vicar's request, we were also blessed with an Episcopal nun, Sister Grace, who humorously became known as "Sargent Grace." Her bona fides consisted of chevrons on her habit ripped from the sleeve of a witting police officer. She ran interference between sometimes unruly construction workers and oversaw the clergy Rota for the daily Eucharist. She was central to the morale of the whole operation, just being there in her habit and having a "no nonsense" approach to chapel management.

As the weeks unfolded, our volunteer pool continued to grow. The Episcopal Church's General Theological Seminary stepped up to offer support services. One of their administrators, Mary Morris, mobilized a team of five people who took calls and coordinated volunteers, supplies, and requests for visits from dignitaries. Meanwhile, I was charged with interfacing with the leadership at Trinity, who seemed to have different ideas about what our ministry should be doing. I felt as if I were standing in a breach—a wide chasm between the leadership of a historic institution and an emergent community responding to the urgent needs of Ground Zero that could change in a moment. It was like riding a rocket that was doomed to crash. I just didn't know where, or when. I remember vividly sitting in the sacristy one evening talking with Fred and Courtney. I expressed my concern that we were overstepping an uncomfortable line with our bosses down the street. I said, "In five years, we may have lost our jobs here. But let's get together, have a beer and toast, knowing we did the right thing."

Whether I realized it fully at that time or not, I had crossed over to another understanding of authority and leadership. The crisis of Ground Zero was not a normal situation; normal approaches would not suffice. To my increasing personal peril, I adopted the view that authority was earned by having boots on the ground, serving in the trenches. There was an emerging foreboding tension in my relationship with church leadership; it was becoming more difficult to stand in the middle of what we were doing at Saint Paul's and what Trinity expected of me.

And it was costly: the operation at Saint Paul's was costing $3,500 a day, a statistic shared with the *New York Times*.[6] Trinity itself, though basically intact, also faced massive expenses in cleaning up the main church. I thought this concern about money was strange; donations rolling in from all over the country surpassed our expenses.

At the time, I wasn't sure what to do about the pushback from church leadership. Communication with them was spotty at best. Our chain of command was broken. The only person I interacted with regularly was John Allen, the communications director. We had become close chatting by email on the evening of 9/11, comparing notes about the safety of our friends and staff members at Trinity, parents and children who attended the Trinity preschool, and the future Archbishop of Canterbury, Rowan Williams, who had been visiting that day. John also was getting emails from concerned family members about their loved ones living in Saint Margaret's House, the retirement center Trinity owns located near the South Street Seaport. Once I got their name and apartment number, I would walk over and check on them and report back. In many areas, phones were still down, as well as electricity. I was happy I could do such a little thing that could make such a big difference in relieving worried family members.

Part of church leadership's concern, I now suspect, was that I had assumed authority that I hadn't been given, since they weren't present. Although I was the priest associate charged with the ministries at Saint Paul's Chapel, I served under the authority of the rector and vicar. Their concerns about what they saw as overreach seemed to be confirmed when a comment I offered showed up in the *Wall Street Journal*. Addressing a question about memorials, I said that I thought we should use the trunk of the fallen sycamore tree in Saint Paul's cemetery to create a baptismal font as a memorial to those who died on 9/11. I said it would help us to "remember what happened and to grieve. We could use the trunk to make a memorial to the dead juxtaposed with the new life of those being baptized in the years to come." I thought it was a beautiful way to remind people of the importance of taking our baptismal vows seriously, to love and serve, and to respect the dignity of all human beings, while we honored those who died. The *Wall Street Journal* thought it was a good idea too, calling it the "most poetic" of the ideas for memorials being proposed at that time.[7] But I heard through the grapevine that this was seen as evidence that I was overstepping my role—setting policy and making commitments without permission. I see now that I was unbelievably naïve, but I was doing my best in the leadership vacuum.

The tree became a flash point of conflict in my relationship to church leadership, while at the same time it became a topic of great concern for the public. Visitors came from all over pleading to see the tree, the symbol of hope that withstood the blasts from the terrorists' attacks. News networks were clamoring for interviews. When Trinity begrudgingly gave in to MSNBC's repeated requests to do an interview with me, I was explicitly forbidden to speak about the tree, even though MSNBC set up their camera so that the tree was prominent in the background. I did as I was told, but not happily. I gave the interview as the vicar stood nearby, arms folded and looking menacing. It was clear that I was becoming more and more alienated from church leadership. I felt they did not support me or what we were doing, and I had a hard time understanding why, except to chalk it up to the institutional concerns about liability. Control is the mother's milk of such an institution, but control was hard to find in what became the Wild West of Ground Zero. By spring of 2002, even as the devastated tree showed new shoots of growth, I was told that it would be replaced by a Norwegian spruce tree—and it was, the following November.[8]

I didn't set out to become a thorn in anyone's side. But neither could I stop what I believed to be the most important ministry I had ever been part of. It was hard to follow protocol, waiting for my bosses to give me permission to do what I knew needed to be done—with urgency and in real time. Increasingly, I came to believe that the real leaders were those who showed up—who were in the trenches responding to the crises—more so than those endowed with formal titles. Our contrasting views could be summed up in a question I was asked, emphatically, "But, Lyndon, when will it be a church again?!" Under my breath I stammered, "We've never been more of a church."

Regardless of the conflicts and difficulties that followed as the days and months unfolded, I will always be proud that we showed up. When the needs were great, everyone at Ground Zero—sanitation workers, clergy and cooks, cops and firefighters—showed up. Despite horrific memories of the terrorist attacks replaying constantly in the back of our minds, despite our own fears and hesitations, we showed up. With great courage. With great love. At first, to do the somber but necessary task of rescuing any survivors or finding the remains of the dead. And then to do the daily agonizing work of cleaning up the site. Saint Paul's took as its mission to care for those charged with working in Ground Zero. These courageous people were our church. They wore respirators instead of neckties and Kevlar vests instead of Brooks Brothers suits. I felt then and still feel today that this scariest place on Earth was exactly where I needed to be.

In the next days and weeks, there was much talk at Ground Zero about the "miracle of Saint Paul's," asserting that God had placed God's hands over the chapel and protected it from the blast. But, as a theologian, I didn't think that sounded right. It implied that somehow Saint Paul's was holier, or of greater concern to God, than the people who died across the street. But I believed that, if Saint Paul's being spared was a miracle, it was not because we were holier than anyone else, but it was because we had a big job to do, if only we were allowed to keep doing it.

5

Unlocking Anger (and Throwing Away the Key)

Within a few weeks, the Saint Paul's ministry was by far one of the most predictable operations going on anywhere in Lower Manhattan. Getting deliveries of food and supplies, ice and sundry other items ran like clockwork. Restaurants delivered meals at scheduled times, the warming trays were ready to keep the meals hot, and we had plenty of sodas, water, and coffee. (Figures 5.1, 5.2)

But the predictability of what we were doing took place in an unpredictable context. In the middle of serving lunch or dinner, a siren might scream from Ground Zero, and hundreds of people dressed in bunker clothes, camouflage, jumpsuits, or jackets with FBI or ATF printed on the back would scramble and run out of the site. When we heard the sirens in Saint Paul's, we wondered if One Liberty Plaza, two blocks south would fall on us. If the building fell in our direction, Saint Paul's Chapel—and everyone and everything in it—would be crushed instantaneously. Those sirens were like a zero to sixty jump-start for our anxiety.

Meanwhile, hundreds of construction workers were appearing, looking for work or hoping to help. Several men in fire department bunker outfits came to the city, and while most were the real deal, a few were not and that made us wary. One persistent visitor in a wheelchair pleaded with us to allow the Vienna Boys' Choir to perform at Saint Paul's. This request seemed so absurd, given the conditions, that I made the judgment that he might be dangerous.

Figure 5.1 *SPC full-time staff.*

One day he brought a box of promotional materials. This was at the height of an anthrax scare, so I took the box immediately to our outside storage shed at Saint Paul's, just in case. With fear and trembling, and a huge dose of stupidity, I opened the box alone. It turned out to be an authentic appeal, with an abundance of cards and flyers about the choir. Weeks later, I was both happy and relieved to stand alongside the rector, both of us wearing white Vienna Boys' Choir baseball caps, as they sang like angels in the sacred space of Saint Paul's.

Frequent visits by VIPs made life interesting at Ground Zero. Visits by President George W. Bush on September 24 and October 3 meant the whole area was put under lockdown. Secret Service, military, and police units went on to the highest level of alert and we simply couldn't move around. We were scared that the terrorists might hit again. But this was Broadway and the show—or at least the meals—had to go on. And so they did.

Things at Ground Zero were extremely tense for weeks after the attacks, but there was an enormous outpouring of support and encouragement from the surrounding community. Traveling in and out of the site, we were met

Figure 5.2 *SPC leadership.*

by crowds of people—young and old—who were standing at the barricaded entrances with signs, flags, and banners, offering bottles of water as they waved and cheered. Their support both surprised and touched everyone, especially the construction workers. Courtney tells the story of one man who got home and found his wife looking at him strangely. "What's wrong?" the man asked. "Look in the mirror," she answered. His otherwise grimy face was marked by clean lines where tears of overwhelm had fallen when he experienced the kindness and affection of the cheering crowds.[1]

As time passed, it became increasingly clear, to both the men and women who were working at Ground Zero and to us, that there would be no rescue of survivors. Day after day, workers faced gruesome sights, some of which involved retrieving bodies of people they knew and cared for. Their grief was enormous and inconsolable, and they brought it with them into Saint Paul's.

One afternoon as I was looking over the crowd resting in the pews at Saint Paul's, I saw a construction worker sitting in a pew, alone and slumped over in a pew. He wore heavy brown coveralls and had placed his hard hat by his side.

"Are you OK?" I asked, after I had sat quietly beside him for a few minutes. He shook his head, unable to speak. "Whenever you're ready," I said. He spread his hands helplessly.

Gradually it came out. "We were working, clearing out the crap, and there it was."

"What was it?"

"An arm. A woman's arm. Perfect. Didn't look like anything was wrong with it. Just an arm. Lying there." He stopped. When he spoke again, it was in a whisper. "An engagement ring. On her third finger. That poor girl." And then he sobbed.

This was a man whose masculinity had likely been formed around his not crying, around his ability to take whatever came his way. And now there was nothing he could do but weep for the young woman whose life had been cut short. There was anger, too, at those who had committed this atrocity. I then realized that we had to get ready for far more than simply filling bellies or providing a place of rest. We needed help from clergy and counselors with experience and training in pastoral care, especially pastoral care in the context of disaster.

We appealed to religious orders in the city and then, in response to this need, Bishop George Packard, in charge of Armed Services, Prison, and Healthcare Ministries for the Episcopal Church, declared a "Hundred Day Mission" for his department. George and his staff heroically recruited, trained, and organized volunteer clergy from all over the country who began to appear, listening to and comforting those who came to Saint Paul's as well as the Ground Zero site. George's leadership was a godsend.

Mary Morris, assistant to the dean of general seminary, who had started out organizing volunteers for the Seaman's Church Institute, recruiting from among the seminarians, ended up coordinating the volunteers from parishes, businesses, and other institutions. Only a few days after September 11, she needed three full-time helpers to do this task. Volunteers poured in, twenty a shift, two shifts per day, all needing to be told what to do, where to go, and what to say to those they were serving. We eventually accumulated a roster of over 15,000 volunteers. I was bemused to learn that volunteers had to be told that they couldn't bring a dog or cat to Ground Zero, that they had to wear suitable clothes and boots, and that you absolutely could not bring your children. What, I wondered, did these good-hearted volunteers think was going on at the World Trade Center anyway? Someone once asked Mr. Rogers how we should talk to the children about 9/11. He said that we should encourage the children to keep their eyes on the helpers. The love present in Saint Paul's was so strong maybe they wanted their children to get a glimpse of the good of humanity, not the worst. (Figure 5.3)

My devotion to Saint Paul's was difficult for my family. There were many concerns about conditions at Ground Zero, particularly about the noxious air I was breathing. I felt I needed to spend more time at home but felt equally urgent about being at Saint Paul's. It all felt like I was losing control, not an emotion I relish even in the calmest of times. I was overwhelmed. I began to feel as though my head was in a giant vise tightening.

The collective emotional energy surging through the site and through Saint Paul's Chapel could swing from the jubilation of experiencing an amazing concert, along with delicious food, to the devastation unleashed by

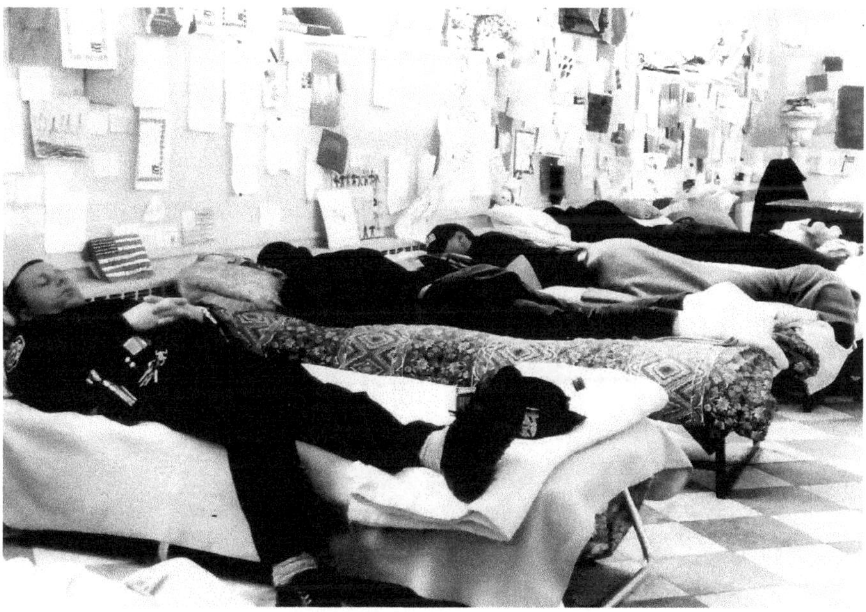

Figure 5.3 *First Responders sleeping in SPC.*

finding new groups of bodies being uncovered. I'll never forget the story of the firefighter who came to the site every single day to look for his firefighter son who had not been found. Three months to the day of the attacks, he found his son himself. But he did not stop there. The next day he came back to the site to dig for the remains of other people's sons and daughters. All the agonizing highs and lows that unfolded every day in relentless grief, bouts of anger, depression, and despair were balanced at times with a deep sense of connection and some days, even joy as our community deepened its bonds of affection for one another. (Figure 5.4)

This intense bonding, born of the singular mission of the workers at Ground Zero and our attempts to support them in this mission at Saint Paul's Chapel, solidified our community. In the intense emotions we felt about our mission, the staff and volunteers at Saint Paul's Chapel became an in-group that was suspicious of any out-group that threatened the mission. Those out-groups were anyone who sought to change or deter us from what we were doing. At first, this was the Health Department shutting down our food service. And ultimately, for good or bad, Trinity Church leadership at the time, the top of our

Figure 5.4 *Prayers offered by Chicago Firefighter Chaplain Bob Ossler.*

organizational structure, came to be the most threatening out-group. We felt they tried to countermand what we were doing: workers shouldn't sleep in the pews, we shouldn't have such an elaborate food service, we should not burn candles, we should not put children's letters on the wall, we should not allow the fence at Saint Paul's to become so thick with the grief of people who came, leaving a remembrance or memento to a loved one. The church should be a quiet place of prayer and contemplation, not a full-service mission. Food should be scaled back to coffee and donuts, not hot meals and sandwiches.

The food service was indeed extravagant—and free—but their critique angered me. I felt that, given the sacrificial tasks these men and women were doing, no food item was good enough, especially since it was all amply covered by unsolicited donations. To me, church leadership's objections seemed trivial and incessant. As I reflect, I know it was not the case that they were wrong and we were right, or vice versa. It was a complex urgent situation in which the normal protocols of the chain of command broke down. The reality was that there were different and competing ideas of what Saint Paul's ministry to Ground Zero should be. As I was at Saint Paul's Chapel and Ground Zero almost every single day for 8 1/2 months, I felt strongly, passionately that the mission was more important than any damage that might be done to Saint Paul's, the institution, or wounded egos—mine or theirs. Their objections that I saw as trivial concerns, especially in light of the gravity of the context, upset me deeply. When the rector accosted me for accepting a donated drink refrigerator (because our antiquated electrical wiring might not be able to handle it), I was furious and frustrated. I knew the wiring was fine but said nothing. As it turned out, it wasn't the drink refrigerator that bothered him. I perceived it was that I didn't get his approval.

For Thanksgiving in 2001, two months after the attacks, the Waldorf Astoria made us an offer it would be hard to refuse: they wanted to cook Thanksgiving dinner for the workers and their families and serve it at Saint Paul's, for free. I was told by the vicar, "absolutely not." He said that these workers were being paid double time on the taxpayer's dime to work on holidays. They should eat their meal and get back to work quickly.[2] I was livid. Thanksgiving Day came, and we did it anyway as they ultimately relented. This decision became one of many nails to be driven into my professional coffin.

My sense was that the more the conflicts accumulated with me dodging their requests, church leadership saw me more and more as out of control and unwilling to meet their demands. Whenever I went to meetings at Trinity, I felt a searing disdain from leadership and some of the staff. I had crossed a line, maybe more than once. Perhaps one of my mistakes was in not finding ways to create more opportunities for church leadership to participate in the work at Saint Paul's. But deep down I resisted this because I was afraid it would be shut down. They didn't spend much time there, and that lack of involvement was at the root of our problems. My anger and contempt were not helping.

It seemed that once I unlocked the place in my heart where anger resides, it flowed continuously throughout the daily tit-for-tat with church leadership. I felt that our mission was vitally important, more important actually than my outcome or fate. I often said to myself that the person who wins the chess game is the one who can think of the greatest number of moves in advance. That became a mantra I recited under my breath. I was angry, but I had to keep my anger in check.

So, what about anger? Was it right for a priest of the church to become so angry? Was it appropriate for me to bristle and seethe when I was confronted about serving too much food? About a drink machine? Let me say a little bit about anger. Anger can be a healthy emotion when it is constructive, such as when anger summons the energy you need to defend yourself and others. But anger can be destructive when it becomes embedded in your psyche and turns into emotions such as revenge fantasies where you have a strong desire to "make them pay." This desire for revenge is something we all feel from time to time. It's healthy and normal. Psychologist J. Everitt Worthington, retired professor at Virginia Commonwealth University and leader in the field of the scientific study of forgiveness, discovered in his research that when a person contemplates revenge, the pleasure pathways of the brain light up—the same ones that light up when eating chocolate![3] This adds a new perspective on the idea of "sweet revenge." But the problem with revenge, in a quotation often attributed to Mark Twain, is "there ain't no future in it." The problem with destructive anger is that it is caustic; it's like battery acid that ultimately eats through its container. Destructive anger can destroy your soul—and it nearly did mine.

One of the things I have learned about anger is that it is one of the ways we express grief. I was angry when church leadership criticized what we were doing, but deeper down, my anger toward church leadership and their anger toward me, I think, was born of a shared unremitting grief that what we had hoped for ourselves, our church and our families, was cast into a dustbin of depression with the terrorists' attack. The world had changed. People had died, people dear to us were gone. Not only did the emergent creative ministries we were developing have to be paused; they were over. Individually and collectively, we felt a sorrow that what we had hoped would come to pass in the future, what we worked so hard to achieve—would now never happen. My heart sinks even to write this. Prior to 9/11 we had healthy disagreements and different ideas, but at that point we were part of a thriving team, working together to accomplish something. After 9/11, grief and frustration turned to anger and became a wedge between us. I had a hard time working through my anger, while my grief longed for proper acknowledgment and expression.

Behind anger might be fear, anxiety, overwhelming stress, outrage at injustice, jealousy, sadness, disappointment, and loneliness, as Brene Brown has pointed out.[4] All those emotions are responses to the frustrations of the noes life was giving me, including not being able to continue my grand experiment in liturgy driven by contemporary music and art forms; feeling the weight of the world on my shoulders urging me to respond in some constructive way to the 9/11 disaster; the ongoing pushback I got from church leadership for doing so.

What I have learned about the noes in life is that you can protest as long as you like, but it doesn't change what happened. You can spend a decade in resentments, being loyal to your suffering. It's a choice. I have also learned, though, that the best way to deal with a no is to grieve the loss, forgo blaming others, and make peace with it. In short, to learn the practice of forgiveness. Otherwise, you are arguing with your life. The reason this is futile has been expressed in a pithy quotation that is widely shared but often attributed to comedian Lily Tomlin: "Forgiveness means giving up all hope of a better past."

I had been given a no from life and I didn't have a clue as to what to do about it. I had been given something I didn't want. I didn't get something I wanted. I hadn't yet learned the importance of finding peace with that no.

In those heady and dark days at Ground Zero, I didn't yet have the skills—or the luxury of time—to process my anger in a healthy, constructive way. I had spoken often about forgiveness as a priest, but I didn't really understand it, and I certainly didn't know how to do it. But I learned.

6

The Grievance Begins

Responding to bureaucratic pushbacks from outside of Saint Paul's while managing the ongoing ministry within it felt like dancing on a tightrope that kept undulating and changing tension, minute by minute. The rapid action that urgent, critical needs on the ground dictated never seemed to align with what might satisfy church leadership. The constant stress led to anxiety, which bred insomnia and subsequent exhaustion. When I did sleep, I was bombarded with dreams that recounted the nightmare we had been living in and manifested my worst fears for the future.

One re-occurring dream featured body parts strewn across the devastated landscape of Ground Zero, scattered in the dirt, or were tangled up in the twisted steel and detritus. Other times, I would dream of being called before various iterations of church leadership, each gathered to belittle, denigrate, and ultimately dismiss me from my position. I also had panic dreams of logistical crises unfolding in the day-to-day operations of Saint Paul's: Had I sent someone to get milk for the nighttime coffees that sustained workers like a warm hug? Would the 4 a.m. delivery of breakfast arrive on time? Are we sufficiently stocked up on socks, raincoats, parkas, Band-Aids? Do we have enough Mentholatum for the workers to smudge it inside of their respirators to mask the unbearable scent of decaying bodies? Each dream surfaced my truest nightmare—that somehow, I would lose the battle to keep Saint Paul's mission going when it was still so desperately needed.

When I was serving at Grace Church, before coming to Trinity, a friend had commented to me I was the "Ice Man." I think it was intended as a compliment.

Somehow, when faced with challenges or adversity, I could usually keep my head. Even when all about me were "losing theirs and blaming it on me,"[1] she had said. But now, that sense of grounding was rapidly dissipating, like the ice in my sweet tea on a blazing August day. While I maintained a relatively smooth veneer, my inner world was in turmoil. I was becoming irritable and impatient. I lacked the skills to navigate a difficult marriage. I was an absent and sometimes impatient father. Not even the volunteers at Saint Paul's were immune to my occasional outbursts. My dreams did what they could to warn me, to provide a biopsy, a glimpse of the emotional tumors beginning to grow in my psyche. These were troubles that I had no ability to excise or treat, so I turned instead to nightly doses of Benadryl hoping that would help me sleep as dreamlessly as possible. At this juncture, my grievances grew like mold on a damp log in a rain forest, and this toxic blight, in turn, took a significant toll on my mental health.

Eventually, through a generous contribution by Lutheran Disaster Relief, I and countless others affected by the traumas of 9/11 were given access to EMDR therapy. EMDR, short for Eye Movement Desensitization and Reprocessing, is particularly suited to trauma victims because of the way it helps you reorganize and process your memories. An EMDR experience for me typically went something like this: the therapist would have me place headphones in my ears while instructing me to relax to the sounds of ocean waves gently crashing on the beach. Then he would slowly move a wand from side to side in my field of vision. After a minute or two of focusing on the movement, he'd ask me how I was feeling. Finally, speaking of my distress (this was therapy, after all), he would ask where I felt it and what it looked like. In what part of my body? In an organ? A limb? Was there a texture to it? A color? A few minutes later, with my eyes closed, and my brain would transport me into surprising and sometimes dramatic places in my imagination, kind of like a dream sequence in a movie beginning to play on a big screen in the cinema of my mind. This was accomplished through the combination of bilateral stimulation from the wand movement, ocean sounds, and the guidance of my therapist. It helped me to process and integrate the painful memories in a way that allowed me to feel more balanced and present in my life.

During one particularly vivid session of EMDR, my imagination took me to a hospital emergency room full of angst and stress. With a degree of detail that felt painfully real, I watched as the patient suddenly began to code. The cacophony of erratic beeps and whistles of the machines prompted the doctors and nurses as they shouted and responded to commands. A crash cart burst onto the scene. The patient was in serious trouble. And, as I watched the drama unfold, as my focus slowly became clearer, in shock, I saw that the patient was me. Only, of course, it was me. Time slowed as the doctors tried to save me, each loud beep, each alarm signal pleading for a response. But none came. In terror, I then noticed the walls and ceiling begin to shift, closing in around us. Time was running out. Just when I began to feel overwhelmed with anxiety, my therapist gently invited me back into the present moment. It took several minutes, but the visuals on the screen of my mind dissipated and faded to black. I opened my eyes, exhaled deeply, and was once again present and conversing with my therapist about what I had experienced.

The imagery of this ordeal was reminiscent of a classic scene in Star Wars, when Luke Skywalker and his companions, while rescuing Princess Leia from the Death Star, dove into a trash compactor to hide from the dark side's clone troopers. Little did they know, as they fought to save themselves from being crushed, that there was also a monster in residence just under their feet. Similarly, I had been crushed by my inability to deal with the challenge of irreconcilable demands. I felt squeezed by the garbage compactor that was the command-and-control structure of church leadership. There were a few monsters, too. EMDR therapy became a healing catharsis for me, a way for my brain to surface images like these while trying to process and integrate the trauma they held. EMDR therapy gave me clarity that my ongoing nightmares had not. While the dreams and anxiety had helped me see that I was in danger, I had no recognizable possibility for course correction until much later. I realized that both the stress and dangers of working at the Ground Zero site, because of compounding traumas in addition to the toxic air, could literally kill me. But I didn't have a clue as to what I could do with that knowledge, other than what I was already doing, and working with my therapist.

The clash between the demands of church leadership and Saint Paul's ministry intensified as the winter months arrived with more bodies being discovered on the site. Opportunities as consoling as a comforting Thanksgiving dinner (catered by the Waldorf Astoria) required battlefield decisions. Soon, everything church leadership asked of me risked tripping the hair-wire trigger of my growing reactivity. I became obsessed with keeping the ministry at Saint Paul's open at all costs and felt the need to play defense to do so. I wanted to protect the staff, the volunteers, and the vital ministry we were offering to the Ground Zero workers who relied on our support. They would come in from the cold, wiping tears from their eyes in response to something they had just seen or experienced, and we would offer them a haven to process their grief and find some measure of peace. I wasn't going to give that up without a fight. I just wasn't sure why it required a fight to begin with.

To be clear, my anger was not that I had been inconvenienced or even that I had been sabotaged while trying to host Thanksgiving dinner. But that I had found a way to reimagine the original dream of the Saint Paul's Initiative—of building a church community that helped people, that gave sustenance to the hungry and comfort to those afflicted. Naturally, I felt protective of that. It was a ministry that meant something, as measured by theologian Emil Brunner's idea of the church: "the church exists by mission the way a fire exists by burning."[2] Those of us working at Saint Paul's caught a glimpse of what the church could be: an agent of change for good in the world, ever-widening and ever-deepening the sphere of divine love and reconciliation, even as the world itself was on fire.

I often speak about "9/12" in the way rabbinic scholars might talk about the acts of God: This happened, but then the better happened as a response inspired by God. 9/11 happened, covered by every media outlet in the world. But another important story has always been the story of 9/12: how we got out of bed every morning after the attacks, responding with courage and compassion, and an urgent drive to rescue any and all survivors. We were, as I would often say, practicing the fine art of radical hospitality.[3] My greatest fear was not for my own life or circumstances, but that somehow church leadership would impose a no onto the yes that I felt God was calling our church to be.

I was not going to let them take this away from the workers and the city, the country and the world. I was not going to let them take it from me. At least, that was my thinking.

As a forgotten middle child growing up mostly without a father, as an Enneagram 3 seeking attention, as a dreamer deeply intoxicated with a missional understanding of the church, I was in too deep.[4] The work at Saint Paul's did wonders for my ego. I can now acknowledge the dangers of that dynamic, but simultaneously, the work itself was so much more. The church was becoming relevant, becoming real for so many who longed to see such a day. During the Christmas season in 2001, *TimeOut Magazine* declared that getting a shift volunteering at Saint Paul's was greater than getting highly sought-after tickets to see the Broadway musical *The Producers*. We even had a Jewish volunteer asking if his child could be bar-mitzvahed at Saint Paul's. How could we not fight for such an extraordinary community?

One night, weary after a long shift, I stepped into the N&R subway across the street from Saint Paul's for a late commute home. The subway was practically empty, the platform placid with a less frequent arrival of trains that time of night, the air still for wont of activity and people. One or two other riders waited with me, while a saxophonist played from his own world. He riffed on the notes from the quixotic hymn "The Impossible Dream" from the musical *Man of La Mancha*, broadcasting them gently into the void of the train tunnels. The mellow tune echoed, filling the space with the energy of a knight-errant longing to somehow meet the pressing challenges of his time. The sax player offered a musical meditation, and my mind conjured the lyrics:

> "To dream the impossible dream
> To fight the unbeatable foe . . . ."

Standing there in a moment of sublime beauty, I couldn't believe it. This was my song. I have always been seduced by that dream, ever since I heard Jim Nabors (who portrayed Gomer Pyle on TV—"Shazam!") sing it when I was a child. In that moment, I was floored. How could God or the universe or my lucky stars provide for me such extraordinary encouragement—just when I needed it the most? With tears welling up in my eyes, I nodded to this subway minstrel my deep gratitude and respect for his gift, a blessing worth a thousand times more than the $5 I dropped into his basket. The muse I didn't know I needed had arrived.

I was still humming along when the next train approached in the distance. The moment of timelessness shifted back into time—Kairos returning to Chronos, a sense of an eternal moment dissolving into the everyday—his parting notes left in me a swell of pride and the inspiration I needed to redouble my efforts in leading Saint Paul's. As the subway doors opened, in my own world, I sang the final words with gusto, out loud: "to march into Hell for a Heavenly cause." Other riders on the train, startled, looked up nervously for a moment, then shrugged and let it go. This was, after all, a subway in New York City. I smiled sheepishly and sat down.

Day after day at Saint Paul's, I felt we fought the good fight, marching on behalf of our heavenly cause. But we had no idea that a substantial and surprising frontal assault would soon appear. At about the same time, every year, the church performed an audit on one of its departments—a thorough evaluation that involves, among other things, questioning every aspect of the work carried out in the previous year, and evaluating it relative to its mission and goals. The strategic objective is to see how things are going and how they can be improved, to lay the groundwork for gains in efficiency and productivity the following year.

In February 2002, the vicar announced that Trinity's yearly audit would be of the Ground Zero ministries of Saint Paul's Chapel. It seemed strange to me that Saint Paul's would need to be audited, since by the very nature of things, I could see no future for our Ground Zero mission beyond the aftermath of 9/11. Were we seriously planning to do another World Trade Center type relief mission once the clearing and recovery operation at Ground Zero was over? Of course not. More than that, I found it ridiculous that I was required to participate in this audit while already working twelve hours a day. In hindsight I can see the benefit to administering some kind of audit at this critical juncture, but in the urgency that was my everyday life at the time, it felt counterproductive. In my head space, unfortunately, I could only see the Breed audit as a threat. With my grievances occupying more and more real estate in my mind, I couldn't see this as anything but harassment. In my limited perspective, born of trauma, i did the best I could. I wondered if this was the beginning of the hit job that my nightmares had been warning me about.

Soon after it was decided that Saint Paul's Ground Zero mission would be audited, a member of the committee came up to Saint Paul's with a six-page, double-spaced questionnaire in hand to give me. In some ways, it was a boilerplate evaluation. Much of it, I felt, was irrelevant to an ad hoc operation like the one at Saint Paul's, and there was a significant concentration on financial management: Were there bookkeeping manuals? Were there lists of procedures? What checks and balances and financial controls were there? To be sure, the Saint Paul's mission was expensive, about $3,500 per day as the rector confirmed in the *New York Times*.[5] But as the final report would confirm, the donations significantly outpaced the expenses.[6]

I felt that it was as if, the day after 9/11, we were supposed to have taken an administrative day, with time to write out several different operating manuals before doing anything at all—as if anyone could have known what would be required of us or what might unfold. No one knew beforehand that we would end up getting food from hundreds of suppliers so we could produce nearly 3,000 meals a day at the mission's height. Or that we would find it supportive to host three concerts a day. Or that we would need to provide not only supplies but foot care, massages, and other services to the workers whose brutal task seemed as though it would never end. We had, early on, developed a mission statement with procedures and protocols, as best we could. But none of these things could have been predicted, yet the inquiries seemed to presume, at least to me, that it all should have been planned for and budgeted and executed to logistical perfection.

In addition to the templated questions that most audits include, there were pointed ones as well. A series of questions about the donation boxes located in Saint Paul's seemed especially prosecutorial in tone: Who was in charge of these? Who emptied them? Who recorded the amounts? Who carried the money to Trinity Church? I'd been extremely careful around those boxes, realizing that even the remotest possibility of abuse needed to be considered. Even so, the answer to every single one of these questions was the same: Trinity Church's security staff. No one on Saint Paul's staff had anything to do with donation boxes. Adding perceived insult to injury, I was given the questionnaire late one afternoon, with an expectation that I have it completed by the following morning. When I protested, given that I had already worked such a long day with still much more to do, I was told I could just write short answers in the margins and that I needn't worry about complete sentences.

I'd had my differences with church leadership, but nothing like the unfairness I felt in this audit. Its tone felt prosecutorial, crushing, like the trash compactor was finally succeeding in its work. The whole business of this inquisition felt like interrupting a surgeon in the middle of an open-heart procedure demanding to know what size shoe the patient wears. And when the report was finalized and issued, I was mortified to find my responses to the questionnaire I was given was reproduced as "Exhibit A" in the final draft of the report in my opinion inferring that it was an example of my lack of cooperation and inability to manage the operation. In great contrast to the inspiration I felt born of my quixotic visitation in the subway, with the publication of the Breed Report, I don't think I've ever felt so alone.

I worried that the Breed Report's release would be devastating for our team's morale, so I only shared it on a "need to know" basis. I hadn't wanted to share it with the staff who'd been working so hard for so long, because it didn't have anything to do with the real Saint Paul's—the living, breathing Saint Paul's they'd created. It classified the thousands of children's letters hanging on the walls and pews, lovingly sent by young people from all over the world, as fire hazards that needed to be discarded. And while everyone working at Ground Zero worked in a toxic context, the report disregarded the spaces for healing that we'd created with a blanket declaration that the ministry was a threat to public health—what I felt were statements accusing me of dereliction of duty, as though we were the risk and not the respite. In addition to accusing me of dereliction of duty, infraction of rules, and negligent paperwork, it named liability, fire safety, public health, housekeeping, and security issues as reasons that "consideration should be given to a total shutdown of operations . . . to return Saint Paul's to its ministry as a beautiful chapel."

I shared concerns for safety; it doesn't have to be either/or. But now I could only ask what could be more beautiful than to retreat to the tender comfort of encouraging letters from children after a day spent digging for the remains of the dead? The "Dear Firefighter" letter from the little Claudia Fischer in Scarsdale, NY, had proven priceless (and has since proved to be timeless). What could be more beautiful than a cup of hot cocoa served with kindness and love, to warm both heart and soul? That NYPD officer Gail Douglas described as an "experience of Heaven in the midst of Hell." What could be more beautiful than a podiatrist lovingly tending to the wounded feet of men and women who worked in the longest burning fire in US history? George Washington's box pew served as the podiatry station, unquestioningly its greatest use in hundreds of years. What could be more beautiful than a cot outfitted with a teddy bear, pillows, and a blanket, all lovingly placed by volunteers who knew the healing power of a good nap and a loving embrace? What could be more beautiful than the banner calling us to COURAGE? Jessica Stammen and other art students at Cooper Union crafted these for us as more than decorations, much like the elementary students in Michigan who assembled their handprints into a giant American flag. Again, I ask, what could be more beautiful?

The cards and letters from heartbroken family members of loved ones lost on 9/11 were not hazards to be discarded. They were relics, elegiacally displayed as an acknowledgment of our collective unmitigated grief. Instead of seeing fire hazards, we saw icons—sacred marks of hope and beauty. These icons were signs of life standing against the carnage and death embodied by Ground Zero just a few yards away. They were sacramental—sanctifying our beloved community, inspiring us to carry on.

In short, the Breed Report felt like the monster under our feet. It felt to me like the manifestation of a hydra—a mythical sea monster crouching in the mystical waters of Greek antiquity. The hydra had multiple heads, with the ability to regenerate more. For every head that is cut off, the hydra will grow two to replace the severed one. And for every perceived attack on the mission of Saint Paul's that we addressed, two more seemed to take its place. The walls and ceiling of Ground Zero were closing in, and it felt like hungry beasts of destruction were roaming through our sanctuary. I was in a crisis that I neither knew how to diagnose nor address. I couldn't conjure any artful ways to navigate this unfolding catastrophe.

Again, Fred Luskin explains that one understanding of forgiveness is making peace with the word no. We get many yesses in life but, to be sure, every one of us will also get some noes: you didn't get the job, the marriage didn't work out, your mother got cancer, you got cancer, the hurricane destroyed your home. This is part of the universal human condition. And even if you live a charmed life from birth forward, you will, like everyone else, get the ultimate no from life when death finally arrives. Or, to rephrase it with a bit of levity that has been attributed widely, one comedian conjured: "the biggest problem with life is that none of us is going to get out alive!"

When we get a no from life, instead of making peace with it, often we tend to push back, forming a grievance. This is a very natural human response. A grievance is created when something happens that we didn't want to have happen or when something didn't happen that we wished would happen. A grievance is incomplete grief. Instead of grieving our loss, going through its stages (Kubler-Ross) and finding acceptance, in grievance we often look for and fixate on someone or something to blame. And usually, there are plenty of options.

At this acutely painful time of my life, a monsoon of noes had threatened to drown me alive, starting with the event of 9/11 itself. It was one of the most dramatic and decisive noes anyone could receive. And I was one of the lucky ones, in contrast with those who lost their lives or loved ones that day. Compared to this grieving community of people, my losses were insignificant. But while in comparison my losses were not extreme, my losses, nevertheless, were significant for me. The no I received was the death of a dream, a loss that had devastating repercussions. The chance to lead the Saint Paul's Initiative was one of the most extraordinary opportunities I had ever been given. That brief moment of service had reaffirmed my belief in a world of hope and love, a cosmos full of potential and possibilities. That world now felt gone for me, and I hadn't fully grieved its passing before being thrown headlong into my post 9/11 world of crisis and urgency. Like many people struggling with grievances, I didn't have the luxury of time or space to heal. Life rarely unfolds in orderly sequences. While the pre-9/11 Saint Paul's Initiative had ended, in its wake, a new community emerged. We found another way to be the church, another way to live out our baptismal commitment of love and service. But now the succession of noes that followed—and kept coming—threatened to turn the lost dream into a veritable nightmare.

Because grievance stories, by their very nature, are one-sided, I judged anyone who disagreed with me as wrong. To be clear: I had good reason to feel wronged by the actions of church leadership. But I had no power to do anything about that. As I process my experience, looking at what I did and what I could do, I can see that I tried making sense of what happened to me by playing the blame game. And there were plenty of legitimate options for placing my blame. But what it took me so many years to understand is that when you blame, *you stay the same*. I can't change the past, including how I felt or how I responded at the time. But using the tools and insights of forgiveness, I can begin to untangle the Gordian knot of grievance that had become my life.

While I had a legitimate right to feel wronged, psychologically understood, blame can be seen as a defense mechanism that helps us avoid confronting our own heartache by projecting responsibility onto another person. Blaming becomes a way to temporarily relieve ourselves of personal accountability and still maintain a positive self-image. But in the long term, it's not a successful strategy for living your life. In 1968, psychologist Dr. Stephen Karpman created a social model called the Karpman Drama Triangle that includes three roles: rescuer, persecutor, and victim.[7] The rescuer is always seeking to help, the persecutor often carries a negative energy that stifles relationships, and the victim always finds himself at the mercy of others. The victim's story is all about "what they did to me."

To be sure, most of us have been victimized in some way by life or circumstances, but it is up to us to decide whether we will adopt the toxic and weak mental framework of the victim. The biggest problem with being a victim is that we give up our power and agency. No matter how circumstances might change, the victim is resigned to accept, unhappily, whatever "they" do to him. This mindset is poisonous. Nelson Mandela, the former President of South Africa, once said that "Resentment (i.e., not to forgive) is like drinking poison and waiting for your enemies to die."[8] The problem was, in my victimhood, I drank a lot of that poison. And if I am honest, it tasted good. But every time I took a sip, a part of me died.

In contrast to the victim of Karpman's drama triangle, another role has been identified by one of Karpman's colleagues, David Emerald. In his social model known as The Empowerment Dynamic, the role of creator rises heroically above life's challenges.[9] Creators assess their challenges, cut their losses, and take responsibility for their lives. Overcoming and forgiving the changes and chances of life, the creator courageously rises—again, like a kite—against the wind, not with it. Facing these provocations, the mentally and spiritually tough creator decides where to put emphasis. No better example of a person who could have remained a victim but instead chose the heroic path of creator is Nelson Mandela. After being imprisoned for 27 years, he was released and became one of the most important political figures in the twentieth century as the president of South Africa. Becoming president, he chose not to focus on the grievances that would provoke a bloodbath at the hands of the oppressed, but to seek solutions that would make South Africa a vital and viable country.[10]

In our forgiveness work, the role of creator is synonymous with "hero"—the protagonist. While the victim is always a minor player in someone else's story ("look what they did to me"), the hero claims agency and charts a new direction for himself. There is a whole body of research supporting the idea that if you change your story, you will change your life.[11] The problem is, once you're in a victim's spiral, it's nearly impossible to contravene the gravitational pull to chart a new, more constructive, life-affirming course.

But unbeknownst to me, the work of forgiveness was beginning to lay a claim on my life. If there was one day at Ground Zero and Saint Paul's Chapel that was more prescient than others, it was the day Michael Lapsley, a South African priest and exemplar of forgiveness, visited with us. Father Michael was one of the first white clerics to stand against the Apartheid regime in South Africa that President Mandela and Archbishop Tutu stood against. Joining them in the call for an end to the cruel, racist practices of the South African Apartheid government, he decried the context in which citizens were ranked in order of importance: white, brown, then black. This practice of discrimination and the vicious methods used to enforce it were horrific. In 1990, in repayment for his stance against Apartheid, Father Michael received a bomb in the mail that brutally severed both arms and blinded him in one eye. It was a barbarous and savage act visited upon a truly heroic man.[12]

I asked Father Michael to preside at our daily Eucharist at Saint Paul's. As I got to know him, I came to have the deepest respect for him and the way he presented himself to the world—no blame, no self-pity, no grievance—all with a wicked sense of humor to boot. When he joined us for lunch and was offered a cup of split pea with ham soup, he gently ribbed the server for such a challenging option given his disability. "Really?" he said with a twinkle in his eyes. With the server's face aghast, Michael followed quickly with, "No! I'm kidding. Let me have it. I'm starving!" He then masterfully navigated the consumption of split pea soup from a Styrofoam cup, using hooks for hands.

I marveled at this extraordinary man who, despite all his challenges, was still fostering a light and loving heart. His sermon that day continues to resonate powerfully with me: it was about moving from being a victim to living victoriously through the power of forgiveness. Forgiveness? How could he speak of forgiveness after such brutality and suffering? I thought I knew a bit about forgiveness as a priest myself, but I didn't have a clue as to what strange superpower he was summoning. It was beyond my comprehension.

While personally stewing in grievances that paled in comparison to any he could have rightfully claimed, I assisted Michael at the altar. There, amid the cacophonous sounds of daily life in Saint Paul's Chapel, we once again offered prayers and blessings in this hectic haven of sacred busy-ness. Because of the potential dangers of snoring competing with the communion service, firefighters and police officers and other ground zero workers self-designated the first sections of pews to be off-limits for napping when the communion service was happening. But the continuous crinkle of cellophane-wrapped sandwiches from the popular local supermarket, Zabar's, the pop-fizz of soda cans being opened, walkie-talkies squeaking and squawking, and urgent conversations whispered in the shadows—these were additional sacrament experiences of our blessed community. Even so, time stood still yet again as I assisted at mass, in total awe.

Father Michael lifted the Eucharistic host with prosthetic arms, cradling the body of Christ in the hooks that replaced his hands. When this man of sacred wounds and an unscarred heart reverently elevated and broke the bread, the quiet, jarring crack sent chills down my spine. I was spellbound. A visceral sense of the broken body of Christ's love permeated my own brokenness that day in a way that I didn't and still can't find the words to express. It was truly a mystery. The healing work of forgiveness had presented itself to me. Much later, I learned that we are not able to forgive until we are ready.

I had been given an invitation, but clearly, looking back, I was not yet ready to respond.

7

Indulging the Revenge Fantasy

After the Breed Report, I felt completely vulnerable. The men who held power over our future, whom I'd admired and been so honored to work alongside, I felt would not tell me the rules of the game, let alone why I seemed to be losing the latest round of play. Case in point: Back in October, the rector had insisted I stay in touch with him directly, emphatically waving his telephone as he said to "Call me!" if I needed anything. Now, he wouldn't even speak to me without the vicar present, admonishing me for not knowing the protocol better when I requested a time to update him on the state of things at Ground Zero.

I thought I'd gotten used to the enigmatic inconsistency of such large-scale systemic politics, but honestly, I was completely taken aback. I had finally decided to ask him for advice on dealing with the structural issues that separated Saint Paul's from Trinity and him from me. I wanted to talk about a *reasonable* end scenario for our ministry, with adjustments that reflected the current state of things. And because I believed the rector felt positively about my leadership even if he didn't approve of everything I did, I wanted his guidance on interacting with the vicar. Technically, that meant I *was* attempting an end-around. But I was desperate, and I believed he had welcomed such communication. What I didn't realize, nor understand, at the time is that no one knew the rules of this game. It was entirely new, and none of us, top management included, had any idea of how best to respond to the unfolding crisis before us.

Soon after my chain-of-command faux pas, I was summoned to meet with both the rector and the vicar in a formal capacity: they wished to speak with me at 74 Trinity Place—HQ. A pall of dread fell over the whole of Saint Paul's as everyone, including me, fully expected that I would be fired. The leaders of our mission had even begun to strategize about the fallout. How would the staff respond? The Ground Zero community? The media? Most importantly, how would we keep our services running? How would we keep our blessed community alive? For whatever reason, I clung to keeping this ministry going at all costs, like a sacred talisman, without realizing the receipts would soon come due. The support of our staff kept my underinflated psychological inner tube afloat, but I continued bobbing through waves of panic and peace while I held on for dear life, fearing at any moment I might drown.

Before I left for the meeting, I sat for a moment in the same sacristy where Mahalia Jackson had flooded my headphones in preparation for the planned worship services just before 9/11. Her soulful renditions of "You'll Never Walk Alone" and "Precious Lord Take My Hand" once again gave me a sense of courage and resolve. I took out one of my Trinity business cards as I hummed bits and pieces of the melodies, running my thumb over the embossed "three-hundred-years-old" logo. Without pausing to think why, I turned it over and wrote the words "I am a Free Man." Then I placed the card in the shirt pocket just over my heart and began my procession to the tower of power—the oak-lined office on the twenty-fifth floor, where the rector had watched in horror as the events of that fateful morning collapsed the world around us.

With my heart pounding in my throat and one hand discreetly over the card in my pocket, I was ushered into what had all the trappings of a "come to Jesus" meeting. Between Mahalia and my note to self, I felt prepared to meet whatever comeuppance they had in store. I might not survive as an employee, but I would survive with my honor and dignity as a human being intact. I had done the best I could in such extreme circumstances, and I would remain free to continue doing my best no matter how those circumstances changed. However, absolutely nothing had prepared me for the first salvo to fire as a *consultation* rather than a dressing down.

They wanted *my* advice. What date might *we* consider for the closure of Saint Paul's mission? When could *we* begin scaling operations back? What were *our* objectives for the work for the next few weeks? What thoughts did *I* have? I was flabbergasted. For the first time, I felt that my input was welcomed—that I was on a team rather than working against one. Unfortunately, I had no definitive answers for their queries. Things were indeed slowing down at the site, but that could change on a dime. Looking at the ceiling, trying to pluck out some significant date, I floated Easter. Easter, it was.

Easter was about two months away and, in my mind, seemed like an eternity. Provided there weren't any further traumatic discoveries at the site, it seemed like a safe bet for closing the ministry. Surely, all the bodies would be recovered by Easter. Then again, I have been known to miss a projection or two. Back in September, the vicar cautioned me about getting too involved in the work at Ground Zero. He said, "Lyndon, if you're not careful, you'll still be doing this work at Thanksgiving." My dismissal had not aged well: *There's no way we'll still be doing this by Thanksgiving*. Now that Thanksgiving had come and gone, I added the provision that, if needs changed before Easter, we'd need to reconsider. They accepted my terms with a sense of finality that let me know they would hold me accountable for that end date, and so they did. The Breed Report was Exhibit 1 in the argument for closing Saint Paul's, but now these arguments were accompanied by a timeline and frequent reminders that I *myself* had agreed to close Saint Paul's Chapel on Easter.

I regretted the date almost immediately.

I hoped to maintain the camaraderie I'd felt when the "come to Jesus" ... into a consultation, but my updates about the site were not ... ness as my projected closing date had. As Easter ... had in fact changed, and we were down ... out 3,500 at the height of our food service. ... at our work was far from over. Many of the ... Chapel, and their spiritual and psychological ... as ever.

While our mission at Saint Paul's was to support the workers at Ground Zero, their work was now to clear the site of the many remains left to account for. Dirt and debris would be carefully searched for signs of humanity, then hauled off to a garbage dump on Staten Island.[1] Ground Zero workers were finding more and more bodies in the decimated twists of metal, sometimes uncovering large groups of victims who had huddled together in their final moments. The closer the workers got to the bottom of the pit, the more the trauma of these discoveries compounded against the grief-filled knowledge that so many more would never be recovered and identified, giving some measure of closure. By late winter, we were running out of dirt, and their pain was visible, palpable, and searing. In my amateurish attempt to process this grief through song, I wrote the refrain, "250 thousand tons of steel couldn't compare to the weight we'd feel if we didn't do our best to try and find the rest . . . we're not leaving until the job is done . . . gonna keeping searching, gotta find everyone . . ."[2]

The work, the brutally cold nights, and the approaching end of the ministry drenched the site with a collective depression, seeping into every last corner like a storm surge after a king tide. A burly construction worker would begin sobbing in the dinner line; police officers once again sat in the pews at all hours, holding that thousand-yard stare; firefighters were, at times, inconsolable. Some took it out in anger, some in drinking. Others were terribly, dreadfully quiet. The workers desperately needed encouragement and support. Meanwhile, we were implementing a plan to replace our four-meals-a-day food service with coffee and donuts.

I frequently spoke to the vicar about these concerns, reminding him the agreement was that we would consider revising these plans based on the urgent needs at the site. I explained that the new conditions made it impossible for us to close at Easter, that we were needed now more than ever. He agree
with me that the pastoral needs accompanying the recent finds made the
rationale he had heard yet for keeping Saint Paul's open. I hoped that
our concerns would be passed up the chain of command, since I wa
to convey information directly to the rector myself. In the comp
of the institution, however, these conversations never seemed t
top. Or, if they did, nothing happened.

Several weeks into Lent, during a Sunday morning service at Trinity Church, the rector announced that Saint Paul's Chapel would in fact close at Easter. He reported that, on December 31, Trinity had received a notice from the city's Department of Environmental Protection that the Chapel had to be thoroughly cleaned. That all the banners and letters and cards from children must go, all the food service and supply tables needed to be removed, all the cots for sleeping disassembled, and all the walls and floors needed to be scrubbed of any remaining residue. And plans were being made to do just that. A few days later, the vicar commented in the *New York Times* that, once the Chapel was thoroughly cleaned, it would be opened to minister to the "urgent, unique, spiritual needs of a community that is recovering but still grieving from the terrible tragedy."[3]

I felt like I'd been kicked in the stomach. While initially I had been part of the decision to close SPC on Easter, I had hoped my petitions to keep SPC open would have been heard and accepted. It was as if all my pleading was for nought.

None of the concerns I had expressed created their hoped-for results. The announcement came without consideration of my interim updates or with any advance warning. I only found out when folks came up to me at Saint Paul's after church that Sunday asking, "So what's this about us closing?"

On Palm Sunday morning, I began the Eucharistic liturgy for the 8:00 a.m. congregation with a heavy heart. I felt privileged to preside at the service for this beautiful, beloved community on one of the high holy days of the Christian liturgical calendar. The day is associated with the color red, representing the Passion of Jesus, and was the theme of the worship that day. So, with little optimism for the future, I donned one of the most spectacular vestments I have ever seen or worn: the red patch chasuble of Saint Paul's. (Figure 7.1)

Early in the Ground Zero operation, a Roman Catholic friend of Saint Paul's had gifted us this chasuble and stole, one that his mother had made for him on the occasion of his ordination to the priesthood. As it sat hanging in the corner closest to the sacristy of Saint Paul's, someone on the night shift started adding patches to it. One by one, signifiers of the various ladders, brigades, squads, units, and companies serving at Ground Zero were safety-pinned to the thick

Figure 7.1 *LH in Red patch chasuble.*

red fabric. Before long, the chasuble became heavy with the representation of all who worked so hard at the site. Patches were added by the day, a touching point of pride for the groups of men and women who came from near and far to contribute their efforts. It was a beautiful outward sign that their work was connected with the healing work of God. Its weight on my shoulders became a physical manifestation of the profound responsibility I felt in caring for these extraordinary human beings.

At the beginning of every liturgy, I got my bearings by connecting visually with the HOPE banner, a sacred icon of inspiration made by schoolchildren in Charlotte, North Carolina. Against a bright yellow background, the word "hope" was spelled out in many colors and surrounded by the precious multi-colored handprints of children. I had always wanted to have this made into an altar frontal, since for me there was no more important message to be imparted from Ground Zero. "Dum spiro, spero." My mother inhabited this hopeful belief in God's love and mercy and she passed it along to her children. I can still remember the strength in her voice as she would remind us of this. She insisted that God would never leave us or forsake us, and that somehow God felt our pain, and deeply cared. Often, when reminding us of this, she would say, "Look at my arms. See the goosebumps? God is here with us now." With a child's wide eyes, sure I was witnessing some kind of mystical incantation I couldn't understand, her words took root in my heart. The experience grew over the years, becoming a kind of spiritual mantra for me—an insistent belief that God has compassion for us, literally meaning to "suffer with" (cum-passio) us in our sorrows and brokenness.

Only, that morning, as I adjusted the chasuble and turned to gaze toward the gallery in the back, all the oxygen left the room as I discovered the banner was gone.

In Dante's disquisition on Hell, there is a sign at the entrance of the fiery pit: "Abandon hope all ye who enter here."[4] I truly felt like we had been going through Hell, but I hadn't realized that we'd stopped there. In that moment of profound sadness, I wondered when hope had abandoned us.

Yet, on that same day—March 24, 2002—unbeknownst to me at that time, an explosive article had been published featuring the staff, volunteers, and workers who had all expressed their anger, dismay, and immense grief at the announcement that Saint Paul's would be closing.[5] Trinity's director of press relations, John Allen, had given permission for the New York *Times* reporter, Tina Kelley, to do the story, and she gathered quotes from many of those who came to the Chapel regularly. One firefighter was quoted as saying, "Good things usually don't last anyway." Mike Bellone dug deeper: "We feel like we're being orphaned . . . how many bones and arms and hands can you pick up in a day before it gets to you? You come in here, and they put a smile on your face. They help you keep your faith." Most tellingly of all, Rob Schwarz, a priest friend who would brace himself at Saint Paul's before many a shift at the temporary morgue, declared, "This church has never been holier in its whole history. This is what it means to be a sacred place. To close Saint Paul's on Easter is like rolling the rock back in front of the tomb."

Without realizing what had been set in motion and without knowing where the HOPE banner had gone, I continued the liturgy. I wondered if I too might soon be gone. Dejection and despair swirled in my head like a tempest out on the Hudson River, matching the mood of the day's readings. Palm Sunday is about a parade that goes bad. In the beginning of the liturgy, the readings from Luke's gospel (Lk. 19:28-40) show Jesus arriving on a humble donkey as the crowds gather and throw palms on the ground before him. Initially, they shout hosannahs and celebrate his coming by saying, "Blessed is he who comes in the name of the Lord." But by the end of the reading, the very same crowds shout for his crucifixion.

Finally, at the sharing of the peace, I departed the inner sanctum behind the altar rails and moved out into the congregation for customary greetings, offering a handshake or a hug to the people in attendance. That's when I realized the HOPE banner wasn't gone at all—it had only been moved—closer to the altar. There, having left the sanctuary and joining the people I cared so much about, hope had found another way to surprise me.

From then on, it became clear that hope lived in and with the people. Doug Rice, one of our loyal congregation members and a tireless volunteer, was one such man. Having just returned from a trip to Mexico, he whipped out a twenty peso note from his wallet and bet me that we would stay open. I accepted, and we put the twenty pesos in a hymnal where it remained until the end of the operation.

The publication of Tina Kelley's article sparked a groundswell of protest. Rumors flew about possible picketing of Trinity during Holy Week services and on Easter Sunday. There was even talk of workers marching to Trinity offices to stage a sit-down strike. I had no idea if this was true. I didn't want to ask. However sympathetic I was to the possibility of protest, I expected I would be wrongfully blamed for having orchestrated such actions, even if my dejected attitude might have fomented them. I had never felt closer to Jesus on Palm Sunday and his journey toward Jerusalem—I, too, felt like I was riding a slow donkey to my demise. Even so, volunteers and clergy constantly called Trinity to complain about the closure. If the rector and the vicar got half the letters and calls that I got, and I'm sure they probably got thousands more, they could see a clear opposition emerging. The shutdown of Saint Paul's would not happen without a public spectacle.

We were demoralized, but the job of relating to the workers and those grieved by 9/11 was too important simply to slacken our efforts. If Saint Paul's had to

They wanted *my* advice. What date might *we* consider for the closure of Saint Paul's mission? When could *we* begin scaling operations back? What were *our* objectives for the work for the next few weeks? What thoughts did *I* have? I was flabbergasted. For the first time, I felt that my input was welcomed—that I was on a team rather than working against one. Unfortunately, I had no definitive answers for their queries. Things were indeed slowing down at the site, but that could change on a dime. Looking at the ceiling, trying to pluck out some significant date, I floated Easter. Easter, it was.

Easter was about two months away and, in my mind, seemed like an eternity. Provided there weren't any further traumatic discoveries at the site, it seemed like a safe bet for closing the ministry. Surely, all the bodies would be recovered by Easter. Then again, I have been known to miss a projection or two. Back in September, the vicar cautioned me about getting too involved in the work at Ground Zero. He said, "Lyndon, if you're not careful, you'll still be doing this work at Thanksgiving." My dismissal had not aged well: *There's no way we'll still be doing this by Thanksgiving.* Now that Thanksgiving had come and gone, I added the provision that, if needs changed before Easter, we'd need to reconsider. They accepted my terms with a sense of finality that let me know they would hold me accountable for that end date, and so they did. The Breed Report was Exhibit 1 in the argument for closing Saint Paul's, but now these arguments were accompanied by a timeline and frequent reminders that I *myself* had agreed to close Saint Paul's Chapel on Easter.

I regretted the date almost immediately.

I hoped to maintain the camaraderie I'd felt when the "come to Jesus" meeting turned into a consultation, but my updates about the site were not met with the same openness as my projected closing date had. As Easter approached, the situation at the site had in fact changed, and we were down to about 1,500 meals a day, from about 3,500 at the height of our food service. But it was also becoming clear that our work was far from over. Many of the workers were still sleeping at the Chapel, and their spiritual and psychological conditions were just as tenuous as ever.

While our mission at Saint Paul's was to support the workers at Ground Zero, their work was now to clear the site of the many remains left to account for. Dirt and debris would be carefully searched for signs of humanity, then hauled off to a garbage dump on Staten Island.[1] Ground Zero workers were finding more and more bodies in the decimated twists of metal, sometimes uncovering large groups of victims who had huddled together in their final moments. The closer the workers got to the bottom of the pit, the more the trauma of these discoveries compounded against the grief-filled knowledge that so many more would never be recovered and identified, giving some measure of closure. By late winter, we were running out of dirt, and their pain was visible, palpable, and searing. In my amateurish attempt to process this grief through song, I wrote the refrain, "250 thousand tons of steel couldn't compare to the weight we'd feel if we didn't do our best to try and find the rest . . . we're not leaving until the job is done . . . gonna keeping searching, gotta find everyone . . ."[2]

The work, the brutally cold nights, and the approaching end of the ministry drenched the site with a collective depression, seeping into every last corner like a storm surge after a king tide. A burly construction worker would begin sobbing in the dinner line; police officers once again sat in the pews at all hours, holding that thousand-yard stare; firefighters were, at times, inconsolable. Some took it out in anger, some in drinking. Others were terribly, dreadfully quiet. The workers desperately needed encouragement and support. Meanwhile, we were implementing a plan to replace our four-meals-a-day food service with coffee and donuts.

I frequently spoke to the vicar about these concerns, reminding him the agreement was that we would consider revising these plans based on the urgent needs at the site. I explained that the new conditions made it impossible for us to close at Easter, that we were needed now more than ever. He agreed with me that the pastoral needs accompanying the recent finds made the best rationale he had heard yet for keeping Saint Paul's open. I hoped that meant our concerns would be passed up the chain of command, since I was not free to convey information directly to the rector myself. In the complicated maze of the institution, however, these conversations never seemed to make it to the top. Or, if they did, nothing happened.

close, we wanted to take its ministry "outside the walls." Several staff members had joined me in hatching a plan to continue the relief ministry begun at Saint Paul's with a nonprofit that we were calling the 9/12 Foundation and, later, the 9/12 Community. Since it would be very complicated and a possible conflict of interest for me to lead this effort, it fell to the members of my staff who, we acknowledged, would soon be out of a job anyway due to their temporary work status. We hoped to be operating by Easter night—one week later—at a location that we hadn't yet found but fully trusted would materialize.

In one such staff meeting, tucked into our makeshift conference room upstairs, I began our session in my gravest tone of voice, thanking them for their hard work and for helping us reclaim our humanity in the face of a violence that sought to strip us of it. I told them that, in my gratitude, I had brought something to encourage them in our work. Then I slowly pulled out of my jacket pocket a Jesus action figure doll I had just bought at a funky little shop a few blocks north of us in Greenwich Village. Brandishing him with a flourish, I exclaimed that "Action Figure Jesus" was on our side. Their expressions turned from puzzlement to smiles, and with nagging groans of "*oh Padre . . .*" more than a few eyes rolled at my corny attempt at humor. Someone later commented that 10,000 comedians were out of work and here I was trying to be funny. But there was no doubt in my mind that even an action figure Jesus would have been flipping illegal burgers at the Barbeque on Broadway and washing the blistered and traumatized feet of the men and women whose work boots had burned in the hellish fires of Ground Zero.

Meanwhile, other wheels were turning. Someone interceded on our behalf, calling the New York City Department of Design and Construction, asking for their help. In response, Commissioner Kenneth Holden of the DDC sent a letter to Trinity requesting that the Chapel remain open.[6] In response, the vicar acknowledged spending a sleepless night worrying about the situation. But the rector was, by my estimation, truly surprised by the public response to the announcement of the closing. He even came to Saint Paul's, angry to see that I had not yet made plans to stage the closing. But the work of Saint Paul's mission was not even slowing, and he seemed unaware of the continuing, urgent needs of those working in the Pit. This, in turn, surprised *me*. How could he, as rector, be so out of touch with the reality on the ground?

On Monday of Holy Week, the day after Tina Kelley's article rocked all of Ground Zero, I was on a conference call with lawyers discussing the 9/12 Foundation when an urgent message came up from Trinity by walkie talkie. Once again, I had been summoned to 74 Trinity Place. This time, I was to report *immediately*. I cut my call short and left in a New York minute, just as requested. As soon as I arrived, John told me, with no trace of irritation or guile, that they had decided to keep the chapel open. They also needed a comment about this decision from me for the church's press release, and I was as shocked as I was elated to contribute and, at the same time, wary about what might come next. With faltering trust, I gave them a statement that would be faxed to the chapel that same afternoon: "We are delighted that we are able to respond to the request of the City of New York to keep the doors of Saint Paul's open to the police officers, firefighters and rescue workers as they complete their tasks at the site."[7]

With the release in hand, I rang the bell in the sacristy that was typically reserved for the beginning of the Eucharist. I then read the announcement out loud as everyone in the Chapel burst into cheers and clapping. The musicians made a joyful noise. Hugs were shared. Police officers surrounded and embraced Sister Grace. A construction worker in filthy Carhartt coveralls lifted Katherine Avery off her feet and swung her around in circles. The only thing missing from our celebration was the champagne!

To add to the festivities, Martin Cowart, our food service manager, received a middle-of-the-night call from a very generous man in Hawaii, not asking us *if* we would like to have fresh fish and fresh orchid leis, but informing him that they *would be* arriving. Martin made arrangements to get a truck to the airport, not knowing exactly what was coming or when, and the gift of aloha turned out to be thousands of beautiful orchid leis and hundreds of pounds of fresh tuna, *plus* pineapples. Martin masterfully figured out a way to prepare the tuna, and anyone within the orbit of Saint Paul's Chapel on Easter 2002 was adorned with a beautiful orchid lei. The televised coverage of the Pit on Easter weekend shows many of the workers wearing leis that they had received from Saint Paul's.

More than flowers bloomed on that Easter Day. The whole of Saint Paul's was gaily bedecked with leis, banners, posters, paper chains, and origami cranes. Our congregation wore their Easter best and Kevlar vests—some bright and shining, others covered with dust and dirt, and all sharing in the hope that Easter brings. I spoke that morning of the sacrificial love shown in the plenitude of financial donations we'd received, the offering of time by our volunteers, and the hard work done by rescue and construction workers. Adding to our celebration, a retired NYPD officer brought his 5-month-old twin daughters, Isabella Rose and Emma Elizabeth Guagliardo, to be baptized. "It's a joy," their father said, "not only to bring them into the family, but to do it under such adverse conditions. It's a feeling of resurrection."

Perhaps the only sad note that weekend was the news that Sister Grace had been requested to return to her training at the convent in Boston. Before she left that day, Sister Grace and I went for a walk outside, into the graveyard that surrounds Saint Paul's. She wanted to show me the miracle of new birth that she spotted in one of our trees. Across Church Street, the Pit now seemed orderly and organized, although the roar of the cranes reminded us of the final clean-up efforts that remained. The graveyard at Saint Paul's Chapel had been cleaned as well, though the trees were still dusty, with pieces of debris still held in their branches. There she pointed to two birds busily building a nest next to a twisted section of Levolor blinds, repurposing paper they'd found that had once been in offices. They were chirping happily as they made their home out of the detritus. It was such a beautiful hopeful sight for me. I took this opportunity to express to Grace my enormous gratitude for her service and courage as her time with us was coming to an end. There in the graveyard, full of emotions, we remembered together how things looked in October when she'd joined us: the smoke, the devastation, the sirens screaming, the filth, and the acrid smell of the site. But, most importantly, we gave thanks to God for the love that sustained us all. Our Lenten season had been long—201 days from our "Ash Tuesday" to the day that Easter became real for us. Sister Grace, barely having begun her novitiate (training) as a nun, had shown up right after 9/11 with the biggest heart imaginable as she went to work supporting the sacred work we were doing together, all of us, at Saint Paul's Chapel. It was hard for me to imagine Saint Paul's without Sister/Sargeant Grace.

Looking back on this powerful moment, as the future of the Ground Zero ministry of Saint Paul's was reasonably secure, I truly had gotten everything I had asked for. The mission was spared. It would continue at the level of services I wanted, full speed ahead. Indeed, I was euphoric about keeping the ministry going, comforted that we could continue to serve. But the euphoria was fleeting, tainted by grievances I couldn't let go of, memories of subterfuge I couldn't forgive, nightmares I couldn't shake.

In all honesty, even the celebrations that week had been diluted by the growing list of grievances I had begun to harbor. Take, for example, the day that I signed off on the press release and rang the bells in the chapel. My ecstasy in announcing to a cheering crowd that Saint Paul's would remain open had just about the shortest life cycle imaginable. Later that very afternoon, the vicar called me to yet another meeting. This time, I was asked to devise a plan to scale down the food service to coffee, donuts, and bagels.

As the Spirit would have it, that *same evening* I got a phone call from Edwin Moore of the Federation of Protestant Welfare Agencies who, in conjunction with the New York Times Neediest Fund, declared that they wanted to underwrite the entire expense of the food service at Saint Paul's for the remainder of the operation. *What were the odds?!* I knew about the New York Times Neediest Fund but had no idea that it could be allocated for a ministry such as ours, or that there was even such a thing as the Federation of Protestant Welfare Agencies. In the end, the *Times* and the Federation of Protestant Welfare Agencies wrote checks totaling nearly $200,000, covering the food service expenses at Saint Paul's from Easter until June.[8] This generosity assured that we could finish our work in the same style and manner that we had begun: a loving and generous expression of radical hospitality offered with deep gratitude for the workers. The ministry at Saint Paul's had dodged yet another bullet, and truly, God had wiped the tears of sorrow from our eyes and replaced them with tears of joy. The dream was alive again. The community had been spared—yet another time. I asked Edwin to fax that commitment in writing to Trinity so it could be considered at the next morning's budget meeting, then I bellowed out for Martin and Katherine and Sister Grace and anyone within earshot: "Y'all won't *believe* this!"

It was hard to metabolize such rapid-fire switching between emotional extremes. How can you go from joy to depression and back to joy in the span of a few hours? I was extremely happy to reach so many highs, but I didn't have the emotional skills to let the low moments go. My victim's narrative was only dormant, not released. I showed up on September 12 and almost every day after that to oversee an operation that grew to over 15,000 volunteer shifts served, 12 hours at a time, for months on end, and I wanted them to acknowledge me for my work. I wanted them to express gratitude for the way I had led the mission.

To be as clear as I possibly can be: it was all of us who did the work, not just me, and I had no desire to take undue credit. I simply wanted, as a neglected son of an abusive father, to hear my spiritual fathers say, "Well done, Lyndon."

But it was not to be.

In fact, the most painful act of disrespect that I felt was yet to come. Later that spring, in 2002, Trinity TV produced a highly promoted documentary on the mission of Saint Paul's, and it was widely anticipated. The premiere debuted at The New York Historical Society, and it seemed the whole city—influential community leaders, church leaders, academics, politicians, and people of good will—came out for it. For 22 minutes, the gathered crowd watched the story of this great work of healing and mercy. I joined them in eager anticipation. Surely the forgotten child in me would finally be acknowledged. Minute by minute, my heart sank in humiliation as I realized none of it had been enough. I was not in a single frame. Not starting the operation, not overseeing it for close to nine months, not scarred lungs, not PTSD or depression—none of it was enough to earn even a single frame of recognition in their film.

Over time, my grievances descended deeper into the emotional no-man's land of a revenge fantasy, a barely contained rage that hovered over even the good times like a ghost roaming a wasteland of wrongs at a grievance convention. I wanted to stand up for myself; I was proud of the work that I did and couldn't understand why they weren't. I wanted to let folks know that I had been slighted—but as the revenge fantasy grew, so did the malice in these desires. In the absence of the love I had hoped they'd display, I decided I wanted to shame them, not only for the struggles we faced to keep the chapel open, but for what I was convinced was an ongoing attempt to humiliate *me*. I couldn't help taking things way too personally. I couldn't let go of the fact that I had to fight so hard for our mission—a community clearly inspired, in my opinion, by the compassionate teachings of Jesus—against a church leadership team supposedly adhering to the same principles.

But the heat of battle, the haze of grievance and the fog of my own intransigence blinded me. I couldn't see what my need to be "right" was costing me. Ultimately, I wanted church leadership to apologize to me for what my ego saw as a series of blatant wrongs because it was, to my understanding of forgiveness at the time, necessary to my ability to move on. To forgive an offender, they had to first make an apology, express remorse, and if necessary, make amends. Far from expressing contrition or making an apology, church leadership didn't even see my dilemma as anything important enough to acknowledge. I felt disposable.

Why did I feel this way? Was it just an ego trip of acknowledgment I was looking for? Why did it upset me so much that I felt church leadership was working to erase me? If it's recognition I wanted, then the whole world had already acknowledged my work. I received distinguished alumnus awards from all three institutions of higher learning I had attended. My work had been applauded in the *Christian Science Monitor* in their "People Making a Difference" column.[9] Countless articles in the *New York Times*, The *Washington Post*, *Time Magazine*, and many other smaller regional papers and news outlets had acknowledged me as the leader of the ministry at Saint Paul's Chapel. We even had a song dedicated to us on the national radio program, *A Prairie Home Companion*.[10] Why was that not enough?

If I didn't get acknowledged for successful completion of a mid-level project or giving a good sermon, I could get over that. But I was putting my health at risk to do heroic work (that I am proud of), and events like cutting me out of the Saint Paul's story at the New York Historical Society felt like a malicious mendacious assault to erase me. There were many articles and events, with many glad conversations about the miracle of Saint Paul's, but these glowing generic references were incomplete, and each time I heard them, they stung. Why? Because they cut me out. I wasn't the be-all and end-all of the ministry at Saint Paul's Chapel, and I'll be the first to say that. But to be painfully clear: the Saint Paul's ministry didn't rise up out of the ether, it didn't create itself *ex nihilo*, and it certainly didn't miraculously run itself, as it was insinuated countless times. I started the 9/11 outreach by gathering a small group of volunteers in the scary lonely days (no other Trinity clergy were there) following the 9/11 attacks that grew into an enormous cohort of 15,000 volunteers. And for the next 8.5 months (over 240+ days), I showed up to oversee the ministry, to guide it along, and to keep people safe. I'm not saying I was perfect, or that I didn't make mistakes. But I felt I was under assault in an unjust strategy to erase me.

And later, after leaving Trinity/Saint Paul's for the Cathedral of Saint John the Divine, this painful diminishment continued. Upon my arrival, the dean asked the rector for a comment about my work for the cathedral newsletter. What he got back was "Remarkable. Unbelievable. It affected hundreds of volunteers. He was trying to ride herd on chaos and he handled it very well."[11] At first glance, this comment should be seen as complimentary, but for one—like myself—who was looking for negative inferences, what I saw was an example of what the ancient philosopher Favorinus describes as being "damned by faint praise."[12] With over 15,000 volunteers serving over half a million meals, our efforts obviously touched more than a few hundred people. Feeling "damned by faint praise," I tried to take it as yet another bitter pill to swallow, an assault on my character. I never believed the adage "No good deed goes unpunished" but I was beginning to. I tried to move on as best I could, but I was angered by what I felt was the pettiness of the rector's response.

To leave out or withhold acknowledgment of one's work, or to "damn by faint praise," is usually an attempt to humiliate the person in question. Favorinus held that being damned by faint praise is a backhanded way to diminish the person in question that is malicious—more harmful even than harsh critique. Already in a vulnerable place, these unkindnesses hurt me deeply. If that was the intention, they worked. I was devastated. I couldn't help but wonder what I had done to make myself such an object of scorn.

I felt left out in other ways too. When significant events happened or dignitaries visited, even though I was a subway ride away, I wasn't invited. To honor the amazing work of Saint Paul's Chapel's ministry to Ground Zero after 9/11 with President Bush and President Vaclav Havel, the person who started and oversaw the amazing ministry that was being honored (me) *wasn't invited.* In 2004, a significant photographic tribute to the rescue mission of Saint Paul's, entitled "Unwavering Spirit,"[13] was developed inside Saint Paul's, and countless visitors flocked from all over the world to see it. Using several of the photos I had taken and happily shared (without attribution), in the few photos in the exhibit that included me, I was listed as a "volunteer." A *volunteer*!

But why did these unkindnesses wound me so deeply? For so long? And why couldn't I let them go? The short answer is that the people whose influence held great sway over me—my spiritual fathers—I felt would not acknowledge my work. I could shrug it off and pretend that these perceived slights didn't hurt me, but I would be lying. For a while I tried gaslighting myself, telling myself that it didn't really matter. But it did. Profoundly. For an "achiever" who longs for external validation to feel successful, this unwillingness to acknowledge me felt like a disowning. Research shows that when individuals feel unacknowledged, the brain understands this as a potential social threat, leading to the release of cortisol and adrenaline, a physiological stress response.[14] The stress hormones of cortisol and adrenaline took the place of the dopamine and oxytocin my nervous system longed for and caused significant physiological stress and damage to me.

One of the reasons I couldn't let this diminishment go was that I felt that if I did, then what happened to me somehow didn't matter. Or, that how I was treated was somehow OK. To be clear: it does matter and it's not OK. But what I didn't understand at the time is that forgiveness is something we do for ourselves, and it is not dependent on the other party apologizing or even acknowledging any perceived transgressions. It would surely be helpful and life-giving if they did. But, as Lew Smedes said, forgiveness is "setting a prisoner free and realizing, after the fact, that the prisoner was you."[15] Because of my inability to process adequately my anger over being diminished, I was not only in prison; I was in emotional solitary confinement in a supermax lockup.

The most ironic part of it all was that I perceived myself to be free, even as my anger continued to build more and more silos of unforgiveness around me. Each time I felt insulted as a leader or felt that my character was assaulted by those I'd once aspired to follow, I believed my defensiveness to be born of righteous anger, and it was as headstrong as it was persistent. That place in my heart where I carried this wounding was closed off. It was a place so compacted that the energies of life for new beginnings were nearly impossible to generate. When I wrote "I am a free man" on that business card, I wanted to project myself as tough, untouchable by the assaults. But the truth is, I was hurt. Deeply. And some part of me had begun to fantasize about hurting them back.

I know the idea of a revenge fantasy in the context of church life seems contrary and unsavory. But it is as human and natural as the day is long. How many stories can you think of in which that satisfying moment of vengeance is achieved? *Yippee-ki-yay!* as the actor Bruce Willis might put it.

Movies about revenge are beloved because we find a certain catharsis in them. Any person, even a priest, who carries a grievance and nurtures a victim's narrative can be seduced by a desire for revenge. We appear to be hardwired for it, as Professor Everitt Worthington has pointed out.[16] According to the National Institute of Health, one psychological benefit of a revenge fantasy can be a temporary sense of restored power and control, allowing someone who feels wronged to mentally "punish" the perpetrator, potentially alleviating negative emotions like frustration, humiliation, and anger by imagining a scenario where justice is served, even if only in their mind. It essentially provides a sense of closure or balance after experiencing a perceived injustice.[17]

This desire for revenge, in hindsight, was understandable. My life had long been out of control, and by hating church leadership, I was able to regain a (temporary, false) sense of control. I thought that I wanted justice to be served, but in my short-sightedness, I had come to see justice as "just us"—things that needed to be done *just our way*. And I was blinded to the beam in my own eye: my festering resentments prohibited any positive constructive way to move forward with my superiors.

Revenge is the very opposite of justice. Revenge is motivated by anger, fear, and hatred. It is emotional and subjective. Justice, on the other hand, is objective and rational, motivated by compassion, empathy, and understanding. Revenge spirals into endless cycles of give and take, while justice seeks to bring about closure. Revenge is about seeking retaliation; justice is about seeking balance. I wanted revenge. I wanted them to suffer. I didn't have any particular kind of suffering in mind, except maybe a measure of humiliation that came from them being shamed for what I felt was pettiness and subterfuge. I wanted them to be found out for what they had done, and in my revenge fantasy, I wanted the world to agree with me that their actions were un-Christian and cruel. But that didn't happen. And because of these desires for revenge, my heart became hardened, making it difficult for *anything* beautiful to grow there, let alone justice.

Revenge fantasies can make us feel better in the short run. They enable us to marshal the energy to see beyond our sense of despair and victimhood. But if we hold onto them, over time, revenge fantasies only cement our connection to the offender in a way that ensures that our own sense of victimhood continues, with all the bitterness and depression it ever had. A Chinese proverb says that the person who seeks revenge should dig two graves. Lew Smedes said, "The problem with revenge is that it never evens the score. It ties both the injured and the injurer to an escalator of pain. Both are stuck on the escalator as long as parity is demanded, and the escalator never stops."[18] A desire for revenge causes us to fixate on the hurt and make a caricature of the perceived offender, perpetually defining him by the perceived wrong. Neither of these will help build a more beautiful peaceful world. But when we are able to forgive, foregoing revenge, as Smedes continues, "you cut a malignant tumor out of your inner life."[19] At this point in my journey, I had neither the knowledge nor the ability to do this. I knew well the Gandhi quotation, "An eye for an eye leaves both eyes blind" but, ironically, I just couldn't see it.

Prolonged revenge fantasies create an illusion of optimism: *if only they would . . . then we could set things back on their proper trajectory*. But optimism is a passive mimic of hope, and there's no future at all in revenge.

Hope, on the other hand, is action-oriented. It requires agency and determination, and it expects us to actively work toward a desired result. To be a person of hope is to move forward, continuing to do our best—despite our challenges—to make a difference in the world.

John Wesley's Methodist dictum has always been an inspiration for me: "Do all the good you can, by all the means you can, in all the ways you can, in all the places you can, at all the times you can, to all the people you can, as long as ever you can."[20] But clearly, if I am expending my energy nursing a revenge fantasy, I am far from doing the best I can.

8

The Last Day (Unenforceable Rules)

With the final cleanup mission at Ground Zero completed, June 9 marked the official closure of Saint Paul's Chapel's mission to Ground Zero. As it approached, we made our plans to say goodbye. On June 5, a warm Wednesday afternoon, we set aside time for folks to share their thoughts about what Saint Paul's had meant to them. We had microphones galore, and dozens of media outlets were present for the occasion. Anyone who wanted to do so was invited to speak. There were anecdotes about the comfort they had found while working together through such a trying time. There were speeches honoring our work and acknowledging our necessary closing now that the work was completed. Tender and touching comments came from the hearts of a dozen or more people, with most preferring to express their gratitude one-on-one and peer to peer rather than engaging a microphone.

One of our regulars, a construction worker named Tom Geraghty, offered a particularly poignant reflection. He shared that he had lost his sister-in-law in the attacks, and after which, he had cursed God. How could God allow his sister and 3,000 innocent others to be murdered in such a horrific way? Where was God, and why had he abandoned us? But, Tom said, his visits to Saint Paul's had warmed his heart and brought him comfort. The loving connection he shared with volunteers and other workers brought him a measure of peace. Then he offered his own unforgettable paraphrase of the words of Jesus in Matthew 25. Eloquently rephrasing the words of Jesus, he said, "When I was hungry, you were a little café on Broadway. When I was exhausted, you were a bedroom. When I was at my wit's end, you were a therapist's couch. When I needed inspiration, you were an art gallery and a concert hall. Thank you."

I stood watching, tears streaming from my eyes, while the whole Saint Paul's team was similarly affected. What more could anyone say? What more could I have wished for our little church and our work in the face of such a big catastrophe? His comments confirmed my deepest hope for Saint Paul's: to clothe the beleaguered, help heal the sick, feed the hungry, and give hope to men and women who worked daily in the hell of hope's absence. As I saw it, we had truly been the church as Jesus might have envisioned it.

The next day, after saying our media-public good-byes, I walked over to Ground Zero to join the thousands of people who'd come for the formal closing of the WTC site. It was a clear, beautiful spring day with a brisk wind blowing across the sixteen acres of cleared ground. So different from the war zone I had witnessed the morning of September 12, 2001. Different from the site I found myself visiting constantly—whether paying pastoral visits, performing last rites on body bags, or delivering supplies. Although I was happy to see the clearing was done, I was painfully aware that the hopes of so many firefighters and police officers to find the remains of all the dead, particularly their brothers and sisters in arms, would not come to fruition. We had finally run out of dirt. This cavernous hole in the ground, however pristine, symbolized the gaping hole in our hearts. Through our hearts ran a huge river, continuing through the subterranean caverns of the city and snaking in and out of all our consciousness; its name is grief. It occurred to me that it would take years, maybe decades, to redirect that river and fully recover. To this day, I am reminded of a comment made by Tom Synan, one of the faithful chaplains at Ground Zero: "Jesus didn't say 'Blessed are those who have closure'; he said, 'blessed are those who mourn.'" We need to look, not for closure—what is *closure*?—but for healing." *Amen Tom.*

At exactly 10:29 a.m., the same time that the North Tower had collapsed, a fire engine bell rang the traditional signal for a fallen firefighter: four sets of five rings. Then, as a single drum beat a cadence, fifteen people representing twelve agencies and groups carried a stretcher that was empty except for a folded

American flag. Representatives of the FBI, ATF, the utilities, the families of the lost, and all the multitudes who'd worked on the cleanup formed a single line on each side of the six-story ramp as the stretcher was carried to a waiting Fire Department ambulance. All of us gathered there watched quietly, thinking about the thousand people for whom fire, explosion, or collapse left not a trace to be found.

After the stretcher was placed in the ambulance, a bagpipe band, pipes silent, marched slowly ahead of a huge truck carrying a single 58-ton steel beam covered with black muslin and an American flag. Beneath the muslin were painted farewells, including the numbers lost from the New York Fire Department (343), Port Authority police (37), and New York Police Department (23). The truck began its slow climb up the same ramp, accompanied by a single police officer in dress uniform. When the truck reached the ambulance, it stopped, taps were sounded, and pipers played "America the Beautiful." Then, after a pause, the crowd burst into applause, a slow quiet ripple of hands clapping that went on and on, unlike any I'd ever heard before. Thousands of people mournfully, thankfully, applauded as the work came to an end. Bravo. Well done.

After the truck and the ambulance drove away, I returned to Saint Paul's Chapel wanting to cry but unable to find tears. I felt relieved that we were able to serve these courageous men and women throughout the entire recovery phase. I felt overwhelmed as I thought about the next few days in the life of Saint Paul's Chapel. I felt anxious because I knew that I too would soon be saying goodbye to Saint Paul's and all the things we were able to accomplish there.

For all the grandeur we felt for the eight and a half months we served as a respite center, the chapel now seemed kind of flat—the way your high school feels the day after graduation. What's next? How do you keep up with your friends, fellow graduates who have shared the deepest life experiences, people who you swear you'll keep in touch with but deep down know you won't? A flood of memories washed over me, and as I sat in a secluded pew in the silent chapel, I found my tears. I wept as I gave thanks to God for this rare and extraordinary privilege of being part of such a resilient community. I had been given a glimpse of the kingdom of God, and I knew it would haunt me for the rest of my life. Once you've tasted fine wine, it's hard to go back to drinking anything less.

At noon that final Sunday, the sacristy bell rang as it had every day since our world fell apart. With a grateful heart, I donned the hallowed red patch chasuble that had become such a symbol of our work together and led the congregation in the Eucharist for the last time. I looked out on the congregation and thought about the profound journey we had traveled together. We had dipped our toes into the waters of a great mystery, and each one of us, to a person, had been transformed by it. "Blessed be God, Father, Son and Holy Spirit. And blessed be God's kingdom now and always. Amen."

That afternoon, we held a celebration of our community, this time with the roles reversed. Firefighters, police officers, and construction workers took a turn serving the community of servants that had so caringly served them for so many months. Gail Douglas, the police officer who had helped so much in making access available for our incoming supply trucks, was surrounded by a huge group of volunteers who had gathered to enjoy her warmth and spirit, as she shared her experiences and expressed her gratitude. John Misha, the lovely retired firefighter with the biggest heart ever, came to give us a hug while we wiped tears from the corners of our eyes. It was a reunion of sorts, a family reunion in which we genuinely enjoyed everyone who came. There was the beloved staff who helped make this whole experience possible—Katherine Avery, Martin Cowart, Courtney Cowart, Fred Burnham, Diane Reiners, Carter Booth, and Dennis Fisin. Pamela Wells, who'd started the music program at Saint Paul's, and Ralph Faris, who'd carried it on so magnificently after her, gathered with us, as did our utility infielder volunteer, Barbara Horn, along with Susan Weinman and many other volunteers from all over the city and country. Mary Morris and a host of the clergy volunteers who'd helped were there, along with chiropractors, massage therapists, and mental health workers. The rector and the vicar, and other Trinity staff members, including the cleaning and security teams, Mike Borrero, Jim Doran, and Tom Morgenstern, came to the Chapel to join us for the closing.

After we'd enjoyed our meal and each other's company, Francis Ginzburg, a gifted opera singer, sang "Amazing Grace," and after that, someone asked

Ralph Faris to accompany Francis as she sang "Ave Maria." Ralph had not played it since he was 13 years old, but it flowed out perfectly nonetheless, a beautiful and sacred moment that none of us present will ever forget. Next, some volunteers asked Ralph and the small band of musicians from the Arts Healing Cooperative, "Can you play Hatikvah?"

"Hey," Ralph said, "Every New York musician can play Hatikva."

When he finished, he asked, "What would you like next?"

"Hava Nagilah"—and "Let us rejoice" it was, as the band swung into action, pounding it note for note. Saint Paul's Chapel, from the start of its 9/11 mission, was foundationally interfaith and all faiths. B'nai Jeshurin Synagogue had brought the largest number of volunteers to serve. Rabbi Gelman, from Long Island, a member of the "God Squad," had joined me in offering a service of Hanukkah for his congregation. I'll never forget his sermon, a sermon in which he expressed his reserve about the commercialization of the miracle of the lights, but stammered, visibly moved, that this year of all years, in a Christian chapel no less, he truly felt the spirit of Hanukkah. It was breathtaking to experience the interfaith reality of Saint Paul's, as volunteers from all over the chapel felt the energy and began to gather from the gallery, from the sacristy, from the porch outside where they were reminiscing, all to join in the sacred dance. As the music grew wilder, they danced faster and faster, panting and sweating. Our ministry had begun with a conga line and now would end with the hora, that same spirit intact. All around the little chapel that stood, the community of beloved volunteers and workers whirled and bounced and ducked and roared with laughter, defying the powers of death. *L'Chaim! ("To Life!")*

Eventually, the music tapered off, the family members and Ground Zero workers began to depart, and my thoughts turned to other things. As with each wave of emotion throughout this journey, an undercurrent pulled at me in the form of one repeating question: *Why?* Why did this have to be so hard? Wasn't it challenging enough to try to respond to a crisis of gigantic proportions? Why did I have to spend so much time and energy just trying to keep one step ahead of attacks threatening Saint Paul's closure?

This questioning was intensified by the next bit of work to be done—that night, we had to take all the icons down. The vicar had scheduled a team of cleaners to come to Saint Paul's the very next morning to remove any cards or letters, banners, and memorabilia in order to do a deep clean of the place, and if any of it was to be preserved, it would be our responsibility to do so. I resented that, to say the least. Couldn't we at least have a day to breathe? After 270 days of a 24/7 operation? But a dedicated team of volunteers joined me in pulling one last all-nighter to take down the cards and letters from children, the banners of encouragement from all over the world, and the sacred items of remembrance hanging on the walls and fences of Saint Paul's.

Ralph Ferris stayed with us after the music ended and worked alongside us through the night. While taking down and lovingly cradling these sacred mementos of our time together, I was reminded of the liturgical practice of stripping the altar on Good Friday. Many churches observe this liturgical ceremony as a conveyance of sacred heartbreak and despair upon the death of Jesus. The experience mirrors the act of taking Jesus from the cross to the tomb, conveying that all is lost. More than just a speed bump on the way to Easter Sunday and the resurrection we now know is coming, it's a reminder that in our human experience we must go through the dark night of betrayal and despair, the hopelessness of Gethsemane and the crucifixion, without any knowledge of what might be on the other side.

My ruminating mind landed on the memory of a talk I had given at the Mind-Body Institute at Harvard Medical School back in December 2001. I hadn't a clue what to say back then, so I did the kind of thing I used to do for worship at Saint Paul's before 9/11: I made a video. I compiled the images that I and others had taken of the tender, overwhelming moments that happened every day at the Ground Zero site—scenes of men and women facing extreme conditions as they sought to find any survivors and then, ultimately, the remains of the dead. The video contained images of some of the very items we were removing, set to a song that had touched me deeply, "It's Not Easy (Being Me)" by the group, "Five for Fighting."

The narrator of the song is a vulnerable Superman in the midst of an existential crisis. He confesses that he actually doesn't like to fly, and that it's absurd for people to think that he doesn't have feelings or fears, even if he is a so-called "man of steel." He divulges that his mission—to protect humanity from bad actors and evil villains—is very difficult for him because he carries with him an unresolved grief of "a home that I'll never see," since Superman's father sent him toward Earth before his home planet Krypton was destroyed. He continues his unburdening soliloquy plaintively assessing that even heroes have the right to bleed and to dream.

Finally, in the bridge at the end of his existential aria, Superman takes a deep breath, straightens his cape, and reassures the world that he's got our backs: "You can all sleep sound tonight. I'm not crazy, or anything . . ." This tender confession felt emotionally resonant with the first responders who showed up in a crisis and were catapulted to hero status after 9/11, without acknowledging the painful price they would pay then, and now are paying, with their health's decline. Even today when I watch the video, I feel a lump in my throat and my eyes go watery. And at the Mind-Body Institute in December 2001, I don't think there was a dry eye in the audience.

In my own way, I, too, had identified with this wounded Superman. In fact, for my birthday in June 2002, over ribs at one of my favorite BBQ joints in Soho, my staff gifted me with a Superman t-shirt, although by then I identified more with the experience of kryptonite than with any heroism. That night felt like Good Friday and we "stripped the altar"—and all of Saint Paul's had surely become an altar. Working with Ralph that night I remembered the time I shared with him the video I made for the Mind-Body conference. Ralph said he had heard about my presentation and would like to see it. I happily complied. When it was over, he asked me what I thought of the strings. I said they were transcendent—pure emotion, and essential in conveying the experience of a vulnerable Superman. Ralph's reply shocked me: "Thank you," he said. Unbeknownst to me, Ralph was the violist for the recording. Ralph's participation in this song was more than just serendipity or chance; he himself knew the emotional truth of this song through his own heroic service to our friends and colleagues working at Ground Zero. I felt, and still feel, a deep bond of affection for Ralph, a brother who did everything we asked of him. And so much more.

By the middle of the night, we were exhausted, but unwavering. Our fortitude and resolve were commendable. But each time an item was removed, I wanted to cry out to say "no!" and fight the invisible villains of time and necessity who were asking us to unmake this sacred space. Taking the cards and letters from the walls, we could see the prevalence of Ground Zero dust covering the chapel in stark contrast with the clean wall space that had been safely hidden behind the children's masterpieces. I secretly worried about the health of our lungs. We had become acclimated to the presence of that mortal dust; now the facades were stripped away and the walls laid bare. This truly felt like Good Friday. In a right-side-up world, Good Friday comes *before* Easter.

Each item became a visceral reminder to me, not only that a hallowed time had passed, but that my days in leadership of this chapel were over. As the night wore on, I resigned myself to that fate. The depression seeped into my being like a bathtub quietly filling with tepid water with a funny smell. I was under no illusion that I might have any future at Saint Paul's, and that realization left me with a soupcon of sanguinity ladled over a mountain of grief.

Over and over, I ruminated about the conflict between SPC and church leadership:

Why couldn't they see what we were doing as important?

Had they been threatened by what we were doing?

Why couldn't they see things our way? MY way?

What I didn't and couldn't yet say was:

"How could I have done better?"

"What was my part in this conflict?"

But then the thought came to me that "priests should be priests." *Yes!* That was the essence of the conflict I had felt from the start. Making this declaration gave me a small sense of control. It was my attempt to navigate such enormous grief and my own inescapable vulnerability. Any expectation to the contrary, as many of our friends in twelve-step groups can attest, would be a future resentment waiting to happen. As dawn's early light seeped into our bleary-eyed consciousness, we solemnly placed the boxes of holy artifacts and relics, along with stacks and stacks of over 300 sanctified canvases, into a nondescript white van that Carter and Dennis had secured to take them to storage. I was never told where the storage facility would be. Nor did I ask. It was too painful. I had to let go.

In the days following the closure of Saint Paul's, I was listless, lost. I became more and more intractable in my sense of "rightness." Looking back, my sense of being right was itself an obstacle to working with my superiors. When we need to be right, we often don't allow room for creative exchange or dialogue. Yehuda Amichai, the poet laureate of Israel, wrote a beautiful poem describing this, entitled "From the place where we are right":

> From the place where we are right
> flowers will never grow
> in the spring.
> The place where we are right
> is hard and trampled
> like a yard.[1]

In the place where I was "right," my heart had become hard and trampled, and nothing could grow. No creative collaboration, no impromptu problem solving, no collegial give and take. I don't think I was the only one who shared this problem, but speaking only for myself, I had closed off any collaborative engagements that might have eased my relationship with my bosses and opened the door for constructive possibilities. The chess game was over; the only decision now was to decide how many more moves before I tip my king.

Individually, from the place where we are right, we *don't* have access to the most creative solutions for collaboration. To the hammer, everything is a nail. When we fixate on ideas of rightness, we create what the Stanford Forgiveness method calls "unenforceable rules." Unenforceable rules are rules that our minds create to help bring order to life's chaos, to try to provide a sense of control in the face of life's incredible vulnerabilities: Drivers on the freeway should drive carefully. My boss must treat me fairly. Priests should be priests. These are not bad ideas; they're vitally important. But the truth is we have no way to enforce them as rules. And that's where we get stuck. The longer we hold onto them, the more damage we do to ourselves. If we waited for all the bad drivers to hand in their keys and all bosses to be fair, we'd never drive and we'd never go to work.

Unenforceable rules are the mechanism underlying the grievances that are at the heart of unforgiveness. They are dangerous fictions that can set us back, generate an inordinate amount of misery, and paralyze our joyful engagement with life. When we are only able to see life as it "should" be, we miss out on life as it is. Shoulds and oughts are key indicators that you have an unenforceable rule. By declaring that "priests should be priests," my mind created a demand that anyone working as a priest had to agree with me. I was *right*, after all. I had it figured out. And my own stubbornness, along with the context of the crisis of 9/11, added cement to my already hardened position. But the challenge was, *I too was a priest.*

9

Museum or Mission?

Let me step outside the story for a bit to highlight the path to forgiveness so far. First, we get a no from life—something happens that you didn't want to have happen, or something didn't happen that you hoped would happen. Then our human tendency is to fixate on that. Instead of grieving fully, we subvert the grief process, take things too personally, and form a grievance by looking for someone, or something, to blame.[1] When we take things too personally, every difference is an assault, every conflict, personal. But that's not the full picture. The person who cut us off in traffic on the way to work this morning did not set his alarm and leave home in time to catch up to us and cut us off. When we take things too personally, blaming is a natural by-product. Blaming is a very natural human process and is necessary when assessing who is at fault in a conflict. For example, did you hit my car? Or did I hit yours? Whose insurance will pay? Blame is important for assessment, but after twenty years if you are still miserable in your life because of blaming a bad ex or a manipulative mother or an ungrateful boss, something is askew—you've spent too much time blaming.

And once we've assessed who's to blame, emotionally we contemplate our revenge. Everyone does it. It's natural. It's very human and it's useful. Just the thought of getting even helps restore some sense of emotional balance. But the desire for revenge is a phase, not a place to consecrate a basilica. To be sure, forgiveness is not saying that no one is at fault for the no we get—or give. Forgiveness does not mean we give up our right to seek justice. But as I have pointed out, justice is different from revenge. As a strategy for moving forward, blaming has a limited shelf life. Blaming keeps us stuck and the glue is our revenge fantasies. And when we blame, we stay the same. Blame is the fuel for making and maintaining a grievance. Blaming feels like revenge.

And if blame is the fuel of a grievance, then unenforceable rules are the catalysts, the spark plugs. They're our hope to keep the world safe and in our control. Unenforceable rules precipitate grievances. If we didn't have an unenforceable rule that life should be fair, then we wouldn't be as devastated when we find out it isn't. Unenforceable rules are our attempts to deal with the incredible vulnerabilities of life as we try to create some measure of safety. They can be identified by the use of the words "should" or "ought": my spouse *should* be faithful to me; my boss *ought* to treat me fairly; drivers on the freeway *ought* to drive safely; my father *shouldn't* get cancer. These are all important values, but what do we do when they are not followed? We have no way of enforcing them. When one of our unenforceable rules is violated, we can grieve the no we've gotten, seek recompense or justice, if possible, which is our right, and move on. Or we can stay stuck. Being stuck in blame and grievance is its own level of Hell, a spin cycle in a cosmic drying machine that overheats, runs up the power bill and uses sandpaper for dryer sheets. How long we stay in this hell is, to some degree, up to us. Not completely over your ex cheating on you? Or your neighbor continually parking in *your* parking place? Put another few dollars into the dryer and hop in. Take another spin in the grievance machine. Not enough? Take another year. Or two. Or fifteen. It's your life and you have agency to decide how long you stay in the spin cycle of blame. But it's hot, uncomfortable and, most likely, you'll shrink.

But there is a more excellent way: forgiveness. And while forgiveness isn't exactly a "Get out of Hell Free" card, it certainly helps. In fact, it's one of the few things that does. There can be no future without forgiveness as Archbishop Tutu said. In the forgiveness process the next step after identifying your unenforceable rule(s) is to see that your subjective opinion is not, and never is, the full picture. Forgiveness is not "forgive and forget." It's "forgive and remember differently." The way we remember differently is to acknowledge that reality is bigger than our subjective opinions of it and so to move forward toward health, we must seek a bigger perspective. We do that by acknowledging that our adversary is not evil and that we are not pure.[2]

One of the most important steps on the journey to forgiveness is to realize that your subjective experience is not the whole truth. We each only see as best we can from our own limited perspective. To reclaim our life through forgiveness requires seeing the bigger picture. Having said that, I didn't set out to be a thorn in the vicar or rector's side when I joined the staff at Trinity. And I didn't set out looking for people to antagonize. I had nothing but the fondest hopes for a partnership when I began work at Saint Paul's Chapel. I was elated to join the staff of such a powerful and esteemed church organization with its worldwide reach and impactful presence, under the leadership of Dan Matthews, the sixteenth rector of Trinity Church, a storied church of two hundred and ninety years when he began, and John Howard the vicar, his chosen second in command. Trinity Church is an influential church in the world and Dan and John were the church leaders who brought me on board to join the team.

Trinity has always been held in high esteem in my mind. I remember, as a seminary student in Sewanee, TN, receiving an announcement about the upcoming "Trinity Institute" in my student mailbox. Trinity Institute was courageous and brilliant, probing the borderlands between science and theology. I was so excited to learn about the institute's work of exploring the relationship between an ancient faith tradition and the very latest developments in modern understanding. I still remember holding that flyer, taking it in with a big smile and thinking to myself that, one day, maybe I could attend a Trinity Institute in New York City.

After moving to NYC in 1995, I attended my first Trinity Institute conference in the spring of 1996 and never missed a single Institute after that. I was immediately curious about a church that would sponsor such an offering. The vision of this kind of ministry, exploring the frontiers of Christian thought, Anglican spirituality, and pressing humanitarian issues of politics, justice, and contemporary communities, became a gold standard for me in how I dreamed of doing my own theological work.

Trinity has a powerful presence on Wall Street as well as a significant global reach for its influence and ministries. Trinity grants disburse millions of dollars each year to impact positively humanitarian and faith-based projects around the world. Right after I moved to NYC, I applied for an opportunity to travel in Africa through a Seminary Commission on Mission (SCOM) grant. I planned to spend a month exploring Uganda and Kenya, doing research on the experience of the church in East Africa. I was accepted and happened to be visiting Nairobi in July 1997 when the workers in Nairobi planned a strike for better wages.

It was called the "Saba Saba Saba March," meaning the seventh day of the seventh month with the year ending in seven (1997). The emphasis on seven is a reference to the Biblical sabbath, a day of rest. Unfortunately, the government decided to crack down on the workers, beating them as they retreated into the cathedral, where I was staying, and then tear-gassed the cathedral. This made front page news in the *New York Times* even before my family had heard from me.[3] The staff at the guest house suggested that I leave before a possible martial law went into effect. They took me to the airport where I caught the first available flight, which only went as far as Zanzibar—one of the most exotic places I'd even been to. I found hospitable accommodation at Saint Monica's Lodge, the Christ Church Cathedral guest house in the old Stone Town section. When I checked in at the accommodations desk the staff was delighted to hear that I lived in New York City. With a big smile, their next question to me was, "How is our dear friend Dan Matthews?"

Halfway around the world, on an unforeseen stopover on my journey, I refrained from telling them that NYC was home to 8 million people and that I didn't know Dan personally (at that time, anyway). Instead, I chose to respond, "He's doing very well, thank you, and sends his best regards."

I had followed Dan's ministry for a long time by that point, having distinguished himself as one of the great preachers and leaders of the modern Episcopal Church. I remembered hearing glowing stories of his leadership as rector of the large parish, Saint Luke's in Atlanta, Georgia, as he advocated for support of the homeless. I had even, on occasion, borrowed from his plethora of engaging sermon illustrations. While in seminary, I was placed at St Paul's in

Chattanooga, Tennessee, for my church internship. Dan's son, Danny, served there as well, a recently ordained priest at the time, who was more than kind in looking out for me.[4] One day, I remember riding with him to lunch as he picked up his mail. He was excited to find a package from his father—tapes of recent sermons that Dan often shared with him. It touched a tender place in my heart to see the beautiful love of father and son, working together in the noble cause of sharing the Good News of God with the world. Wistfully, I wondered how a paternal love such as that might feel.

One of my greatest heartbreaks during the rescue mission to Ground Zero is the loss of a sense of comradery I had felt initially from both vicar and rector. In my naivete, I couldn't fathom that we might have different ideas about how to respond to the crisis of 9/11. They were significantly more cautious than I was, and I am sure my leadership at times caused them distress. As my naivete has slowly grown into some measure of maturity, I've tried to work on my own vision until I could see more objectively, giving them the benefit of the doubt. They were human and had made decisions and actions that I disagreed with, just as they had many times made decisions I agreed with. But in the disagreements, I felt that my spiritual fathers, like my own father, had let me down. I didn't have the opportunity to understand the complexity of the circumstances they were facing.

In searching for a bigger, more objective view of the experience, one question I might ask is how did I let *them* down? How did my work, my actions after 9/11 run counter to their views or plans? They were generally in support of the work at Saint Paul's but seemed resistant at times to embrace any ideas I had for moving things forward. They were not present at the Chapel when many decisions needed to be made. In the complexity of the ongoing crisis at Ground Zero, things changed fast.

How did I frustrate their objectives? Some of it was because of my naivete—I had just joined the staff and hadn't yet learned the new language of the corporate ways of this church. But some of it was also born of my determination, my deliberate actions to guide the post 9/11 ministries at Saint Paul's in the way I thought best. To say that I can be hardheaded and driven would not be a surprise. It's hard for me to imagine how upsetting it must have been for them when I assumed the authority I wasn't given by my church contract. And to step out into uncharted territory after 9/11, the way the needs on the ground dictated. It was probably hard for them to imagine the predicament I faced in doing so. It was a crisis no contract could foretell; responding to 9/11 wasn't exactly in anyone's job description.

But for me to forgive and remember differently means trying to understand my part in the conflict and ways I acted that made things worse. When we "march into hell for a heavenly cause" we carry with us a whole lot of self-righteous judgments and opinions. How did I antagonize my superiors? I am sure there were countless ways. I have a placid exterior most of the time, living agreeably with those in my community. But when it comes to differing aims, when I become invested in one side or the other, I can be a fierce competitor. When the stakes are high, my competitive streak intensifies. At Ground Zero after 9/11, every day was game seven of the National Basketball Association world championship series. And I was fiercely protective of the work we were doing.

I hadn't taken the job at Trinity so that I'd build up these grievances and then be fired—I joined to partner with them to make a difference in the world. Correspondingly, they didn't hire me only to turn around and release me—their genuine hope was that we'd work together to accomplish great things for the kingdom of God. They entrusted a great treasure to me, and I was honored.

As I have matured, I see now that, at Saint Paul's Chapel after 9/11, there were competing concerns. The vicar was an earnestly pious man, a man of deep evangelical faith. He always wanted me to "seal the deal" in my preaching so that those present would give their hearts to Jesus. It is understandable that turning Saint Paul's Chapel from a prayerful Georgian chapel into a social services delivery center might offend his piety—a piety that preferred for Saint Paul's Chapel to maintain its role as a beautiful sanctuary where people connect with God spiritually, through quiet reflection and prayer.

In contrast to what I'd told the folks in Zanzibar, I still didn't know the rector that well personally since I was a relative newcomer on staff. But everything about him, at least as I understood it, seemed to be in support of the work of Saint Paul's after 9/11. What I didn't know, since I was the youngest priest on staff and the lowest person on the hierarchical totem pole, was the background level of concerns he undoubtedly addressed every day—dealing with a demanding vestry and powerful corporate officers, considering concerns of both liability and damage to a historical sacred building, financing for operations, and the media frenzy that attached to Saint Paul's immediately after 9/11. I can only imagine his own sleepless nights.

Nevertheless, it took a long time to widen the scope of my perspective to consider any of this. Unfortunately, this is the reality for most people. I was stuck in my grievance story, bound by chains of resentments that threatened to choke the life out of me. But forgiveness isn't possible until we address these resentments and grievances head-on, in two distinct ways. First, to understand them as subjective: a highly personal interpretation, driven largely by our ego's need to defend itself. Second, to consider the bigger picture: we widen our perspective by looking at our grievances more objectively—with a view to a broader understanding that is less ego-centered, more humble, and more inclusive.

Often when I teach forgiveness classes I start with an exercise on grievances to illustrate these points. A common grievance that many people share is the upset that comes when someone cuts you off in traffic. Our first reaction is that the person is a jerk and should receive a ticket for terrible driving. By the end of the exercise, however, I have widened the perspective on the so-called "jerk" (who cut us off in traffic) by being curious and asking questions. Who in fact knows the motivation of the man? Who's to say that the guy isn't a pediatric surgeon who has just been called into the hospital to perform emergency surgery on a child to save her life? We can't say one way or the other. Widening the perspective on this driver, giving him the benefit of the doubt, is exactly the thing I needed to do with regard to my feelings toward the rector and the vicar. And until I did that, I was not able to escape the chains of my own victim's narrative, that kept me imprisoned in bitterness, resentments, and misery—in a word, Hell.

Understanding this subjective/objective dichotomy is essential for releasing resentments and finding healing. When we acknowledge that our viewpoint is subjective and seek to understand things from a wider, more objective sightline, we take things less personally and are humbled to accept that we don't possess the full truth. Recognizing this opens our hearts and enables us to embrace the path of forgiveness more readily. Doing this, we widen our perspective, and we deepen the possibility for healing.

A more objective way to frame this specific conflict is through a systems approach. Fred Burnham, Saint Paul's Chapel's beloved "Monday night guy," was passionate about this. With advanced degrees in both science and theology, Fred fearlessly navigated the in-between places where my concerns and Trinity's concerns overlapped. One night, he came to Saint Paul's and asked for some time to have a conversation with me about the "emergent" properties of the Saint Paul's mission. Fred saw in the Saint Paul's mission the emergence of a "self-organizing system" which, according to his thinking, arises from the creative interplay between two contradictory forces he referred to as "order" and "freedom."

Fred explains: "In the new sciences of chaos and complexity, a self-organizing system is a collection of random material entities that come together suddenly and begin to act as a single organism. These 'complex systems' develop a remarkable adaptive capacity that allows them to shift on a dime in response to critical changes in their immediate environment."[5]

That certainly was true of our mission to Ground Zero. On any given day everything might have changed. In fact, every morning as I went to Saint Paul's I assumed everything *had* changed. That prepared me for the day. Fred continues: " . . . These systems thrive at 'the edge of chaos,' that fine line between their collective order and the freedom of their individual parts. If there is too much order in the system, then routinization, stagnation, and death will follow. If there is too much freedom, then anarchy, discord, and chaos result. Therefore, the critical life force within every complex natural system is this dynamic balance between order and freedom."[6]

Objectively, the delicate dance of order, freedom and chaos, of Trinity and Saint Paul's mission to Ground Zero was hammered out with fear and trembling, a desire to serve, and the hope for a better day. Whether Saint Paul's was a museum embodying the order passed down for centuries of dignified service, or a mission responding to the critical challenges following 9/11, it was a ministry made up of fallible, opinionated, headstrong, kind, compassionate people.

10
Compounding Traumas

With Saint Paul's closed, I was given the equivalent of a "desk job" sewing up loose ends pertaining to Saint Paul's and helping cover regular services at Saint Paul's and Trinity. Walking around on eggshells, I assumed any minute could have been my last on staff. But in a corporate structure as large as Trinity's—with a men's shelter, a retirement home, daily masses to cover, diocesan opportunities and tasks, and support for a convent—there were endless ways to "bide my time."

What I really needed was some time off to process my feelings and to grieve, and to relax a bit. In her beautiful generous spirit, Courtney invited my family, along with other friends from Saint Paul's, to join her at her family's home in Provence in the south of France for a week. We were elated at the prospect. Neither Kirsten nor I had ever been to France, and we were excited to go. Margaret, too, was elated. Even at her young age, she was proficient in French, having taken the language in school every year since second grade. The exquisite beauty of the South of France was medicine for our souls. Drinking in the loveliness of the sunset in Luberon Valley, I could relax with these wonderful friends and feel a sense of joy returning.

But it didn't last long. Returning from France, I had a conversation with the rector about my future goals and what kinds of things I might be interested in doing. This conversation had the feeling of an exit interview in which the exit (mine) had not yet been established. Was he asking so he could help me get a job? Or to get rid of me? Both? He certainly carried a lot of weight in the church and could have opened doors for me if he was willing, but unfortunately, I still carried many resentments and felt no sense of safety in that relationship. He might have been giving me a boost in restarting my life and career, but in my defensiveness, it had the feeling of me getting squeezed out.

The first anniversary of 9/11 I felt a complex mix of emotions: great sadness for those who died, and families affected, grief for ourselves and staff as our jobs and lives had changed, anxiety about the future as there were rumors of war with Iraq, and an already consuming war in Afghanistan. There were in-depth questions circling in the wider community—how do we adequately commemorate this great loss? We had a simple memorial the morning of 9/11's anniversary at Saint Paul's Chapel, and I was involved in the commemoration at the former World Trade Center site. But at the National Cathedral in Washington, DC (where I am a fellow of the former College of Preachers), there was a significant memorial service offered, not only remembering the dead and the families affected, but also honoring first responders, crisis workers, and volunteers who gave so much of themselves for 8.5 months. Courtney, Fred, and I were invited to attend and speak. Courtney and Fred attended, but when I sought to clear this with the vicar, I was not allowed to go. It was clear to me: if I chose to go anyway, there would be a cost.

I was angry, and I had a right to be angry. And ultimately, I didn't fully understand the extent to which I was damaged, the degree to which the anger had possessed me. Often despondent, I felt uncomfortable at work and preferred to hide out in my office. I was avoiding people. I didn't have patience for small talk anymore, and I couldn't find my normal spark, without it turning into rage. I knew I was wounded. But I didn't have a clue as to how much, or, again, what to do about it.

Strategically, one prospect that came to mind—both to get ahead of the endgame I felt was looming *and* to shut the world itself out: going back to General Seminary to finish my Th.D. I had been languishing in ABD Hell ("all but dissertation") since 1998. I had a fond relationship with the faculty at the General Theological (Episcopal) seminary in Chelsea, and the faculty was kind to award me the Dean's Medal for Exemplary Service for my work leading Saint Paul's. So, negotiating a kind of trade for my leaving, I suggested to John that I might want to go back to school and asked if I might receive financial support to help make that possible. This proposition was accepted, and with gratitude for modest financial support from Trinity, my departure was announced on Sunday morning, October 13, 2002.

Reporting on this for the *New York Times*, Dan Wakin observed that the news of my departure was met with audible gasps from parishioners.[1] A frenzy of emotional responses quickly gave way to applause and then a standing ovation. Feeling seen and appreciated was as soothing to my soul as a sunset in Provance. Wakin added that the announcement "also provoked whispers that church officials did not fully support the relief operation, and, by extension, Father Harris." Neither the rector nor the vicar was present at church that morning to field questions about my departure.

The plan to go back to school didn't include an arrangement for a place to live after vacating Trinity-sponsored housing. Serendipitously, with the Dean of the Cathedral of Saint John the Divine in Harlem, James Kowalski, I was able to work out a half-time consultation as "Consultant for Urban Ministries" in exchange for housing. My excitement matched my relief. The community at Saint John the Divine was just what I needed—a progressive faith community deeply engaged with creative arts and liturgies.

My family and I were happy to be at the cathedral. We were allowed to participate in the refurbishment of an already beautiful apartment in Morningside Heights on the lower edge of Harlem. Kirsten's impeccable sense for decorating and interior design brought in butter yellows and hunter green and gunmetal gray, along with pleasing floral patterns for cushions and drapes, and a checkerboard floor for the kitchen. All created a pleasant sense of home. The view from Margaret's bedroom overlooked the cathedral's rose garden, with stunning views that gave her such delight. Our two dogs were thrilled to ramble with peacocks on several acres of green space. The vibrant neighborhood was brimming with heavenly restaurants, including the Hungarian Pastry Shop across the street from the cathedral. Their peach Danishes alone were responsible for putting 15 pounds on me the 2 years we were there. The neighborhood managed to balance a hip urban grittiness with an old-world vibe, with elite educational institutions like Columbia

University and Union Theological Seminary surrounding us. Urban arts balanced with a sense of political seriousness.

The cathedral was right at home as an anchor for this neighborhood, an exemplar of spiritually progressive values and peace culture. It has been affectionately referred to as "Saint John the Unfinished" because Bishop Donegan (serving during the urban crises of the 1960s, from 1950 to 1972), halted work refurbishing the cathedral to instead disburse the funds to organizations supporting the urban poor and needy. Every New Year's Eve, the cathedral hosts a great "concert for peace," with 5,000 attending—usually with Joan Baez singing an encore of either We Shall Overcome and/or Amazing Grace.

I had long admired the creativity and ingenuity of this amazing place. One of Duke Ellington's pianos, a Steinway baby grand, had been placed in Saint James' chapel, on the south side of the cathedral's interior. The jazz musician Paul Winter had won a Grammy for his hauntingly beautiful "Missa Gaia" written for the cathedral's celebration of Saint Francis. The cathedral's Artists in Residence program included the extraordinary Phillip Petit, the French tightrope walker who had walked between the towers of the former World Trade Center. On occasion, when there was a reception in the parish hall, he would string a rope across the gallery and dance on it over our heads. And it was thrilling to get to bless everything from donkeys to hedgehogs to elephants during the cathedral's majestic celebration for the feast day of Saint Francis. Under any other circumstances, my time at the cathedral would have been a dream come true. But I was stuck emotionally. I was depressed.

Also, during this time, the minor celebrity I'd found from 9/11 led to speaking invitations and expenses-paid trips all over the world. I was invited to speak in Barcelona, Montreal, Mumbai, South Africa, and Australia. I also helped plan a cultural exchange that took 9/11 family members to Beirut, Lebanon, to meet with families who had lost loved ones in their civil war. The sponsoring partner in Beirut was the Garden of Forgiveness, led by peace activist and psychotherapist, Alexandra Asseily. Alexandra would become my mentor in developing plans for a similar non-profit, the Gardens of Forgiveness, advocating for a garden of forgiveness at Ground Zero. On our visit, Alexandra asked, "What is my responsibility for peace in the world? My responsibility is to become a better ancestor for my children. How do I do that? Forgiveness."[2]

In preparation for the trip to Beirut, I pulled together a dynamic group of individuals and board members to start a non-profit, the Gardens of Forgiveness, in affiliation with the Garden of Forgiveness in Beirut. Our vision was to create such a garden at Ground Zero - a place where one could think about all the horrors that can happen to us as human beings, but then decide to opt out of the futile cycle of violence and revenge. Our dream ultimately crashed on the shores of the antipathy of many New Yorkers who, at the time, were clearly not ready to forgive. While we had success in supporting and dedicating other such gardens, our dream for the former World trade Center site never came to fruition. I was in over my head, and it was an effort I ultimately could not sustain.

The entire decade following Saint Paul's oscillated between such a fever pitch of inspired activity and an equally deep sense of depression. It didn't matter that I was in a new and exciting place in my life. The conflicts and traumas of 9/11 had taken root in my soul and were continuing to grow into their own burgeoning garden—one full of agony and resentment more than forgiveness—my own personal Gethsemane that I watered with my incessant flow of tears. For every dream opportunity I was given as a priest, my PTSD and trauma countered as cunning saboteurs. It was like running one of the most important races of my life, only to find out the course moved through pluff mud on the banks of a river.[3]

Since my ailments were traceable to my work following 9/11, my therapist encouraged me to apply for workers' compensation. I wasn't so sure. Although I knew I wasn't up to par, I wasn't ready to accept that I was incapacitated. Plus, the process itself seemed belittling in its necessary objectification of my work and how I spent my time. What felt like great schemes for "reimagining the city" and pursuing peace in the city and in the world amounted to little more than fantasy through this lens—castles in the sky—with a particular focus on the lack of traction I'd been able to secure. My ideas were good, but I soon found out why they never got anywhere. And why I was broke.

After several evaluations over the years by Mount Sinai in NYC, and with clinicians affiliated with the World Trade Center Health Registry, I was diagnosed with PTSD, major depressive disorder, several things wrong with my sinuses and lungs—chronic sinusitis, chronic rhinitis, extrinsic asthma—GERD. I was prescribed several medications for these ailments, and Lexapro for the depression. While it took the edge off harmful emotions, I spent the next 12 years in bondage to Lexapro. I was never closer to a complete breakdown than in the moments when I couldn't afford my medication, or wasn't sure if my prescription would renew. Later, I found out that one of its side effects is suicidal ideation. So even as it took the edge off my anxious state, it added its own fears and, unfortunately, also took the edge off every other feeling I might have had. My spontaneity dissipated. My emotional highs were muted, and my emotional lows were numbed.

It took a few years, but I applied for workers' compensation, and a court recognized that the damage to my health was caused by breathing toxic dust for 240+ days and the trauma I had experienced during my constant presence at Ground Zero. Judge Regina Jabbour also declared her appreciation from the bench, acknowledging my courage to serve the workers at Ground Zero—to feed them, to stay with them, to breathe their air, to see their sights. In a surprising and touching unprecedented moment, she then left her bench and came down from the dais to shake my hand. Her decision made me the newest partially disabled case of the World Trade Center Volunteer Fund, and her recognition had met me in my deep, unspoken need to be seen.

Clinicians have a term that seems to fit this stage of my life well: *cascading collective traumas*. What I needed most was to take a time out for healing, but as I kept moving, the traumas of my life were adding up like merit badges for a boy scout going for his Eagle award. I didn't know what else to do to address my pain, so I kept running away from it. Maslow might assess that I'd had a peak experience that changed my life, and before returning to "normal life" I would need to grieve the loss and integrate the experience. But the collective nature of the traumas I had faced needed to be acknowledged within a safe, loving, supportive group, as well as a caring, trauma-informed counselor to help me reenvision my life. To put it mildly, that did not happen.

My grief was both complicated and complex. Complicated in that my quest for healing from the great tragedy of 9/11 was awash in negative emotions toward my former bosses. Complex because there were so many inputs of grief to navigate. The grandiose schemes I had created were unskilled attempts to cope, assuring myself that I still had something important to contribute, something I desperately needed to believe. I depended on the self-imagined, magnificent lie I repeated to myself as a mantra: that New York City *needed* me—my ideas, my passions, and my leadership. As an Enneagram 3, this need for success is not surprising, and my helper tendencies were operating at full throttle. I wanted to see myself—and be seen by others—as someone making a difference in the world. The wounded ego needs that fed this ambition prolonged my suffering. But even if I had known this at the time, I'm not sure what I could have done about it. Of course, I couldn't see any of this then. The protagonist in any tragedy is blinded from his demise until its savage denouement consumes him. *Cue: Rigoletto's final angst-ridden scream.*

The decade of my life that needed to be focused on healing was instead rife with increasing disintegration. I was in denial about my need for help and help was scarcely to be found. The cracks and fissures in the foundation of my marriage had only been amplified by the trauma of 9/11, and we were both unhappy with life. Our marriage born of love and youthful optimism, had, over the years, struggled. I had a constant fear, as a priest, of being judged by others because things weren't perfect, but the truth was that our marriage wasn't working. It's not unusual for a couple under such intense stress and pressure from ongoing trauma to divorce. But it's hard to tell which side of the decision is more painful—before the decision or after? Even though I was the one who left, I was listless, anxious, and worried. I wanted something more, I wanted something else in life, but at what price? If you painted my interior life at the time, it would resemble Edvard Munch's "Scream." Compounding the pain of our separation, my mother-in-law died that same year, and my own mother's death followed thirteen days later. Just when I thought things couldn't get worse, the reality of becoming an orphan crept up on me.

Though my marriage didn't survive one thing that abides from it is the precious child born of our union, our daughter Margaret. She will always be the apple of my eye and the joy of my heart. Wise beyond her years. I'll never forget a concern Margaret expressed one evening over a plate of pasta: "Dad, it's really important to feel your feelings." Her admonition has haunted me ever since. Because of custodial arrangements, I was not allowed to spend time with Margaret on the Easter Sunday following our split. That afternoon, on the day of our Lord's resurrection, I sat on the floor alone with my back up against a friend's borrowed sofa, crying my way through a huge box of Kleenex. Whether I wanted them or not, my feelings had found me. She soon lovingly sent me a beautiful quotation from Pope John Paul II: "Do not abandon yourself to despair. We are an Easter people and Alleluia is our song!"[4] At a time when I struggled with darkness, Margaret's gift was light for my soul.

I was also incredibly lucky to have such loving and generous friends in my time of dire need. I found solace sleeping on my friend Dana Newman's couch shortly after the divorce. When Fred Luskin's father died, leaving his home on Long Island vacant, he generously allowed me to stay there for a while. I soon began another relationship, a carefree and healing chapter that would last for 3 years. Her kindness and humor helped me to fall in love again with being alive. But because I remained my tortured, unbalanced self, I lacked any ability to make a commitment. When she left, the sunshine went with her. When it was clear that the relationship was over, the grief hit me like a tsunami, and I thought I might drown.

I was hurt, and, in my neediness, I was sometimes callous with others. I pursued a series of relationships, trying my best to find the love I needed. Only, the love I was seeking—a love large enough to honor the pain of my trauma, great enough to look with compassion upon my mistakes, kind enough to see myself within the extraordinary mystical turning of life, and hopeful enough to see *myself* embodying sunshine—was love for myself. Another portal had opened for me to engage the work of self-forgiveness, but I wasn't yet able to walk through it. And so again it passed me by, like an estuary draining into the ocean at low tide.

Ever trying to reclaim the highs I experienced at Saint Paul's, I allowed my imagination to run wild when my friend Susan Crowson invited me to consider a part-time opportunity at Saint John's Lutheran Church on Christopher Street in the West Village. The position came with modest housing and, with the support of both the Episcopal and Lutheran bishops, expanded to become a full-time position. Believing I was ready, I relinquished the financial support I had received from workers' comp and began to dream of becoming whole again.

The board and staff at Saint John's happily blessed my ideas, and before long, with my friend Meg Braun's guidance and partnership, we created the Christopher Street Coffee House, a place where rising singer-songwriters would find a supportive venue to hone their craft—just a few blocks away from Café Wha? where Bob Dylan and company had launched the sixties. We offered yoga classes. We created a jazz mass with settings inspired by John Coltrane's exquisite jazz suite "A Love Supreme" led by the talents of Juilliard students who have now become famous jazz musicians, Sharel Cassity and Michael Dease, along with a cohort of their friends, and my long-time friend and pianist Peter Moffit. Peter's daughter Nina was our singer, a young virtuoso on the rise. On Sunday nights, the sanctuary of Saint John's became the West Village's newest intimate jazz club, with selections from Stevie Wonder, Jimmy Heath, Wynton Marsalis, and our band's own exquisite compositions, all woven into the context of the sacred liturgy of Eucharist. Even in my compromised emotional state, I've never been more inspired to share the message of God's love than after prayers offered over the signature jazz riffs of John Coltrane's "ba-du-ba-dum, ba-du-ba-dum."

We soon ran with another idea I had: to commemorate Kristallnacht, a sober remembrance of the devastating "Night of Broken Glass" that had moved forward the Nazi reign of terror in 1938. My talented friends at Saint John's, with their significant connections in the arts world of New York City, recruited Ashley Tuttle, the former principal ballerina of the American Ballet Theatre, to perform a gut-wrenchingly emotional "dance of the broken glass."[5] The choreography was inspired and her dance, of course, brilliant. It ended with three bricks thrown through actual glass that we had placed in the sanctuary of the church. Those in attendance were shocked, to say the least, by the sounds of actual glass breaking. And that was the point. It's so easy to anesthetize ourselves to history, even when it is horrific as Kristallnacht. I felt my ideas were valued and supported. But my healing was still a work in progress.

The connections found within this beautiful community were remarkable. New friends that I got to know through our coffee house at Saint John's expressed interest in the role of forgiveness for healing communities. These included Daniel Neiden and Phil Sauers, and Daniel's mother-in-law, who was the highly respected Holocaust survivor turned peace activist, Luna Kaufman.[6] Luna would later connect me to the work of Yad Vashem in Jerusalem, and I would have the privilege of collaborating with them to address anti-Semitism in church communities.

For the tenth anniversary of 9/11, Mayor Bloomberg announced that more room was needed for family members of 9/11 victims and that first responders should not come down to Ground Zero. While I could appreciate the needs of the family members, I didn't want the day to go by without significant honor for these heroes I had spent so much time supporting. So, my small team and I planned a major production specifically in their honor.

With Pete Seeger as our headliner, we lined up as many stellar musicians as we could, including Spook Handy, David LaMott, and South African bassist Bakithi Kumalo, Paul Simon's legendary bass player. When I first heard my friend Sharon Benson's song, "You Rescued Me," months before, I knew it had to be shared in a big way, and we included her as well. We called the concert "Love Wins," and my dear friend and Gardens of Forgiveness board member, Mary Tufts, connected us to NYU to book a space to host it. Another Gardens of Forgiveness board member, Monica Willard, was also the NGO representative at the United Nations for the United Religions Initiative. She spread the word, and we had a full house. SUNY professor Dr. Benjamin Luft, a medical researcher on the traumatic impacts of 9/11, teaching at Stony Brook University's Renaissance Medical School, screened a section of his compelling new documentary of interviews with first responders entitled "9/11: An American Requiem."[7] There were even parrots—the so-called "Parrots for Peace" from Woodstock, NY, founded by Gloria Waslyn. It was a touching and glorious tribute topped off by an unexpected gift from Pete Seeger. Pete, who sang "We Shall Overcome" at the famous 1963 March on Washington, sang it on the tenth anniversary of 9/11, and added a new verse: "We shall learn to forgive someday."

I've held on to that memory as a talisman of hope ever since that day, through good times and bad, while secretly hoping that I might learn to forgive as well. There were many exciting events at Saint John's, and I had such great joy in sharing them. But while these precious moments of joy adorned my journey, they ultimately wouldn't save me from the miles of growth left ahead of me.

In the lead-up to the tenth anniversary, feeling isolated and lonely, I'd had a romantic interlude with a parishioner, and when confronted about it, I lied. Even as we planned and celebrated the "Love Wins" concert, I found myself in the midst of an excruciating church trial. It didn't go well for me. The bishop's assistant, Andy Dietze, had told me early on in the proceedings that the bishop would depose me if I lied at any point. Long, excruciating story short, I did. And he did. I lied because I didn't feel safe enough to tell the truth, or to acknowledge my brokenness.

I was fired from my job at Saint John's and was refused any public contact with the church community. This included a concert that my friend Martyn Joseph was soon to give at our coffee house. I treasured Martyn's music and was eager to hear songs from his new, widely acclaimed album, *Under Lemonade Skies*. Crestfallen, I had to miss the concert. But that night, he dedicated a song to me from his new album, entitled "Brothers in Exile." The wistful, melancholic song had one verse in particular that gave voice to the agony of separation I was feeling:

> "Living out here means nostalgia burns strong
> For the forests of Eden where we used to belong
> But we couldn't remain there, that was a land we outgrew
> But the wilderness she gives a far-reaching view
> To brothers in exile"[8]

This song has been part of my soul's music ever since, marking the nadir of my journey. Being deposed decimated my sense of identity and purpose in life. I never opened the bishop's decree that came by certified mail until a decade later. I had already gotten the email. I knew what it said. Seeing that was enough; I didn't know if I would ever breathe again. I was sure that the sun would not, in fact, rise again the next morning. Lyndon, as I knew him, died that day, leaving every last part of the life I'd tried to put together in ruins, smoldering.

I loved being a priest. I loved officiating weddings, attending family celebrations, visiting the sick in the hospital, encouraging parishioners in their struggles, celebrating with those who were joyous, weeping with those who wept, and especially preaching and presiding at the Eucharist. I loved being a part of a structured community that allowed my creativity to flourish. This was a tragedy for me, and it would take years for me to hold that awareness in my consciousness without the need to convulse with pain, burst into tears, or hyperventilate in a panic attack. Being a priest had been my identity, and that fateful day initiated a split in my psyche that ravaged my mental capacity like a hurricane attacking a 12-foot john boat lost at sea. Trauma compounding upon trauma.

Looking back, it's not surprising that I failed to such a significant degree. This does not excuse my actions or choices but helps me understand them. Research confirms that anyone suffering great trauma has a much higher possibility of making significant life mistakes. And the truth is, many people have lost their credentials. Medical licenses have been revoked, lawyers have been disbarred, clergy have been deposed, and a significant number of people have been incarcerated.[7] These revocations leave an indelible mark on one's professional record and limit the possibilities for work. When I was deposed, I lost my identity as a priest, I lost the opportunity for employment in my preferred line of work, and I lost the image of myself as the person I had always wanted to convey.

At this point in my journey I descended into what psychologists call mortification—a searing shame based on loss of identity or status. My being deposed became a carefully guarded secret that I hid from myself as well as from others—something that I couldn't bear the thought of sharing. But deep down I knew it was inevitable that people would come to know my secret shame, even before I could metabolize it. It was a time bomb, prickly and dangerous, packed with fear, hypocrisy and deception. It promised ruin for my life, shattering everything I held dear.

My depression became so intense that I experienced physical, bodily pain that felt like I had been beaten to within an inch of my life. My shame was unbearable. These triggers led me easily into dissociation and isolation, a coping skill I'd found helpful through life's earlier challenges. I saw clergy friends' posts on Facebook as though they were from family members I had just lost through a divorce. Their family gatherings continued without me. Contact with longtime friends fell away, and the silence was deafening. I felt "ghosted." When courageous friends did reach out to me, I pushed them away. The man who had been raised to be a "good boy" had made career-ending, identity-shifting mistakes, and it was unbearable to live with that shame. Brene Brown distinguishes between guilt and shame. Guilt is "I did something bad." And shame is "I am something bad." I had both. I began to wonder if there was any good reason left to live. I couldn't imagine ever showing my face in public again. The trash compactor had locked me in, and a legion of monsters was devouring me, one prickly bite at a time.

Many claim that the downfall of clergy is a "messiah complex," but I was consumed by what I called a "pariah complex." I no longer fit. I felt shunned. The dream I had for the church as an ever-widening sphere of an ever-deepening reconciliation felt like it no longer had a place for me.

Who are you when your foundation is ripped away?
What do you do when your life falls apart?

My most insidious and tightly held unenforceable rule was not simply that priests should be priests—but that *I had to be perfect*. That I could never make a mistake.

Ten years after 9/11, everything I had worked for was in ashes. My final moments living in NYC were spent in the loneliest seemingly godforsaken place on Earth: the rundown Greyhound Bus terminal at Port Authority. With two bags of luggage in tow—more than enough room to carry what was left of my diminished life—I waited for the big gray dog to carry me away.

It was a bookend moment, of sorts. Instead of "taking a Greyhound down the Hudson River line" into the city while humming Billy Joel's "New York State of Mind," the tune haunted me as I instead took a Greyhound south, down the unseemly Jersey Turnpike. With New York City in the rearview mirror, I felt like an utter failure. The heights of ecstasy and jubilation I had experienced in my NYC sojourn were matched now by the depths of my despair as I retreated home to family, dreams fizzling like grains of sand through my desperately clutched hands.

A dull ache started at the tip of my Nike-covered toes and filled the hollows of my empty body, right to the top of my throbbing, headache-addled skull. Why didn't I just do what so many others have in such despair—why not step in front of a subway car and claim the infamous legacy of a "jumper"? Or more dramatically, catch a cab to the George Washington Bridge and leap? Why didn't I?

Because I still had hope.
I had a daughter that I love with all my heart.
And I was still a person of faith.
I still believed that God could redeem even the mess I had made of my life.

Saint Augustine once said that hope has two daughters: anger and courage. My anger had run its course, draining me of my life's energy and nearly killing me in the process. Would I ever find courage again?

I had been given so much in my life, but I would never find healing without finding the courage to face what I had lost and the mistakes I had made. To deal with the word "no" in healthy ways. No more denial. No more compartmentalization. No more blame.

But it was November of 2011, and I was sitting alone in a bus station, waiting to leave New York. There, I wept for my mistakes. I wept for all those I had failed. I wept for my churches. I wept for my city. I wept for my family. I wept for myself, remembering that I have been surrounded by loved ones and friends who had been ports of calm throughout my storms.

Welling up from somewhere deep inside, I felt the stirring of a Sikh mantra I had learned from my dear friend Hari Kaur in the yoga classes she had offered at Saint John's. I hummed this mantra as a prayer of love. Love for all who were precious to me. Love for my city. And finally, in its infancy, love for myself:

> May the long time sun
> Shine upon you
> All love surround you
> And the pure light
> Within you
> Guide your way on
> Guide your way on

11

Ain't It Awful Ain't Working

Leaving NYC, I took a Greyhound bus about 15 hours south, down I-95, then I-75 and I-85 to my former city, Spartanburg, SC. There, my older sister Cheryl picked me up for the 30-minute drive to my hometown, Gaffney. Coming home on the "Big Grey Dog" was not my idea of a triumphal return to Spartanburg where I used to live: the parish I served, or the city where I attended college (Wofford), where I had been selected as Outstanding Young Alumnus in 2003 for my work after 9/11, and where, ultimately, I lost my house in foreclosure. The city where I began work as a manager for Milliken and Company, a storied textile company that trained me thoroughly for managing impossible situations. In 1986 I had been selected "Management Associate of the Year" for my division—Textured Yarns. My time with Milliken lasted for 4 years. Showing up to the crisis-laden context of GZ the morning of September 12 was more the production manager Lyndon than Lyndon the priest. It's amazing how experiences earlier in life prepare us for the next.

After collecting me, Cheryl and I stopped by one of my old favorite burger joints, The Beacon, a sentimental dive that never ceases to put a smile on my face. After my chili-cheese a'plenty, and with a tank of their famous sweet tea to go, we set our sights for Gaffney, just 30 minutes north. Driving from Spartanburg to Gaffney is a stretch of road I could drive in my sleep, a well-worn passage of my former life. Nearing Gaffney, on the horizon you discover one of Gaffney's claims to fame—the "Peachoid"—a giant peach-shaped water tower. I always chuckle when I see the sign, "To View Peach, Take Exit 90." As if you needed to take Exit 90 to see this eighth wonder of the world.

My humble return home was full of nostalgia and catching sight of the Peachoid brought back so many memories, like the time our graduating class helped peel peaches for the world's largest peach cobbler, as certified by my childhood bible, *The Guinness Book of World Records*. Every summer Gaffney has a Peach Festival with musicians and artists galore, along with a monster tractor pull, and the grand finale—the Peach Festival Parade.

Gaffney is a small town in the upcountry region of South Carolina. With rolling hills cascading down from the Blue Ridge Mountains, large stretches of farmland, especially peaches, and, at the time I grew up, a small community of less than 15,000 people. Gaffney is known for three things: its football team, peaches, and Andie MacDowell. Our football team consistently is either winning the state championship or in the hunt for it. Gaffney holds the state record for most championships overall at 18. The abundance of summer peaches when I was growing up in the seventies garnered for our town the title "Peach Capital of SC." Each summer the Peach Festival brings in popular musicians from the fields of rock and country, with R&B performers on occasion.

I remembered the time when some of my friends and I mischievously perched along the early parade route in a Cadillac, a tank of a car belonging to a friend's mother, and edged into the parade when there was an unprotected gap. Joining the procession of marching bands, beauty queens, large plastic cows, cowboys on horses, and Shriners on go-carts, we unfurled a peace flag to hang out the window. It was what we could find. We were appropriately stocked with bags of candy, and with great fanfare tossed out our treasures to adoring spectators along the parade route. We howled with laughter, seeing the faces of friends and family, initially greeting us with waves and smiles that soon turned to quizical expressions of "but wait . . . , what??" The Peach Festival precipitated my older sister Cheryl's lifelong disdain for William Shatner. No room for forgiveness here. Shatner was hired to be the parade marshal one summer, and with his galactic smile charmed every single one of us as he cruised along the route. But the next night he appeared on the Johnny Carson show laughing about the "hick town" he had just visited for their parade. Not nice, Captain Kirk.

And when Andie MacDowell became a breakout movie star, it was all Gaffney could talk about. I didn't know Andie, or as she was referred to by her family, Rosie. At the age of 19, Andie's star became luminescent with modeling contracts that took her to New York City and Paris, and to movie roles that propelled her to big screens around the world. Gaffney could not have been prouder of its cherished daughter turned movie star, and in 1992 named a major thoroughfare in town, the "Andie MacDowell Boulevard."

Gaffney has other cinematic accolades as well. The first is what many consider a fun, but dubious distinction: Gaffney is the fictional hometown of Frank Underwood, the US Representative from South Carolina's fifth congressional district who, through corrupt means, claws his way to the top of the political world in the United States, becoming the president. The opening trailer for the Netflix show prominently displays Gaffney's iconic landmark—the Peachoid. They searched the whole country for a fictional villain politician, and they chose my hometown. The other cinematic accolade comes because Gaffney is home to a discontinued nuclear power plant, and the containment pool intended for such use was made available to James Cameron and his crew in 1989 to film the blockbuster sci-fi film "The Abyss," starring Ed Harris. Gaffney is the affiliated home of actresses and Jurassic dinosaurs, giant peaches, aliens from outer space, crooked politicians, and ordinary folks like me.

My nephew Clint welcomed me into his home for a jaunt, and it didn't take long before we made a pilgrimage to Tendal's, a diner/dive on Main Street in Gaffney. I had known it as Harold Tendal's growing up, but hey, if Madonna and Adele can get away with just one name, Harold should too. The fact that Tendal's is a bar made it a hushed favorite for the locals, who preferred not to be seen frequenting a "beer joint" as many were teetotaling Baptists. Tendal's serves one of the most unique hamburgers I've ever had—the burger is round like a meatball, which is what attracted Guy Fieri to Tendal's to do an interview for the show, "Diners, Drive-ins and Dives" on the Food Network.

That afternoon, when Clint and I picked up our order at "the beer joint," it turned into a laugh fest. My shy, tall, and handsome nephew was accosted by the cashier serving us at the register, convinced he was a celebrity. She said, "I know who you are! You're that wrestler on TV! I've seen you! I know it's you." It's hard to describe how many shades of red Clint turned, and being the mischievous uncle I am, I egged it on. Of course I did. "She's on to you, Stone Cold! We'd better get out of here before she calls all her friends and the media!" Clint's mortification was matched by her jubilation, and it continues to bring a smile to my face to this day.

I spent several weeks recuperating with Clint and family who still lived in the area. Returning home, spending time with my family was healing for me. While they had some appreciation for the rollercoaster I had been on since 9/11 in NYC, I was always, first, foremost and always, just Lyndon. Being seen and loved at that level was healing because it helped me remember some of the challenges I overcame and accomplishments I had growing up, and they reminded me that the bonds of family are stronger than death. Always my cheerleader, my younger sister Libby is an extravert off the scale, with enough funny stories to fill a library of books, and my brother Bo is temperamentally her opposite—a quiet, self-sufficient man preferring to live in the country and as close to the land as possible. My older sister Cheryl had assumed the role of family matriarch after our mother's death in 2005. She worked hard, as she has always done, to create opportunities for connection and bringing the family together while I was home.

Being back in Gaffney brought up so many memories of my biggest supporter in life, my mother. A pillar of the community in her own kind and unassuming way, whenever I would meet someone new there, they would almost always say, "Oh, you're Annie Laura's son!" My life had always been influenced by both the centrifugal and centripetal forces of her personality that both drew me in toward her love and propelled me away by her steadfast desire that I remain in Gaffney. I wanted to become the man she had in mind for me, but on my own terms. Still, my Baptist mother's influence was the biggest force active in my becoming an Episcopalian. She brought me up with the vision that I led with at Saint Paul's Chapel: when someone is in trouble, you help them out—and then, if you can, you feed them.

Always the host for large family gatherings, the sweetness of her hospitality was expressed in tangible, delicious form by the wide variety of cakes she prepared: red velvet, coconut, "rotten" coconut (made with cream cheese), chocolate, chocolate marble, orange, hummingbird, and a respectable assortment of cobblers to boot. There would be no end to her delight if she could see the exquisite creations my daughter Margaret makes, now carrying on mom's legacy as a trained and gifted pastry chef in her own right. Being home, being reminded who and whose I am, helped me with another vital step along my journey to healing.

One day while Cheryl and Clint were at work, I drove over to our mom's house to spend some time there by myself. I was glad it was cold so I could justify building a fire. Growing up, we heated our house by woodstove, and it was my chore to stock the wood bin. Sitting by that same woodstove, the fire warmed my body as memories warmed my heart. But almost without warning, an acute flash of shame took my breath away. These episodes would come from time to time, like a thick dark cloak seizing me and smothering me by surprise. This time, it brought with it a spiral of thoughts about how my life had fallen apart. Tears followed, pouring out from some primordial river of dread deep within me. I pulled my arms and legs into a tight ball and sat there in the recliner by the woodstove, stewing in remorse and regret for what seemed like an eternity.

Slowly, as the fire died down, my panic also turned to ash in the spiritual fire of my family's love. It was a love that I'd often felt over the years while communing at that hearth—a love that had always been there for me, even on my darkest days. I came back to myself, remembering that we all must grow up, that the real world is much more nuanced than the one I'd projected as a child. That every single one of us makes mistakes. But becoming a kind, caring, compassionate, and honest man—in spite of mistakes and failures—continued to be my life's worthy goal.

With a measure of fortitude, I accepted that life had handed me challenges. Some I had met with grace, and some I had failed. I thought of the velveteen rabbit in the children's story, who bemoaned her tattered fabric and lost buttons, until she realized they were signs of the love that made her real.[1] Through my own scuffs, challenges, and my failures—and thanks to the love of my family through it all—I was on my way to becoming real. But the dying embers of that fire sparked one more realization before I left that day: I wasn't ready to settle down back at home. The respite had been wonderful. I enjoyed visiting friends and family, as I always have and always will. But my wanderlust for the big wide world was still strong, and my sense of purpose and meaning was still bubbling. I sensed that my journey had many more twists and turns to come. And, to no small degree, I longed for some kind of move that might offer an antidote for my depression.

With just enough money to survive for a year and great hope for rebooting my life, I decided to move to California. I rented a modest apartment in Santa Monica, and in the honeymoon phase of my time in Los Angeles, I found myself making new acquaintances, hiking exquisite trails through the canyons, and soaking up the sun at Venice Beach. Coming from NYC, I needed to get a car, and I found an affordable Volkswagen Cabrio that was made for me, a convertible that met my soul's longing to be free. Driving on the Pacific Coast Highway with the top down on a sunny day, my troubles could hardly keep up. Unfortunately, as I would soon discover, some days they do. As much as you might try to run away from your problems, they always seem to find a way to come along for the ride. Even with the top down.

My strategy for this LA sojourn was that I might recreate myself as a forgiveness teacher and find a way to make a living doing that. That was the full extent of my plans. To some, LA might have been seen as a surprising move. I remembered speaking with a neighbor in NYC before 9/11, as we were walking our dogs (our dog Grammar had the hots for their dog Frieda). When he confessed that he was moving to LA, I was stupefied. "Why would you want to go to *LA*? NYC is the center of the universe. Isn't it?" He mumbled that one of his colleagues thought it would be good for his career. I said, "Well, good luck." A few years later, per the cover of *TimeOut NY* magazine, I discovered that our neighbor Mark's last name was Ruffalo. His decision must have planted a seed of curiosity in me about LA. But when I moved to California to move forward from my failures, I was running from myself as much as running toward opportunity.

Fortunately, I fell into a great set of friends at the Creative Visions Foundation, and especially Kathy Eldon, its founder. I had met Kathy in 2006 at the United Nations. She was the emcee for that year's Human Rights Awards ceremony, and I was asked to give the invocation. I dropped by to visit Kathy at her office in Malibu shortly after I moved to LA, and she welcomed me with open arms. She had a keen sense of my need for community and connection. She spoke glowingly of me to others, especially about the morning of 9/11, and how I had been instrumental in helping the children in our preschool escape the maelstrom of the terrorists' attacks. She remembered the good work I had done.

Kathy's kindness was quixotic; instead of seeing a depressed deposed former priest, she saw a courageous human being who put his life on the line trying to do good, trying to help people in an unprecedented crisis. It was the kind of love and acceptance I had longed for. With her metaphoric sword, she dubbed me Creative Vision's "Minister for Inspiration, Compassion and Outreach." I felt seen. And loved. I felt like it was one of the luckiest days of my life.

One year later, and before my funds were totally depleted, I found a more affordable place in Topanga Canyon. As a card-carrying idealist, I fell in love with Topanga, certain I had found my new corner of the sky. Topanga is a quirky, offbeat place up in the canyon from Malibu, whose name, given to the area by the Native American indigenous Tongva tribe, means "where the mountain meets the sea." The hiking is spectacular, with a sundown-moonrise trek on the Topanga Lookout Trail being my absolute favorite.

Topanga has historically been a place of revolutionaries, nudists, rock bands, hippies, radicals, and environmentalists. I felt right at home. There are quirky restaurants, funky clothing shops, and public art installations, like the "flying pig"—a large pink flying pig up high on a pole along the Topanga Canyon Boulevard. I haven't a clue as to its history, but the Flying Pig has its own Facebook page and is a convenient landmark when giving directions: "Just go a quarter mile past the flying pig and take a left."

While in Topanga, I was naturally inclined to explore the back to the land movement, and I discovered the work of Bill McKibben in the Topanga library. His book *Eaarth: Making a Life on a Tough New Planet* changed my life.[2]

Already invested in the environmental movement, I had still been woefully uninformed. *Eaarth* noted that, while we had inherited a magnificent planet, we no longer live on that hospitable planet. We now live on Eaarth—a planet significantly compromised by human-created environmental degradation. My daily reading practices took a deep dive into conservation and permaculture, leading me to start Transition Topanga, a conservation group inspired by the work of the Transition movement in the UK. I had a new crusade.

Another benefit of moving to Topanga was that I'd be closer to my dear friend Sharon Benson and her partner Linda. Sharon had been one of the musicians who played in our Gardens of Forgiveness concert with Pete Seeger at New York University. We had lots of fun making music during my California sojourn. Music has been a pathway to healing for me, and Sharon was always an inspiring musical doula.

Joy had begun to spring up from the troubled soil of my life, even if in small doses. Hiking with like-minded neighbors and adventures with Maggie, the cocker spaniel from South LA who had rescued me the year before. The sweeping panoramas of the Santa Monica Mountains, the exotic beauty of the desert wildflowers when in bloom, and the gentle breezes of a temperate western climate—each mystical outing seemed to make time slow down and undoubtedly made the pangs of my grief and regret less intense.

But still, darkness tagged along throughout my time in this sunshine-infused state. My lungs were damaged by the smoke at Ground Zero; I had few financial resources, and I was still struggling with depression and trauma. I was still nursing old wounds and still running from myself. In the immortal words of T. S. Eliot, I was "distracted from distraction by distraction."[3] I was speaking passionately about the power of forgiveness, but I had yet to fully incorporate it into my life.

Each time my new circle of friends asked about my 9/11 experiences, I couldn't resist the temptation to turn my story into a victim's narrative, like I discussed earlier. Sharing a victim's narrative is a ploy to garner sympathy and affection from others. But as I pointed out earlier, whenever a story includes the words or thought, "They did this to me," the teller no longer is the protagonist of his own story and therefore has given up his power, his agency.

I had been playing this game for so long even I was tired of it. Yet, more than a decade later, there I was giving up what little power I had left. Every time I was seduced by the endorphin-releasing game of "Ain't it awful?" my victim's narrative suffocated me.

But honestly, it feels good to complain when something has happened to us. "Do you know what they did to me?" or "Can you believe how I was treated?" It brings others to our side or justifies our disdain. I had many collaborators who, out of kindness, were willing to play a few rounds with me. "Ain't it awful?" is one of the games listed in Eric Berne's *Games People Play: The Psychology of Human Relationships*.[4] It's a kind of script for bad conversations that people love to have. For those recovering from trauma, this is a very natural thing to do. Looking for safety, finding sympathetic friends and colleagues who will open their hearts to hear you is the first step to creating a safe container in which to process our anger and grief. But "Ain't it awful" is not a long-term strategy for success in life.

One person who refused to play this game with me was Fred Luskin. Instead, Fred said, "Lyndon, if you spent only 50% of your time complaining, and the other 50% of your time thinking about your blessings, you might have a happier life." I would always nod in agreement. My favorite quotation from Nelson Mandela is that not to forgive is like drinking poison and waiting for your enemies to die from it. Ten years later, I was still drinking the poison. When would I learn? Playing the complain game I gave up my power. I had so much to be grateful for, as Fred had insinuated. But I was blinded by my own inability to let go and make peace with the noes I had gotten from life. It would take years for me to hear and understand that personal growth comes from taking responsibility for my life. But healing from trauma is not a rabbit-infused race; it's more like the tortoise: it takes time.

Another year passed, and so did my finances. I had to look for other possibilities for housing. My friend Dustin said his sister Kiki had a horse ranch in Agoura Hills, CA, and that she might be willing to allow me to stay in an RV on the ranch. Perhaps I could help care for the horses. Sure enough, Kiki Ebsen and her team welcomed me to the amazing hundred-or-so acres of Healing Equine Ranch, nestled in the Agoura Hills/Calabasas region of the Santa Monica Mountains. Kiki had established a trauma-informed equine-assisted therapeutic practice where humans can encounter the healing presence of horses. Natural horsemanship principles, mindfulness practices, breathwork, and trust-based interactions between humans and horses become a healing balm in service of their mission: to be a sanctuary where rescued horses helped rescue humans. I thought I had gone there to help the former; instead, I became the latter. Cleaning horse stalls in jeans and boots was about as far away as I could get from the Brooks Brothers' suits I had worn on Wall Street or the elegant robes I donned when presiding at mass at Trinity. Those experiences were fading into distant memories as my past, my history, my identity were washing away in the unhurried rhythms of life on a western ranch.

The nights were harder than the days as living on a ranch can be isolating. I had grown used to the nocturnal sounds of traffic and the noisy flow of humanity in both NYC and LA, but here, at night the quietude was pervasive, except for the occasional yelping of coyotes off in the distance. But the ephemeral beauty of the night sky was comforting, with the stars and planets on display like diamonds placed on a lush piece of black velvet. When the moon was full, you wanted to ask who left all the lights on. Inside the RV, the local NPR station broadcasted news shows from the BBC in London, in comforting English voices that gave my racing mind comfort and helped me sleep. On the few occasions when a panic attack descended upon me—usually when I ran out of my Lexapro—the night became twice as dark and lonely.

The sands of time slipped through the hourglass of my life as one day's opportunities stretched into the necessities of the next. I began to lose track of time altogether. Between the placid but powerful tides of the Pacific Ocean and the epic skies and hills of the Malibu canyons, I was lulled into a kind of soporific serenity, losing touch with my past and losing touch with those outside of this fragile bubble of domicile in Agoura Hills.

Until one day, when Margaret called me, asking me where I was and what I was doing. She was worried and a bit concerned, adding, "Don't you want to be a part of our lives?" I was thunderstruck. I couldn't imagine how I'd let this happen. Margaret had thrown me a lifeline, and there was no way I was going to let it go.

Not long before that, I had been watering the horses on a particularly hot day. The temperature had topped 103 degrees, and the herd had drained most of their huge trough of water with hours of scorching daylight to go. Refilling the water could take quite a while, given the amount it could hold, and I stood there alone at the trough as the horses wisely sequestered themselves in a far corner of the pasture to enjoy the shade of the towering white oak trees. There the herd stayed, but the leader of the band, August, strode toward me from the far end of the pasture.

I was quite surprised to see him coming toward me at all. Lead horses in a herd are kind of like the cool kids in high school—they don't show a lot of interest in someone who's not in their league. I thought he must be *really* thirsty.

But he wasn't.

He came close to me, still replenishing the water trough, and just stood there, looking right at me. He wasn't in a hurry, and his gaze wasn't angry or fearful. It was peaceful. It felt loving, even. If you've ever looked into a horse's eyes for any amount of time, you'll know how mesmerizing this is. I was moved to tears. Cautiously, I reached to see if I could pet him—something that he had shown no interest in before. Yet, as I moved closer, he gently raised his head, allowing me to give him a "horse hug," with his head over my shoulder and my arm gently reaching up to hug his neck. I had never had any real emotional engagement with August, and I was shocked by his openness to me that day. He always seemed grateful when I fed him, but that was about it. Nothing like this had ever happened before between us.

After a few minutes, he took a slow drink of the fresh cool water from the well and made his way back to his charge underneath the oak trees at the far end of the pasture. I was dumbfounded, unsure of what had just happened. The encounter with August had the feeling of a dream sequence. Was my trauma playing tricks on me?

Later that evening, while cooking dinner in the RV, I turned on my trusty radio to catch the news. It was the twelfth anniversary of 9/11.

12

Painful Acknowledgment

Three years after moving to Los Angeles, I ran out of both money and options. Feeling awkward and humbled, I reached out to Fred Burnham to see if he had any ideas for me to consider. Fred's love and kindness toward me had never faltered, despite the fact that I lost touch with him after moving to Los Angeles. Before that, he and his wife Regan had often pleaded with me to leave NYC and move to North Carolina with them. They had even offered me a beautiful basement apartment in their home, free of charge. I'm not sure why I couldn't accept it, other than the lingering idea that NYC needed me. This illusion had kept me from facing the painful truth: leaving NYC would have meant that I had failed. But if I had to move from NYC, LA seemed to be an attractive option, another adventure. But now, with both NYC and LA in my rearview mirror, the only thing I could see was failure.

Fred and Regan had been genuinely happy to hear from me, so when I came back east for a few days to visit family and gather my bearings, I reached out to them again. They took me to lunch at Luella's BBQ in Asheville, North Carolina—fully aware of my culinary weaknesses. There, over some of the best pulled pork I had had in a long time, Fred told me of his work as a senior fellow of the Institute for Servant Leadership, based at the Kanuga Conference Center, a national Episcopal retreat and conference center named for a Cherokee word that roughly translates to "gathering place." Taking another sip of my iced tea, I had a flashback—earlier in my career, as a priest in the nearby Episcopal Diocese of Upper South Carolina, I had always been energized by the conferences and retreats held at Kanuga.

Fred mentioned that one of his mentees at the Institute for Servant Leadership was starting a regional independent retreat center she called Tigg's Pond. Only 20 minutes away from Kanuga, Tigg's Pond was to be more of a quiet, day-visit kind of place, catering to the needs of interfaith and independent groups. The owner and founder of Tigg's Pond was Posy Jackson, a childhood best friend of Regan's who had visited Saint Paul's Chapel before we closed the relief mission. I remembered her vividly for her cheerful, creative spirit when she visited us at Saint Paul's Chapel.

After some delicious banana pudding—sweet, but not too sweet—our plates were nearly clear when Fred revealed that Posy was looking for ideas and support in generating programming for the retreat center. Given my cruise director approach for offering programming for churches, Fred thought it might be something for me to consider.

The very next day, we went to visit Posy at Tigg's Pond. Tigg's Pond was Posy's masterpiece in the making: 54 acres of land, with a pond, a country estate, a retreat cabin, and an elegant 75-seat venue that she called "the barn." The barn had a rustic but elegant kind of beauty. The cross beams in the ceiling were rough-hewn classics prospected from ancient barns in upstate NY that had fallen into disrepair. Even the floors were spectacular, built from reclaimed barn flooring.

Posy's dream was to create a sacred gathering place for people from all walks of life and spirituality. Her motto, mantra, and email signature were "seek within." At Tigg's Pond, Posy had created a sanctuary for this work, and it looked promising to me.

Posy shared with me that the name she chose for the retreat center, "Tigg's Pond," was named for her spirited Labrador, Tigger, who loved to swim in the pond year-round—even in the winter. Tigg's Pond was fed by the liquid gold of three cool mountain streams, testimony to the land's abundance. I was excited to hear of the half-acre organic garden that took up much of Posy's summer attention. The soil was dark and rich and irrigated easily by a pump from the mountain stream flowing alongside the garden. California had been in a perpetual state of drought while I lived there, but Tigg's Pond was a revelation of the earth's lush bounty.

When I updated friends back in the west, I said, "It's beautiful here. We have water!"

Before the day was over, Posy asked about my life in California, and what I thought about moving to Tigg's Pond. The barn had an efficiency apartment, and apparently, I was welcome to move into it.

The retreat center was conveniently located in Zirconia, North Carolina, about 15 minutes from Hendersonville, and equidistant between Asheville to the north and Greenville, South Carolina, to the south. It was also an hour from my hometown of Gaffney, South Carolina, making it close enough to visit family often without actually moving home. Even more important than the location and how impressed I was by the place, I felt completely safe with Posy. Her easy disposition, maternal kindness, generosity, and sense of humor sealed the deal for me. That day, on nothing more than a handshake, Posy and I agreed that I would join her and be a part of the Tigg's Pond community.

Returning to LA, I said goodbye to friends, and before I knew it, almost all my worldly possessions were in storage. Soon it was time to make the cross-country trek from the City of Angels to the Kingdom of Zirconia.

I had never driven cross-country before, but I had always fantasized about having a VW van with pop-top camper, roaming the backroads of our enchanted lands. Driving east, I pondered a mantra I had internalized from my friends at the Creative Visions Foundation in Malibu: "the journey is the destination." This is the title of a collection of art and poetry created by Kathy Eldon's late son Dan. Dan had also been transfixed by wanderlust, and in his early life he traveled around Africa as a photographer for Reuters, garnering the affectionate title, "Mayor of Mogadishu." Unfortunately, after the US government mistakenly bombed what they thought was council of warlords, in the violence that ensued Dan tragically lost his life.

Planning my cross-country adventure to North Carolina, I thought to myself, I wish I could have known Dan. His love affair with life was inspiring. Undoubtedly, Dan lit up any room he entered, and he enthusiastically embraced every challenge. And, to boot, he was a huge Bob Marley fan, as am I. Dan lived his life to the fullest because he knew, even at his young age, how incredibly precious life is. To this day, Dan's effervescent spirit (Kathy lovingly refers to his spirit as "noisy") stands as a reminder of what Marley's three little birds had to say: "every little thing gon' be alright." I sure hoped so.

When I gave my older sister Cheryl the details of my cross-country trek, she was green with envy. I suggested she join me, and she said she was up for the adventure. Our plans were easily made—she would fly to Albuquerque, where I would collect her at the airport, and we would continue on together. It warmed my heart to think about traveling with her, and to consider that the spirit of our mother, herself an adventurer in life, would also be along for the ride. It was from our mother that we both found our love for the big wide world and our journey east would be a celebration of her continuing love in our lives.

And so, in April 2014, I set out on "the 10" to New Mexico—for some reason, Californians use the definite article when referring to freeways. I forgot that the crack of dawn would be the worst time to travel east across the desert. Nevertheless, with the sun directly in my eyes and my trusty cocker spaniel Maggie the Wonderdog in tow, my hopes were riding on the wind. What was next? How might this unfold? Would I be happy?

As the highway stretched out ahead of me toward the horizon, I had plenty of time to consider my life to that point. I thought back to when I had graduated from Wofford College in Spartanburg, South Carolina, and could get all my worldly possessions into the trunk and the cabin of my pale yellow 1971 VW Bug. Now, more than 30 years later, both my VW Cabrio and a storage unit were full. And nothing had turned out quite like I imagined. The shock of how much I had lost still reverberated for me, but I also felt deep gratitude that somehow, in so many surprising ways, life was making a new path for me. Like a stream clouded by soot and sand when you tramp through, I was waiting for the water to clear.

In Albuquerque, I picked up Cheryl as planned, then we had some lunch and set out for our sojourn, making time for some sightseeing along the way. Our first diversion came just seventeen miles into our 1500+ mile eastern passage, taking us up the magnificent "Turquoise Trail" at nearby Tijeras, New Mexico. It's not really a detour if you consider that the journey is the destination though, right? All was good but I did wonder how long it might take for us to get to North Carolina at such a leisurely pace. We both fell in love with the artists, the colors, the mountains, and the night sky in Santa Fe.

But the highlight of this stopover had to be the Georgia O'Keeffe Museum. O'Keeffe's exquisite vision of the southwest tugged at my heart so much that I wondered what it might be like if I just stopped there to put down roots. The muted landscapes, the brilliance of her flowers, and the sublime panoramas melted our hearts with their beauty. O'Keeffe's masterpieces took me back to an earlier life, in the days before 9/11 at Saint Paul's Chapel and had referenced one of O'Keeffe's paintings, the "Ranchos Church." As I mentioned earlier, beautiful as it was, the Ranchos Church was painted from the rear and didn't exhibit any doors. It reminded me of my presentation to the vestry at Trinity, when I juxtaposed the Ranchos Church painting with my hopes for Saint Paul's Chapel.

We bought several posters at the museum, including the "Ranchos Church," which we were excited to frame and hang when we got to our respective homes. But later, driving through the nighttime desert landscape, Cheryl decided to roll down her window for a breath of fresh air. By mistake, she hit the wrong button, and instead of cracking her window, she inadvertently rolled down the back window. Our prints flew away into the desert night they'd been painted for. Without realizing it, though, I had already lost my connection to the Ranchos Church.

There were many challenges inherent to a cross-country trip in a small car with two people, a dog, and as much of my life as I could pack into the back seat and trunk—and my sister's rather large suitcase. About 1,500 miles in such small quarters bonded my sister and Maggie in a friendship that stands strong to this day.

After many other stops on the road, we finally made it to Tigg's Pond. Arriving, we pried our arms and legs and the rest of our bodies out of my tiny VW, and I found relief at this journey's end. Cheryl met Posy for the first time, beginning a beautiful, loving friendship that lasted until Posy's death in 2023.

I unloaded my things into the beautiful apartment upstairs in "the barn," which had great acoustics and no one around to hear a thing as I played my guitar. Soon, I realized I could crank the amp up as loud as I liked. The apartment had a queen-sized bed with a bathroom, a couch, a desk, and a fridge. None of it really matched, but that was OK. Downstairs in the barn, there was a full-size industrial kitchen where I could cook to my soul's delight. And the back side of the barn bordered a creek that would swell up after a rain, gurgling peaceful sounds that became music for my soul. *We have water.*

In the days and weeks after settling in, I began work in the garden. I discovered the "back to the land" movement in Topanga without realizing that the original movement, from the 1960s at least, had been conceived by the Mother Earth community just 15 miles from Zirconia, in Hendersonville, North Carolina. It was a joy to get my hands in the dirt, seeking to assist in nature's artistry on such an abundant canvas as Tigg's Pond. In all, there were twenty-seven raised beds, measuring 4 feet wide by 8 feet long. We planted cucumbers, carrots, tomatoes, peppers, okra, squash, and asparagus. A whole section of the garden was dedicated to herbs—especially basil. A massive perennial strawberry patch, both delicious and productive, ran between the beds, and a perennial asparagus patch measuring 6 feet by 30 feet bordered the garden on the side nearest the pond. It was more food than we could eat, and we took delight in sharing it with others.

Maggie was in doggy heaven, with so many smells and so many things to chase across all 54 acres. She loved tramping in the edge of the creek—the muddiest part, of course—or sunning on the dock by the pond as schools of sunfish swam up, asking for a treat. On rare occasions, we might glimpse Leviathan: a milky white bottom-feeding carp so large that he more than warranted his name.

To the west of the barn, a pasture begged for attention, green with four-leaf clovers that seemed to wink at me whenever I looked down. Each one felt like a reminder that Bob Marley's three little birds were correct in their predictions. In this pasture, Posy suggested we build a labyrinth.

For the next several weeks, with help from our friends Tarleton Brooks and Roy Harris, we framed and dug a labyrinth modeled after the legends of the ancient pre-Christian Minotaur labyrinth in Knossos, Crete. Our labyrinth at Tigg's Pond became a spiritual tool for our retreatants to go deep within themselves and confront their own demons and seek answers for their lives.

In a nutshell, this would become the metaphor for my own labyrinthine journey at Tigg's Pond. Like Theseus, I too went into the labyrinth to confront demons—only, they were mostly of my own making.

Walking a labyrinth is a bit like fishing. It's great if you happen to catch any insight, but good even when you don't. I loved to spend time out there, especially on sunny days, opening my heart to any available spiritual wisdom while I wrestled with my persisting demons of resentments, shame, and regret.

Just a little bit beyond the north side of the labyrinth, there was a hiking path leading to a small waterfall. Sometimes, I would go to my favorite perch on the creek bank and put my feet into the easy-paced cold mountain water. Other times, I would hike the quarter mile away to the waterfall, where I often encountered trees marked by bear claws, a reminder of the creature-inhabited wilderness we occupied. We had so many bear sightings at Tigg's Pond that the lodge on the property was named Black Bear Lodge. They were just another animal among the many sharing our space: hawks, owls, buzzards, mountain cats, deer, opossums, foxes, and one black snake I befriended and named Jack.

Tigg's Pond was a veritable paradise, if a bit lonely. I had moved from major metropolitan areas to Zirconia, North Carolina—an unincorporated community of less than 5,000 people. At that time, the only restaurant was the Chuck Wagon Grill, a food truck at Roscoe's, the nearby gas station.

Settling into the idyllic countryside and feeling a little bored, I had the bright idea to go cold turkey off my Lexapro. What could go wrong? Talk about wrestling with demons! I found out that the woods are like space—no one can hear you scream. Admittedly, it was not the best idea I'd had. It is certainly not advisable to stop taking Lexapro without medical supervision, and I don't recommend it. It was brutal, especially at first. Insomnia-triggered panic attacks replaced my already disrupted sleep. I would wake up, curl myself into a tight ball, and turn on my radio for the comforting voices of newscasters in the night as I reminded myself to breathe. And to focus on light and the future, not the darkness or the events in my past. I reminded myself that I *wanted* to feel my feelings. In the back of my mind, I often heard the cliché, "You gotta feel it to heal it." After a month of hyperventilating my way through the night, I finally began to glimpse the light of better days. When I could, I worked extra hard in the garden and on various projects that exhausted me, which helped me sleep better at night. And eventually, I was free of the Lexapro.

Still lonely, I decided to see what hiking groups might be active in the area. I found more than I had imagined. Western North Carolina is a hiking mecca, with many opportunities to meet up with fellow enthusiasts. I found a sundown-moonrise hike, like my favorite hike in Topanga, and I signed up for one going to Bearwallow Mountain. It was sponsored by Conserving Carolina, an exemplary conservation group with a terrific track record of success in protecting the natural beauty of the region. The Bearwallow Mountain hike is only about 2 miles long but has a moderate ascent of about 500 feet, making it strenuous but not difficult. The reward is a view on a bald summit with green pasture and a stunning 360-degree panoramic vista of the Blue Ridge Mountains off in the distance. The scenery along the hike was breathtaking as well, with the trail awash in blooming rhododendron and wildflowers galore. The comeliness of the sunset was only surpassed by the ethereal beauty of the simultaneous moonrise, with the twilight promising the possibility of a magnificent field of stars.

But the majestic beauty of the hike competed with the loveliness of a volunteer who introduced herself as Maria. Charming and gracious, with an easy sense of humor, I felt that I was glimpsing Dante's Beatrice. It was love at first sight—for me, anyway. Maria was a regular volunteer for Conserving Carolina, and that night, she took "sweep," the role of bringing up the rear of the hike to make sure no one was lost along the way. Smitten, I walked along slowly, lagging behind everyone so that I could chat with Maria and hear about the hike from her perspective. We had a delightful conversation, and she appeared to be everything I'd ever wanted in a partner. Gorgeous, witty and smart, great sense of humor, outgoing and athletic—the only thing I didn't like about her was that she was engaged. Of course she was. There is no way such an extraordinary woman wouldn't be attached. I left the hike crestfallen, tail tucked between my legs, but I never forgot the encounter.

Returning to Tigg's Pond, I was possessed by a wistful bout of nostalgia. Maria had inadvertently reminded me how tantalizing the emotions of companionship could be. I missed that sense of closeness and the excitement of sharing life with another person. I would think of her often over the next days, weeks, and months with a bittersweet pang of longing. Perhaps my heart had thawed enough to imagine being in a relationship again.

I channeled that energy into my work at Tigg's Pond. Posy had an enormous circle of friends eager to help and participate in events at Tigg's, and they became my dear friends as well. Moving back east to Zirconia had also reconnected me with my greatest advocate, Fred Burnham, and his equally extraordinary wife, Regan. With their home just 40 minutes away, we visited often, and their fellowship warmed my heart. I didn't always get what I wanted in life after 9/11, but I sure got better than I deserved when it came to friends. With Posy, Fred, and Regan in my camp, the odds of reclaiming my life were great and increasing every day.

I took the time to read, research, and write that being at Tigg's offered, then eventually consulted with my friends about developing a forgiveness initiative. I really wasn't able to work with any consistency or determination, and if I had to clock in somewhere, forget about it. But I had visions of what I might become—a forgiveness teacher. Incorporating Fred Luskin's Nine Steps to Forgiveness and Father Michael Lapsley's work at his "Healing of Memories" Institute, I came up with a plan for a Journey to Forgiveness walking trail. It would begin at the barn, moving from the back steps into the garden. With the help of dear friends Roy and Jimmie Harris, we built a bridge across one of the streams. The path would then travel around the lake and make its way to the labyrinth, the culmination of the forgiveness trail. For entering the labyrinth, we suggested Bishop Tutu's forgiveness decision tree that he and his daughter Mpho wrote about in their Fourfold Path of Forgiveness. Their idea, focused on relationships, was to decide whether, after forgiveness, one should renew or release a relationship. Either is acceptable, and both are appropriate. For example, if you have been in an abusive relationship, either personally or professionally, you can still forgive what happened and reclaim your power and agency by forgiving, but we don't recommend returning to an abusive relationship.

And if you are the one who needs to apologize in such a context, following the wisdom of our twelve step friends, amends are to be made, unless to do so might cause further harm. If necessary one can make amends by paying kindness and generosity forward. For example, if for some reason you were not present for a dying family member, you might consider volunteering or donating to organizations that offer solace and support for those struggling with end-of-life issues like hospice. And an important truth for offering any amends is to never repeat the infraction. These ideas were percolating in my consciousness.

As best I could I offered forgiveness classes based on Fred's methods, even though I had yet to commit to them fully myself. The love I felt from this community was palpable and empowering. I was making progress. I was feeling my feelings. I was experiencing some measure of healing. But despite all this love, I could not fully love myself. Despite all my talk of forgiveness, I could not yet forgive myself.

One day, my hope-to-do list included a project cleaning up the edges of the garden. There were clumps of logs and uprooted bushes, along with old hoses, broken planters, buckets, and wooden boards that had previously been used in some capacity in the garden but had long since been forgotten. In the same space, a neglected compost pile was growing both watermelons and tomatoes. It was a veritable jungle.

One pile of detritus had taken on a life of its own, loaded with bugs, bees, frogs, and a snake or two. I decided to tackle it that day, but before I could even get to the items needing removal, I had to whack through a wasteland of weeds. Vine by vine, I made my way down to a second level of rubbish. Underneath it all, I found the edge of a dilapidated tarp. I pulled and pulled to no avail. I had to excavate further and deeper if I had any hope of pulling it loose, cautious to avoid any repercussions. One Herculean yank pulled a large part of the tarp free, but that yank also angered a bee or a wasp or some other violent insect that stung me on the arm. More angry than hurt, I pulled at the tarp with even more force until finally, most of it was free.

I was bewildered. This tarp was huge—larger than any I had seen before. Examining my prize, I found an acronym stamped along one edge: ECVA. *ECVA? What could that mean?* Possibilities ran through my mind, and I was stunned to consider it might be "Episcopal Church and the Visual Arts." Posy, a priest, a visual artist, and graphic designer, was a member of this fellowship of church artists. And at the only General Convention of the Episcopal Church I had ever attended, the ECVA had projected visuals onto a huge screen during their worship services.

I was invited to attend because General Convention was celebrating our work at Saint Paul's Chapel. The work that I had started and led. And photos of me . . . and of my staff . . . and of Saint Paul's volunteers . . . Those photos had been lovingly displayed on that huge screen. Photos that had been taken by my friend Krystyna Sanderson—also a member of ECVA—and later published in her pictorial book, *Light at Ground Zero*.[1] I remembered the pride I'd felt seeing a photo she took of me blown up to life-size and stationed at the entrance of the convention space.

Stung by bee and circumstance, I realized that the crowning achievement of my career as a priest now lay in tatters, decaying in the forgotten rubbish, in the middle of nowhere at Tigg's Pond.

Could this possibly be true? Or was the intensity of my trauma playing with my mind? At this point, I can't say. Either way, that moment became a reckoning.

If you've even been in an automobile crash, you know there is a stunned mental silence before the pain of injury registers. The quiet of that moment of shock is incredibly loud. A void consumes your hearing, and time seems to stand still. My encounter with that tarp became one of those moments. I was stunned. It felt as if my life were flashing before my eyes. As if I myself and all of my life's work had been buried under that tangle of weeds. It broke my heart, and it broke me down.

The bee had stung my arm, and the tarp had stung my soul. My trauma had caught up with me. *Tag, you're it.* I fell to the ground, in shock, unable to weep. The stunned silence gave way to sirens going off in my head. My chest pounded. My head was splitting. I was glad to be alone. I stayed there on the ground, in outward silence while everything inside me was churning in tumult.

I wanted desperately to cry, but I had no tears. I wanted desperately to scream, but I had no voice. In that timeless moment, I questioned everything about myself. Was my life over? Is there any way I could ever do anything worthwhile or impactful in the world? Would I ever be more than just a defrocked priest?

After the extreme overwhelm of the initial shock abated, I pulled myself to my feet and staggered back to the barn. I wouldn't share this with Posy. How could I? It was too raw for me to mention without hyperventilating. I knew how to compartmentalize my emotions on the outside, just like I knew I would survive the sting of the bee. But the sting of the truth hit deeper, where bone meets marrow, and in that moment, I had no idea if I would survive. I spent the next two days in bed as truth and trauma slowly and painfully picked away every bit of flesh from my bones, like ants invading a church picnic. I couldn't move. The only thing I could find to be grateful for was the barn's doggy door so Maggie could take care of herself.

Like Paul on his way to Damascus, I had been blinded by reality, and it broke me into pieces. I can't describe the depths of my anguish; I can only point to a visual example. Albert Gyorgy's sculpture "Melancholie" is a bronze sculpture of a figure sitting on a bench, hunched over, with a giant hole in the center of his torso. (Figure 12.1) I was confronted by this image in one of the myriad articles of grief that I read in order to try and fix myself. The body of the man is created from the thinnest lines of copper, clearly making the case that the most important thing about the man is the void in the center of his being. The head is bowed as completely as possible, heavy with grief. The shoulders sag in despair. The hole, a total absence, represents the all-consuming anguish and grief the artist felt after the death of his beloved wife. My grief, like his, was unapproachable by the construction of words but spoke volumes in its silence.

What do you do when your life falls apart? When everything that brings you meaning and joy is taken from you?

You grieve.

You must.

Grief is different from grievance. Grievance is a kind of incomplete grief that seeks to blame someone else, often fantasizing about revenge. Grief, on the other hand, is acknowledging that you got a no from life and understanding

Figure 12.1 *The sculpture "Melancholia" by Albert György opened my heart to the tears I needed to cry.*

that getting a no is part of the human condition. Grief provides a period of mourning in which the nervous system works to metabolize the loss and to reset itself. Real grief takes time. And honesty. And courage. Grief is both a necessity and a blessing.

When I encountered the tarp in the garden, the real work of grief was beginning to take root in my life. It hit me hard, like a runaway locomotive. Truly I had been dancing around the edge of the labyrinth of my life, but now, I had set foot inside. It felt scary; I didn't know what demons might be waiting, or what I might encounter.

13

Will the Tears Stop?

After my rendezvous with the tarp in the garden, the behemoth of depression would come on like a slow ache in my heart and radiate outward until it consumed my whole body. In those moments, physical pain would crush any desire to move. Even my thoughts hurt. For the first few days, I was seized with this depression in seclusion, avoiding much of the suffering that I believed sharing my shame would bring. In the forgiveness methodology I now teach, we refer to the toxic combination of guilt and shame as "self-attack." Unaddressed, it can lead to isolation and despair. *Check, check, and check.*

Finding the tarp forced me to acknowledge the heartbreaking losses that I'd tried so hard to run from. Whether I was in New York City, Los Angeles, or Western North Carolina, the reality was still the same: my life was a mess. I was catastrophically entangled by grievances and resentments, and every time I tried to reimagine my future, I only saw the travails of my past slinking along. Finding the tarp opened floodgates of grief within me that I had worked hard for years to suppress. Grief that I had tried my best to push away in the form of anger. Grief that, in my anger, I had tried to project onto someone else in the form of my oft-told victim's narrative. These stories caused my nervous system to be constantly triggered, forcing me to run the emotional gamut of fight, flight, freeze, or fawn. Losing my capacity for joy and fulfillment, meaning and purpose. My mental and emotional options were limited, and I became a shell of my true self. And as I found out, this is a dangerous place to be.

Emotional overwhelm has been compared to a shaken bottle of soda with a great deal of pressure on the inside of the bottle. The safest way to release the pressure and prevent an explosion is to open and close the cap in a slow, cautious manner.[1] The encounter with the tarp presented me with a shocking moment of truth, a tragic denouement of my life's aspirations, shaking me up and throwing open the cap. My damaged ego exploded right there in the garden, leaving me shattered and scattered in its aftermath.

Everything I'd ever wanted to do with my life had been embodied in the role of a priest. And here I was, without a job and homeless, but for the kindness of Posy. I had a great job before 9/11, but because I couldn't find a way to make peace with resentments and losses, I couldn't find a successful way to move forward. While all of my losses were subsumed under the heading of my diagnoses—PTSD, depression, and several things wrong with my lungs and sinuses—it did not excuse me from my responsibility for my behavior. In denial I thought: If only I had listened to my superiors, I'd still have a job. I'd still have my health. I'd still be a priest. I'd still have my status in the world.

But then again, if I hadn't stood up to the challenge of bringing relief and comfort to workers at Ground Zero, I would be consumed by regret and shame. It would mean that I failed the great test of my life. For me, it was black and white. That, to me, was what it meant to be a priest. And now, I was undergoing an identity crisis, a psychic split, over losing my status because of my attitude and my ensuing mistakes. Lying in my bed, I didn't know if I could survive if I opened up to Posy about all that. I tried desperately to keep it contained. When I finally emerged to say hello to her, she asked where I'd been. "Just sorting through some things," I said. She didn't pry further, and I didn't divulge. I couldn't. I was paralyzed by the fear that I might start crying and *never* stop.

Intellectually, I knew much of what I needed to do to get on with my life. I was well-versed in the steps to forgiveness, the benefits of forgiveness, and the cost of non-forgiveness. It could not have been clearer. I had gotten a series of noes from life and, instead of grieving them, I kept them alive by blaming others. I held on to my grievances, and they only hurt me—not anyone else. The problem was, although I knew on some level these grievances were detrimental to me, I couldn't let go because I was too loyal to my suffering. But knowing what to do and doing it are two different things. It felt like the inverse of a story comedian Ron White shared. Recounting an unfortunate altercation at a bar, he said, "I might have had the right to remain silent—I just didn't have the ability."[2]

As my anger ran out of steam, even I became bored with my victim's narrative. I began to see the importance of opening a door to my grief. I was horrified that someone might find out that I was no longer a priest, even though at that point everyone already knew. I oscillated between denial of reality and bargaining with life to change the past. This left me on edge in any conversation, constantly prepared to steer the discussion in a different direction. If it came anywhere close to my pain, a paroxysm of shame would cause my heart to palpitate, my blood pressure would increase to a dull thump in my head, and my face would flush. It was as if I could feel the corpuscles in my body flashing red danger signals. Only, instead of sirens, a silence descended. Time slowed down, and all speech turned into barely audible distortions like I was submerged underwater.

Clinical studies say that recovering from trauma means being able to live in the present without being overwhelmed by the thoughts and feelings you have about what happened in the past.[3] Trauma provokes feelings of helplessness, powerlessness, and loss of agency, and compels a drive for isolation. The most important first step in trauma recovery is to re-establish a sense of safety. It took the company of the kind, compassionate friends I had gained at Tigg's Pond to create enough safety for me to take even the tiniest steps toward healing. I would rather have taken a pill (although the Lexapro didn't work) or flipped some switch to fast track my healing, but that's not how it works. Without feeling my feelings *and sharing them*, I had stunted my post-traumatic growth. There is no quick fix. True healing takes time. Little by little, as I began to open up about my grief, I was able to reconsider, and in small ways, relinquish my self-attacks.

During the summer of 2014, I found solace in the busyness of retreats and classes at Tigg's, while trying to keep up with our rather large garden. Fresh corn, tomatoes, okra, and cucumbers provided an almost daily feast as we hosted churches for their own retreats and offered a series of forgiveness classes and talks for a variety of different groups. Posy and I made numerous visits to the nearby Flat Rock Bakery for strategy sessions—as well as for their goat cheese and artichoke hearts pizza with a pesto basil base. *Delicious.* Slowly, my appetite for life was also returning.

That September we put together a commemoration for the anniversary of 9/11 at Tigg's Pond, and I created a display of some of the artifacts and banners that I had. But seeing the banners on display that night Tigg's Pond was a trigger for me. I felt a bit of panic stirring in my heart. I had not encountered these items for years. My challenge was not only visual, but also their smell. The stench of Ground Zero smoke is an indelible sensation that never leaves you once it has made itself at home in your olfactory memory bank. Confronted once again with the odor, I remembered how Ground Zero workers sought reprieve from that smell by smearing Mentholatum inside their respirators. It's funny how our olfactory sense works—how, out of the blue, you can be assaulted by a memory that has the power to shut you down. The smells of Ground Zero bushwhacked me that night and forced me to pause, even for the slightest minute, to whisper a prayer for strength to continue. Fortunately, it was not yet my time to speak, so I had cover for a few minutes before carrying on. Then I was able to continue.

Emotional healing is so complex; it's not straightforward like "step 1, step 2, step 3." Rather, it's more like one step forward, two steps back; or two steps forward, three steps sideways. The next day I laid low, just cherishing time with dear friends who had come to visit. This episode of traumatic triggering was nowhere near the devastation I felt that was prompted by the tarp. I was making progress, and I was surrounded by friends and not isolating. This was an important step.

From time to time, I get requests to speak at a church or to a group or fellowship about my 9/11 experiences and the topic of forgiveness. In 2015, the rector at Saint James Episcopal, Joel Hafer, kindly asked me to preach on the Sunday before Lent and then to offer a series of classes as Lenten teachings based on vignettes from the documentary, "The Power of Forgiveness," which features my work. Joel was the beloved long-time rector of Saint James, and Posy had served there as a pastoral associate for a while.

I was honored to comply. After the service that Sunday morning, while greeting parishioners, I was surprised to be reunited with the woman I thought was the most beautiful hike leader I had ever seen, Maria. I found out that Maria's last name was Lund. When I met her on the hike, I only knew her first name. I couldn't believe it. She was sitting down front where she always sat, as she told me, when attending church with her late mother, Barrie. As we exchanged greetings, I said it was good to see her again and that I hoped she might be able to come to the Wednesday night Lenten offerings. She said that she was planning to. I didn't see a ring on her hand, so I was cautiously optimistic.

For the Wednesday night classes during Lent, I screened successive vignettes from the documentary "The Power of Forgiveness"[4] and offered prepared questions to guide conversations at the dinner tables. Each dinner table constituted a small group, and after initial pleasantries, the conversations would start in earnest. I needed to sit somewhere, so I often took delight in sitting with Maria's groups. We had a conversation on the first night over soup, salad, and breadsticks (it was Lent, after all) and I discovered that she was no longer engaged. And, over those six weeks of Lent, I got up the nerve to ask her to have dinner with me. She said yes. I was euphoric. I couldn't believe my luck. It had only been 231 days since we first met, but who's counting?

After Easter, Maria joined me for dinner at Tigg's Pond. Somehow, I found out that she enjoyed Italian food, that she was vegetarian, and that she loved cheese. I knew exactly what to cook. I made a delicious salad from garden-fresh vegetables and my homemade grapefruit sriracha vinaigrette (don't knock it until you've tried it), followed by a vegetarian lasagna made from roasted vegetables sautéed in a spicy ragu, layered with noodles and as much cheese as I could stuff into the dish. I set a table by candlelight on the porch of the barn, overlooking the pond in the twilight of the evening. We discussed the deep questions of our lives—our hopes and dreams, our pasts and our futures. Fred Luskin had told me that I might be happier if I focused on things I'm grateful for, and I could have filled a whole gratitude journal with that night alone. Close to a year since I scuttled away from that hike forlorn and crestfallen, our friendship began, then grew into romance as easily as one could hope. With her love, I was at a stage in my healing journey where I felt more empowered to open up, to take a risk. The icebergs of grief frozen in my heart were beginning to thaw.

Posy and I had started a coffee house at Tigg's Pond, and Maria enjoyed them as much as I did, especially singer-songwriter Dave Wilcox. I had been a fan of Dave's over the years, remembering one of his songs that got a lot of attention in the eighties, "Eye of the Hurricane." He was great then, but now even better. His well-crafted songs and honey baritone voice melted our hearts. That night was one of the best date nights ever.

Dave is a low-key but charismatic leader and his followers are like an extended family, with cousins galore. They had a yearly "family reunion" weekend at nearby Kanuga. Dave asked me to share a forgiveness workshop for it, and I was happy to do so. On that weekend, we discovered that Dave and his wife Nance have a terrific circle of friends, and I met some of my most dear lifetime friends there. I met Gareth Higgins and his husband Brian Ammons. They invited me to join their Sunday night men's group, a circle of the national men's movement, the New Mankind Project (MKP). Years earlier, I had been initiated into the movement and sat in a men's circle in NYC but, over time, I had fallen by the wayside. This circle of new friends gave me two things I needed desperately: a vision for my own healing and an 8-man personal accountability group that would kick my butt to keep me on track.

Gareth and Brian are both inspiring peace activists, authors, and faith community leaders (Brian served as chaplain to Warren Wilson College in Swannanoa). They also host retreats and workshops on the importance of creating new and better stories to live by. Gareth's book *Corey and the Seventh Story* (co-authored with Brian McClaren) is a kind of children's book for adults. It has the trappings of a children's book with drawings comfortably targeted for young readers, but it is written with an adult's understanding of the popular stories we tell ourselves. *Corey and the Seventh Story* was like a lightning bolt hitting me between the eyes. Reading the book and discussing its themes opened my eyes to a new way of thinking about my journey: I had been stuck in a story—a series of stories—that kept me far from healing. The seventh story, however, and the point of the book, is the story of openheartedness and compassion. It's a story of connection and kindness, for oneself and for others. It was what I needed to hear. It's amazing to think that when we are ready to open our hearts, the universe seems willing to send the needed medicine.

My heart was opening, and I desperately needed to change my story. For too long I had languished in the confines of self-defeating stories, especially the ones characterized by blaming and revenge. In the call to the seventh story, the story of collaboration, compassion, forgiveness, and hope, I heard the words of Father Michael Lapsley echoing loudly: the way to move from being a victim to living victoriously is through forgiveness.

After hearing my story, Gareth and Brian decided to throw a "coming out" party for me, their hetero friend. It was a coming out party where friends gathered just for the sake of hearing me out—my resentments, my failures, my guilt, and my shame. For me, this was church—everything I had hoped for from colleagues and leaders—a community gathered in love, ever-widening, ever-deepening, open to the plight of others. To be heard with ears of kindness and compassion, with a sense of humor thrown in so that I didn't take myself too seriously. It was a healing balm for my soul. I remembered the adage from Paul Tillich—"To love is to listen." That night I felt heard, loved, celebrated, and renewed. Deep down, the new Lyndon was beginning to form.

With my new circle of friends through Brian and Gareth, I had many conversations about grief work. And I was surprised often to find out that I wasn't alone in my struggle. These men were veterans in the ways of grief and had much wisdom to share. One recommendation was to acquaint myself with the ancestral grief work of Malidoma Somé, a West African medicine man hailing from Burkina Faso. Somé lived in the world of West African culture and spirituality, but he also happened to have two doctorates in the healing arts. After doing some searching, I found out that Malidoma offered community grief retreats in Florida. I set an intention to make one. I knew I needed it and made a plan to attend the next one offered in Orlando.

In the summer of 2015, another speaking engagement was on the docket for me—to be the keynote speaker for the annual Christian Formation retreat for the Episcopal Church, held at Kanuga Conference Center. My longtime friend Chris Lynn was chair of the program committee and had presented my work to the committee for consideration. They agreed that as teachers and leaders in the field of Christian formation it would be helpful for church to consider the lessons learned from the response to the tragic attacks on 9/11. I had written a few things about this, including authoring the *Disaster Response Manual* (2004) for the Episcopal Diocese of New York, and giving a talk for the interfaith working group of the National Council of Churches.[5] Additionally, I had published a pertinent article for a collaboration of interfaith chaplains.[6] I was both exhilarated and crushed by the invitation—exhilarated and honored by the invitation to address such an influential church-wide body, and crushed because the previous time I spoke at Kanuga, I had worn the collar of a priest. This time, that collar no longer belonged to me. My new status would be on public display with a group whose opinion of me meant everything to me.

Chris and I had been friends ever since we worked together at the Episcopal Church of the Advent in Spartanburg, South Carolina. I asked Chris to make sure my ecclesial status—or lack thereof—wouldn't be a problem for the committee. Chris called to let me know the committee agreed to have me be their speaker. She understood my embarrassment and was gentle in her care for me. I was both relieved and terrified. My pariah complex, never far away, was rearing its head again. The chaplain for the conference, Bishop Jay Magnes, was also a chaplain to me and encouraged me to stand in my truth, to teach what had cost me so much to learn. As Bishop for the Armed Services, Jay had been at the Pentagon on the fateful day of 9/11 and had been active in helping rescue trapped colleagues there. If anyone could have empathy for my plight, it was Jay.

Each morning, I gave an hour-long presentation on what I thought it meant to find hope in the midst of crisis, even as I struggled to implement that in my own life. Following the presentation, I would retire to my room and with fear and trembling mixed with a few echoes of joy, I prepared for the next day's lecture. I tend to overprepare for speaking engagements, but these presentations felt like the most important presentations of my life. My body was flush with stress chemicals pulsing through it, as I fought off a pretty severe case of imposter syndrome. On the exterior I tried to convey the casual confidence of authority, but inside I heard critical voices lying to me, saying that I had none.

It took copious amounts of raw courage for me to step up to the microphone each day to say anything, since I felt I had little authority to speak. Of course I had already mapped out the whole week's talks, but I was nervous and wanted to make sure I was as prepared as I could be. What I wasn't prepared to do was transform myself into the priest I used to be. That's what my heart wanted, but as I have said, you can't change the past. Nevertheless, this community of Christian educators wrapped their arms around me and inspired me to speak my truth even if my voice quivered. They honored me with their attention, challenged me with their questions, and loved me for who I was, mistakes and all. They welcomed me into the circle of all redeemed sinners as we shared Eucharist, presided over by Bishop Magnes. Maria and Posy took time out of their work schedules to attend at my invitation, and their support helped me know I could get through it.

At the closing of the conference, I shared a song I had written about life inspired by the French tightrope walker I had met while serving at the Cathedral of Saint John the Divine in NYC, Philippe Petit. A poster of him from the movie *Man on a Wire* has had a home on the wall of my study for more than a decade. It's one of my daughter Margaret's favorite movies, and she had me watch it with her. The song I wrote features the concentration of Phillippe Petit, poised between the Twin Towers, 110 stories up, without any safety net. I tried to make the case that if there's anyone who could model what it means to focus on the present moment, it was him. Midway between two towers, 110 stories high, if he looked too far ahead, he might misstep and fall off. And if he looked behind—well, you get the picture. One line goes, "This step, this breath, this moment between life and death, is precious, sacred." Another couplet of lines expressed my aspiration not only for myself but also what I wished for others: "Not looking behind you, or too far ahead, no past to regret, no future to dread." The title for the conference, "Hope in the Midst of Crisis: From Tragedy to Healing through Forgiveness," was exactly what I was desperately trying to accomplish in my own life.

Speaking at this conference was one of the most terrifying things I have ever done. I felt confident and competent to speak to the topic, based on my work, but presenting felt so raw to me—it was almost as if I were standing in front of the whole conference, for the duration, naked, and out on the wire, balance teetering. It's either one of the craziest or the most courageous things I've ever done. I am so glad that I responded to the invitation and found the fortitude to follow through on my commitment. The background noise of my shame at my failure didn't drown out our conversations, but it was a force to be reckoned with. Keynoting this conference was a pivotal point in my development and healing. At this conference, I began to find my voice as a teacher, more so than as a priest. I found an internal authority and calling not dependent upon the conferral of orders by a bishop. I mean no disrespect to those who are so called—as I was. But that part of my life is over, and I needed to open my heart to the life that was showing up for me. When the conference was complete, in my room, I collapsed before I could celebrate.

A few weeks later, Gareth and Brian invited me to go on their retreat to Northern Ireland. Growing up in Northern Ireland in the 1970s, the son of a police officer during the time of "The Troubles," Gareth had imprinted on his soul the vital importance of peace-making. Gareth and Brian offer peace pilgrimages to Northern Ireland, a chance to see the beauties of the Emerald Isle and to hear from leaders on the ground working for peace and conflict transformation. In their kindness, they insisted that I attend their next retreat gratis, and they would find a benefactor to cover my airfare. I couldn't believe my good fortune. Not only was I finding a path to be of service beyond my shame, but I was being welcomed into a new circle of friends who understood me.

They introduced me to a new friend, Bill Creighton, who sponsored the flight. Bill is a kind and generous mensch. I had first met Bill at Dave's annual gathering at Kanuga, but had no idea he would become a benefactor making such an exciting trip possible. Bill is a stocky muscular man, also a musician, whose can-do attitude rarely takes no for an answer. If you've met Bill, you know what I mean. Brian and Gareth, along with Dave Wilcox and Bill Creighton, created an amazing healing pilgrimage through the sacred sites in the North of Ireland, in word and song. It was a healing balm for my soul. I will never forget the vivid beauty of Northern Ireland, its lush green grasses and ancient churches—especially the shrine of Saint Patrick—and so many pastures full of sheep. One day we had lunch in Belfast with leaders from both sides of the former conflict, the "Troubles," and to hear how these leaders were now working together on the City Council of Belfast was so encouraging. While much of the world was still dreaming the impossible dream, these two men were making it happen. They inspired in me a renewed hope for the possibility of peace in the world, and that challenged me to step up and do my part.

Touring the pastoral beauty of the North of Ireland, we spoke often of the sublime work of one of Ireland's greatest poets, John O'Donohue. Gareth had been personal friends with John, and the poet's fingerprints were all over the spiritual presentations on our retreat. A highlight for me was being introduced to one of O'Donoghue's unfinished poems, a stanza I took as a mantra for my life on my own journey to healing:

> "I would love to live like a river flows,
> carried by the surprise of its own unfolding."[7]

14

Seen from the Start

Mother Emanuel AME Church, the oldest African American church in Charleston, South Carolina, was founded in 1817. For more than two centuries it has stood downtown, unsubmissive, on Calhoun Street—a street named for John C. Calhoun, former US vice president turned South Carolina senator, who himself owned more than seventy slaves. Calhoun was known as the "Great Nullifier" advocating for states to nullify any national laws they didn't like—including slavery. He became the political architect for the states' rights movement. In contrast, the Mother Emanuel community has always been a hotbed of freedom energy, working for the liberation and support of slaves and freed slaves. Although Emanuel African Methodist Episcopal Church was disassembled after the Slave Rebellion of 1828, it secretly maintained a network of connections until the church could be re-established following the Union army's defeat of the Confederacy in 1865. When it was rebuilt, it regained its prophetic voice and renewed its actions for freed slaves. Mother Emanuel remains a leading voice for racial justice to this day.

Five days after I had gathered with church leaders at the Kanuga Conference Center to discuss forgiveness and "Hope in the Midst of Crisis," just four hours inland from Charleston, a violent attack was perpetrated against Mother Emanuel and nine of her members murdered. The perpetrator's intent was to rupture the social fabric of the city, region, and country and to start a race war.

Family members of the "Emanuel Nine" had their hearts ripped out of their chests when they heard the news, and the shockwaves of the incident carried across the nation like an emotional atomic bomb. Of course, the perpetrator knew that it would. He chose Mother Emanuel, erroneously thinking that his actions might spark a race riot, his intention. But instead of instigating racial violence, he inadvertently opened the floodgates of love and forgiveness, with a response that was unexpected: they forgave him. Charleston's Mayor Joseph Riley summed it up well: "A hateful person came to this community with some crazy idea he'd be able to divide us, but all he did was unite us and make us love each other even more."[1]

In a shocking turn of events only days after the attacks, the family members of slain loved ones declared their forgiveness for the perpetrator. Not because he deserved it, but because they deserved peace. Amid great pain, they wisely relinquished the most seductive of poisons—the lust for revenge—insisting that if they didn't forgive, hate would win the day. The entire Mother Emanuel community offered prayers for the murderer who had desecrated their sacred community, asking God to open his heart to a new way of seeing things, that he might turn his life around and repent.

When the Mother Emanuel community forgave their murderer, in no way were they saying that his actions were okay, or that what happened didn't matter. Giving up their desire for revenge did not mean foregoing their right to pursue justice through the legal system. Such misconceptions make a mockery of forgiveness. What this community demonstrated—what they embodied—was a master class on the power of forgiveness to transform lives and create the future.[23]

Maria and I went down to Mother Emanuel in Charleston the following weekend to show our support and express our condolences. A large crowd of support had gathered outside during the funeral services for these beloved church members and pastors, some holding signs and placards of solidarity and encouragement. We stood in front of the church with the crowd, in prayer and silent witness.

On that summer day in the Lowcountry, with blue skies, puffy white clouds, and a gentle breeze—the weather belying the solemnity of the day—one sign stood out to me, held in the hands of a young woman: "Love Always Wins #Charlestonstrong." The sign took up residence in my head and heart. *If love always wins, what might I do to be on the winning side?* I was profoundly moved by the tragic loss and the family members' heroic response to it. The work of forgiveness in the world is a serious assignment, a responsibility that, in the depths of my heart, I believed I had not yet measured up to. If all my losses following the tragedy of 9/11 were combined, they were never so great as even the tiniest loss that the Mother Emanuel community sustained. I had experienced 15 years of travail, and much of it was self-inflicted. I had spent too much time focused on my own troubles, licking my wounds, and avoiding true grief. Mother Emanuel refused the seduction of the grievance process; they honored their grief by naming it, feeling it, and then forgiving. I knew forgiveness is a vital tool for conflict transformation, and I believed it was sorely needed in the world. If only I'd had the spiritual strength that these families displayed—to declare forgiveness, forego revenge, and find a path to peace and healing through God's grace. But I didn't. And I still couldn't. *Why was it so hard for me to "let go"?*

Often, when we speak of letting go, it's an oversimplification of a rather complex process. We can't say that the painful experience didn't happen, or that we can magically relegate it to the past. Rather, letting go is a prolonged process of re-evaluating and reframing the painful experience, to see it within a larger context.

My debilitating blockage, the thing standing between me and my ability to let the past go, I soon came to understand was a lack of self-forgiveness. Losing my identity had been a death blow to my ego. Joseph Campbell's quip about embracing the life waiting for us required a radical transition from me. Letting go of my former life and status was a herculean task. It's not the case that I had a choice—that life was gone. I was unsuccessfully trying to hold on to a memory of what was and somehow bring it back to life. But as anyone in their right mind knows, it doesn't work that way. Mother Emanuel's courageous witness precipitated a sense of urgency within me, to get over myself and practice the work of forgiveness as much as I'd taught it. I had been running a race, choosing to carry an extra fifty pounds. What was I thinking? The truth is I was too loyal to my suffering, and I thought the gods of right and wrong might somehow contravene my life and change it back. And while I was waiting for this miracle to happen, I chose to occupy my time by blaming others. But painfully the adage, "If you blame, you stay the same" began to haunt me—even I became bored with the blame games I played in my victim's stories. If I wanted to embrace the life in front of me, I could no longer look to my future and see only the failures and betrayals of my past. Something had to give. But until I could forgive myself for my mistakes, for holding on to my grievances, and for trying to change the past, I would not be able to forgive others. I would not be able to forgive life.

I needed a reframe. I needed to find compassion for myself. I needed to see myself as a person who, like every other person, makes mistakes. I had to give up my ego's desire to be perfect. To be Superman. I had made mistakes, and I had paid dearly for them. Coming to Tigg's Pond, surrounded by loving friends, smitten by a promising romance, I wanted more than anything to embrace the life that was waiting for me. I wanted to move on. I had to let go. Anais Nin summed up my dilemma well: "And the day came when the risk to remain tight in a bud was more painful than the risk it took to blossom."

This transformation was undoubtedly unfolding because the antidote for non-forgiveness is gratitude—and I had so much to be grateful for. I was healing at pace with the growing sense of safety and acceptance I felt. I had moved to Tigg's Pond on a handshake and a prayer, as a declaration of my intention for a new beginning. My hope, my faith, was that I would find the healing my soul longed for. And that's exactly what Tigg's Pond provided. I had a safe and comfortable place to live, surrounded by the natural beauty of the Western North Carolina mountains, and a loving circle of friends who were eager to explore whatever my "next" might be. As far as I could tell, I also had my health—I had ceased the nearly constant hits off my inhaler to help me breathe. I still had disturbing dreams, but they no longer ruined my waking days. And I spent my time caring for a beautiful garden that not only inspired me but also provided a delicious harvest of vegetables, about 40 feet from farm to my table. Taking stock of my life, I had everything I needed. I was blessed.

Now, somehow, I had to find the courage to be present to my pain. Following our visit to Mother Emanuel, I remember sitting with Posy and Tigger, and our friend Thea, sharing the anguish of losing my status as a priest. I opened up about the "pariah complex" of shame that came with it. Through it all, Posy and Thea, always my champions, reminded me that my shame was misleading me. That I am a good person, with a noble cause, and that God has a plan for me. Posy reminded me that we all make mistakes—and that I surely had—but that we are more than the sum of our mistakes. For years, I carried a worn copy of one of her favorite scripture verses in my wallet: "For I know the plans I have for you," declares the Lord, "plans to prosper you and not to harm you, plans to give you hope and a future." Jeremiah 29:11 (NIV).

Even if I had won the lottery, I could not have been luckier when it came to friends. Posy was especially kind to me, her prodigal brother who was coming home to himself. Having endured her own agonies in life, Posy had compassion for me as I struggled to embrace the present moment with joy and awe. To find peace and healing as my life, like a river was unfolding. Concerns about my status, my identity, my understanding of who I was slowly receded like a slack tide at sunset. And things were still changing. Isn't that how life is? You get it all figured out, and you hold it tightly in your hand like a precious stone made just for you. But then it all turns to sand, slipping through your fingers no matter how tight your grip. In tears—both of sorrow and joy—I wondered how the river of my life would twist and turn from here.

In hindsight, my time at Tigg's Pond was less about hosting coffee houses or teaching forgiveness, or any "work" I did; it was about me finding a sanctuary where I could safely fall apart and, through the mercy of God, put my life back together. I needed to stop running, let go, and grieve. And what I needed most of all was to find and embrace compassion for myself. With a circle of loving friends holding me accountable all over Western North Carolina and new romantic possibility with Maria, this promised to be one of the most extraordinary chapters in my life.

One of the cardinal rules in forgiveness work is not to compare suffering. It's not helpful for any of us. My suffering is mine and yours is yours. We all move at different paces toward the cup of healing. But the temptation is strong to compare. When I looked at heroes of forgiveness, I couldn't help but wonder how I missed the mark so significantly. The families of the Emanuel Nine who forgave within a few days of the murders. My friend Jean Paul Samputu, a famous Rwandan singer, lost his whole family in the genocide of 1994—

murdered by his childhood friend. Father Michael Lapsley, the South African priest who lost both of his arms and an eye through political violence. *And still they forgave.* How could the man (me) who courageously improvised in real time to deploy an effort to assist in a catastrophe, be the same man (again, me) who took more than a decade to put into practice the very things he came to teach? I was speaking about forgiveness on a world stage in Rwanda, Beirut, South Africa, Mumbai, and other places in the aftermath of grave atrocities—but *I couldn't find forgiveness in my own heart* for feeling disrespected and betrayed. I couldn't forgive myself or let go of the idea that my mistakes were somehow someone else's fault. If you, dear reader, are looking for a definitive confession of hypocrisy from me, this is it. I was blinded by my ego and too loyal to my suffering. "From the place where we are right, flowers never grow in the springtime." I could grow cucumbers, but I couldn't grow joy in my heart without forgiveness.

The decision to forgive is not once and for all. We don't declare our forgiveness and then shake the dust off our hands and move on. That's not how grief works, and that's not how forgiveness works either. Forgiveness is not just an act or a response to the content of your life's journey. It's a process—a way of navigating the wave and the trough, the agony and ecstasy of your life. Forgiveness is finding peace. It is letting go of the things we can't control and making peace with the noes we get from life. Forgiveness is a daily spiritual practice.

Another lesson I was just beginning to comprehend is that forgiveness does not mean reconciliation. Reconciliation is admirable, healing, and a sacred endeavor—*if* it is possible to do without inflicting further damage to yourself or to another person or group. Families of the Emanuel nine forgave, but they didn't reconcile.

Furthermore, in the Stanford forgiveness methodology, it is clear: forgiveness is something we do for ourselves. It is the very embodiment of self-care—but it is *not selfish.* Taking care of ourselves helps us be the best we can be, not only for ourselves, but for our friends and family, our communities, and the world. Forgiveness is a wellness practice that helps us fulfill Gandhi's exhortation to "Be the peace we wish to see in the world." When we find peace in our own lives, we send forth ripples of peace into the world.

Tigg's Pond had been a refuge, a place where I felt safe and loved enough to let my metaphorical hair down (though mine is usually pretty short). There, I learned more helpful ways to respond to emotional triggers than the ones I had been using. I was turning a corner—finally—and could understand—finally—that I needed to love myself enough to forgive myself for my mistakes. And for my own soul's health, I needed to love myself enough to forgive others. The remembrances of the enemies my mind had perseverated on, ruminated on, for years, was what was thwarting me now, not the acts themselves; actions that happened more than a decade prior. This realization opened a healing portal for me to see things more clearly. Instead of the expected fight, flight, freeze, or fawn responses, I was now finding it useful to become curious. I learned to ask questions of my trauma: "What is this triggered response or memory or dream trying to teach me? How might I honor its presence so that I can begin to unpack it and release it?" Being inquisitive about my trauma triggers allowed me to claim more agency in my responses and a tiny bit more control of my life—both waking *and* sleeping.

Most of my trauma specters visited me in the shadowlands of my dreams. Immediately following 9/11, my nightmares were more focused on the trauma of Ground Zero. Often, I would have troubling dreams conjuring disturbing sights I saw in the pit, or the terror of the workers as they made gruesome discoveries while excavating human remains from the debris. Or I would replay the terror of the second airplane exploding into the south tower of the former World Trade Center as I stood paralyzed by shock, defenseless underneath it. How many times had that fireball erupted in my dreams? I can't tell. While awake, I could use my compartmentalization skills to lessen these internal disturbances. And I discovered that if I took Benadryl for sleeping, I was less likely to remember troublesome dreams the next morning. Sleep had become a liminal world where I was captive to the whims of my REM cycles, a no man's land without the sheriff of my ego to shut down the outlaws of memory.

Over time, there were many other dream variations, but they mostly followed one new narrative arc: I would be serving a new church, officiating at services of Holy Communion, when someone would publicly confront me because of my loss of status, something I had forgotten. Uusually it was a bishop or a church elder wagging fingers at me—sentencing me to return to my dungeon of despair and shame. But now these dreams were becoming less frequent. Instead of four nightmares in a week, I was down to one or two. Little by little, my nervous system was beginning to release the injuries it had stored.[4]

The presenting markers for my diagnosis of PTSD (some clinicians prefer PTSI) include:[56]

- Being easily frightened or startled
- Always staying on guard for danger
- Trouble sleeping
- Trouble concentrating
- Self-destruction behaviors like driving too fast or drinking too much
- Overwhelming sense of shame or guilt.[7]

Recognizing several of these markers in my experience, especially the shame and guilt, helps me find a measure of compassion for myself. Without shifting responsibility for my choices, I could nevertheless realize that my pitfalls were born of injury, injuries that for a long time remained unacknowledged and unhealed.

According to SoCal Mental Health, there are three phases of PTSI and PTSD treatment: stabilization, trauma work, and integration.[8] I had not been aware of this upon my arrival at Tigg's Pond, but I had clearly begun the process of stabilization. Once I could exhale, and with time and the help of loving friends and counselors, I was able to wade through a good bit of trauma work and begin the process of integration. Over time, my nervous system became easier to regulate. Whenever I could reflect from a place of self-care and self-compassion, I was integrating the broken pieces of my past into my new life. It was akin to Japanese art of Kintsugi—using gold to transform broken pieces of pottery into beautiful, unique objects that emphasize both their history and the resilience embodied by their repair.

I found peace in the present, and it was such a gift. At the same time, my courtship with Maria was deepening. We had many opportunities for soul-filled conversations that helped me find calm and look to the future. Did I mention she's a counselor by trade?

Serendipitously, at that time the renters who had been living in the retreat lodge at Tigg's Pond moved out, and Posy insisted that I move in. The lodge is a three-bedroom, three-bath mountain chalet, with a full-length deck overlooking the 54-acre bowl of Tigg's Pond. Sitting on the side of the mountain with sweeping vistas of other mountains and distant valleys is a sight to behold. In the fall, the views from the deck are a rapturous smorgasbord of nature's extravagance—a bouquet of autumnal reds, golden yellows, rustic browns, oranges, and slight purples—all framed by the lush greens of the divinely placed evergreen trees, all accentuated by the crispness of the autumn mountain air. The lodge was named Black Bear for obvious reasons—bears were frequent and sometimes cherished visitors.

I couldn't believe my good fortune. Posy had been rooting for my relationship with Maria to work out, and I suppose she thought it would be good for me to have more space. After my initial reluctance, she insisted, so I gladly accepted. Moving into the lodge was not only luxurious, but it was also incredibly convenient timing—having just made the cross-country trek to retrieve my belongings from storage, I now had a place to put them. Now I had a place to unpack my furniture and personal effects when I brought them back, instead of putting them in storage in the barn.

The decision to collect my personal effects from storage in California was a significant marker: in my heart I was declaring Western North Carolina to be home. As I made plans to bring my worldly goods from my former life to my current one, Maria offered to go with me and turn that chore into an adventure. I had heard the gallows humor that a friend will help you move, but a good friend will help you move a body. But loading up and driving a painfully slow-moving, under-air-conditioned van 2,300+ miles? Across the country? *In August?* Well, that's something more. What could have been a lonely, emotional setback of nostalgia was becoming a future-oriented down payment on my new life.

We flew to LA first to visit with some of my friends for a few days. I was excited to introduce them to Maria, and everyone agreed that I was the luckiest man on Earth. Then we collected the 26-foot moving van that I'd reserved—an exceptionally slow lunker a few years past its prime. Maria's "get'er done" approach to the hard work of loading a van was only surpassed by her fearlessness in taking the wheel of that huge land submarine. As we sweated our way through the day, her warm personality and sense of humor shone through.

For the second time in less than 5 years, I set out on "the 10" headed east. With my past behind me and my future in front of me, Maria and I focused our sights on Tucson, where we would stay with my dear friend Tom Sawyer and his partner Deb Roberts. Tom and I became fast friends on the Ireland retreat while sitting on the back of a bus in Northern Ireland on our way to the shrine of Saint Patrick. As it turned out, Tom, a leader in the health sciences field, was scheduled to give a presentation for the upcoming national Employees Assistance Professionals Association conference—one that Maria, as the president and chief operating officer of First Sun EAP in Columbia, South Carolina, would be attending. Such a coincidence! Tom knew of Maria's leadership in the field and, I would come to find out, she knew about his. Judging by his reactions on that bus to Down Cathedral though, I'm honestly not sure what Tom was most impressed by: me having served in such a dramatic way after 9/11, or that I was in a relationship with such an admired and accomplished leader in the field of mental health.

Two other friends that Tom and I had met on the Ireland pilgrimage, Amy and Kerry Clark, were also in town, and they all joined us at Luby's for dinner—a casual restaurant that featured, to my delight, some spicy Mexican dishes. We were having a grand old time together—margaritas, chips and salsa, chicken-fried steak—until I bit into one of my juicy pickled jalapenos from the salad bar that—I kid you not—spurted juice across the table and right into Maria's eye. It was such a *weird* occurrence that, apart from being mortified, I couldn't help but chuckle. Maria was a good sport about what could have been a test to our budding relationship. *Or so I thought*. The next day, we made a stop to fill our truck with gas on the way out from Tom and Deb's. When I got back in the truck, a rather large, hairy spider descended on me from behind the driver's seat. I was horror-stricken as a large arachnid with a furry leg span of at least

24 inches sprawled across my face. I'm still embarrassed at the scream that this self-identifying "manly man" emitted. Maria had successfully executed her revenge. We had the biggest laugh, and with our new furry eight-legged friend commandeering the way from the dashboard, we set out for the next stop on our pilgrimage: Big Bend National Park in southwest Texas.

If you've ever driven that route or even looked at a map for the drive from LA to North Carolina, you will see that the Chihuahuan Desert is not exactly on the way. We took the detour because Big Bend was a place I had come to love, and I wanted to share it with Maria. In my early years as a priest, I made an annual backpacking pilgrimage with clergy friends who introduced me to the sublime beauties of Big Bend National Park.

Our plan had been to stop at Fort Davis, Texas, then get a rental car for the ninety-mile drive to Big Bend from there. Except there were no available rental cars when we arrived. Faced with a dilemma, we decided to throw caution to the wind and head for the desert. It was a bit of a white-knuckle drive getting our beast of a truck through those mountains, slowly climbing the heights sometimes feeling almost vertical going through the hairpin switchbacks. But we survived—and Maria was enthralled. Mission accomplished. This visit to Big Bend was another step in my journey to healing and feeling safe: I was able to visit a place that I loved and cherished, and to share that with someone who loved it, and me, too. Healing can sometimes be slow and twisted like switchbacks on a hairpin turn through the high desert, but I was on that healing road now, and what's more important—headed in the right direction.

We continued on from Big Bend, with many more adventures along the way. By the time we got to Memphis—and Graceland—I was totally enthralled with Maria. ("Wise men say . . ."). Deep down I began to sense that I knew that she was the one for me, and I wanted to share with her all the places and things that delight me. A week after we began our journey, we arrived at Tigg's Pond. I began sorting my furniture and sorting my life. Soon after that, Maria and I decided to move in together into Black Bear Lodge.

We were each sensitive to the needs of the other, knowing that combining households can be stressful. It had been a long time since I lived with another person. We both had a house full of furniture; she had two cats, and I had a dog. It was a joy and an adjustment. We found great delight in setting up our life together, sharing meals, entertaining friends, and helping all our furry friends navigate our blended family.

Moving to Tigg's Pond had been its own Ground Zero experience in reclaiming and reframing my life. If I could give everyone who is struggling because of mistakes, resentments, or regrets one gift, I would want it to be a place like that. Acknowledging my own unenforceable rule—*that I should never make a mistake*—gave me the freedom to own my story, warts and all. Brene Brown points out that "When we deny our stories, they define us. When we own our stories, we get to write a brave new ending."[9] This means acknowledging and accepting the less flattering parts, not smothering them in shame, but bringing them into the light. What I came to discover is that the more you own the truth of your life, the more resilient you become.

Just as any wound needs sunlight and fresh air for healing, emotional wounds need the fresh air of loving friends. But the bliss of companionship with friends or a romantic partner doesn't mean that whatever was broken in the past will be restored. As I've said, the definition of tragedy I teach in forgiveness classes is that a tragedy is something that is broken and can't be fixed. We can't change the past. We can't withdraw a hurtful comment or action. We can't undo a mistake that has been made. But even though a tragedy can't be fixed, through the mercy of God and in the presence of supportive friends, a tragedy can be *healed*. I was still plenty broken—traumatized and afraid—but in this circle of love in Western North Carolina, I found the courage to embrace the life unfolding before me.

Gabor Maté says that trauma, stemming from the Greek for "wound," is "not what happens to you; it is what happens inside you *as a result* of what happens to you. It is not the blow on the head, but the concussion."[10] That, he says, is the good news—good news because I can do something about it. Tigg's Pond is the place where I drew a line in the sand and decided that I would do that—*finally*.

15

To the End of the World (and Back)

In the fall of 2015, Maria had shared with me that one of her lifetime dreams was to hike the Camino pilgrimage trail in Spain. The Camino de Santiago de Compostela, the "pilgrim way of Saint James under a field of stars," is an ancient spiritual journey that pilgrims have walked for more than a millennium. Established after relics of Saint James the Great were discovered there in the ninth century, it became a major pilgrimage route for medieval Christians looking for spiritual wisdom and meaning for their lives. Hiking the Camino was often prescribed by confessors as an act of penance to atone for one's sins.

Together, we watched the movie *The Way*, in which a father discovers that his free-spirited son tragically died in an accident at the beginning of his journey on the Camino. The father, comfortably ensconced in his life as a doctor, decides to complete the pilgrimage as a tender heartfelt tribute to his deceased son. The film was written and directed by Emilio Estevez, who featured his own father, Martin Sheen, as the protagonist. Through our tears, Maria and I made a pact with each other that we would someday walk this pilgrim's path. It was surely fitting for us to do this—after all, we had met on a hike.

In an added stroke of providence, Pope Francis proclaimed the year 2016 to be an "extraordinary jubilee" or a "Holy Year of Mercy." The Old Testament prophet Isaiah (later echoed by Jesus, Lk. 4:18-19) called for a year of Jubilee every 50 years. In theory, a Jubilee year was a period of restoration through social justice and mercy: a time of forgiveness of debts, freeing of slaves, and return of land to its original owners. With a heart that recognized the epidemic of regret, remorse, and shame that had taken root in the world, Pope Francis's declaration of a Jubilee year in 2016 opened a door for a way in modern times to emphasize forgiveness and mercy for all.

Stating that mercy "is the beating heart of the Gospel," the Jubilee year was set to begin on December 8, 2015, and to end on November 20, 2016. During this period, the great doors of the basilicas and cathedrals would be opened, usually only opened for the great fifty days of Easter, as "a Door of Mercy . . . opened for the duration of the Holy Year."[1] The pope's intentions were clear:

> How much I desire that the year to come will be steeped in mercy, so that we can go out to every man and woman, bringing the goodness and tenderness of God. May the balm of mercy reach everyone, both believers and those far away . . .[2]

To all of us who were struggling to forgive ourselves, Pope Francis offered an olive branch of spiritual care. And it just so happened that the Jubilee of Mercy coincided with the fifteenth anniversary of the terrorist attacks on 9/11.

Through some sort of spiritual alchemy that I'll *never* understand, these two huge concepts—pilgrimage and jubilee—melded together in our hearts into one actionable goal: for us to hike the Camino de Santiago de Compostela in September 2016, timing our pilgrimage to arrive at the Cathedral on the fifteenth anniversary of 9/11. I am convinced that it was divinely inspired, and the mechanics of the journey quickly began to grow in my imagination. Where would we start? How should we prepare? What can we expect? Will it be safe? Where will we stay? What about bed bugs? It had been more than 20 years since my last backpacking trip. Could I still manage to carry the needed provisions on my back?

When I was in the seventh grade, I discovered that one great way to read the latest information about any hobby was to subscribe to a magazine. Plus, every magazine I talked my mom into paying for meant one less magazine I had to sell for the school fundraiser. That year, I subscribed to *Sports Illustrated, Skin Diver, Sailing*, and yes, *Backpacker Magazine*. Although I never made it into the NBA, I have dabbled in the other interests over the years in wonderful and satisfying ways. From *Backpacker Magazine*, I learned that among the cardinal rules of backpacking were that you start where you are, leave no trace, and have a plan.

Starting where you are for the Camino meant accepting myself for where I was in my life at the time. This was a huge endeavor. One of the items we brought from California to Zirconia was my old JanSport backpack—with power bars still tucked inside, though I decided against eating them since they had been there for more than a decade. My backpack was hopelessly antiquated now—some might say "vintage"—an artifact of my pre-NYC life, external frame and all. Physically, I was now thirty pounds heavier than I was on my last backpacking trip. Spiritually, I was even heavier, bringing my wounded and broken self along, in search of healing. This is one of the most common reasons people hike the Camino, so I supposed I was in good company. But I wanted to prepare myself to not only thrive along the journey, but to be strong—and of course to not embarrass myself in front of Maria.

Leaving no trace was an easy one. It's a commitment that Maria and I share, as conservationists and nature lovers. Little did I know, however, that while I worked hard not to leave a trace on the pilgrimage, the pilgrimage would inevitably leave its fingerprints all over my soul.

As for planning, Maria and I happily worked together for months to create a strategy for our adventure. To earn our pilgrim's credentials, we needed to hike 100 km, and there are at least seven routes to the Cathedral of Saint James that can accomplish this: the Camino Francés, Camino Portugués, Camino del Norte, Camino Primitivo, Camino Inglés, Via de la Plata, and Camino de Invierno. Since we are both ocean lovers, we chose the Camino Portugues—the route to Santiago de Compostela starting in Porto, Portugal. We would travel up the Atlantic coast, with beautiful ocean vistas all along the way. With over 25 years of executive management to her credit, Maria has excellent big-picture planning skills as well as the ability to execute on the plan. I deeply appreciated this, and she accepted the "less-than-linear" Lyndon approach too as we worked together to achieve our goal.

We decided to take ten days to accomplish our journey to Santiago, plus a few days to relax and recover, soaking up the beauties of Espana. We gathered information about towns and hamlets along the way to determine where we'd stop overnight. No longer in our twenties, we decided to forego the Albergue experience, staying in the popular pilgrim hostels where everyone sleeps together in large rooms on rows of bunk beds. Hearing that there might be bed bugs confirmed our decision. Beginning in the south, our stops would be Baiona, Vigo, Redondela, Pontevedra, Caldas Rei, Padron, and Teo, before our final arrival in Santiago. We booked inexpensive hotels in each of these towns, with extra nights in the middle of our quest to rest our feet. Flights, hotels, provisions—all these choices required the detailed planning of a bank heist. We shared in this work with joy as we anticipated our upcoming adventure, enthralled by what Goethe described as "holy longing"[3]—the desire to be overtaken by a deeper quest.

In his profound book *The Art of Pilgrimage*, Phil Cousineau sought to recover the idea of pilgrimage from our modern obsession with vacation-oriented travel, where we aspire to "vacate" our lives. In an interview he gave, Cousineau said,

> "Pilgrim" goes back to the Latin "per agrum", and it means to get off the bus, off the train, off the plane, out of your living room and walk through the fields, per agrum. It means putting the sole of your feet to the soul of the world, so it's sacred. . . . The pilgrimage is the journey you can't can't not take. You are at a crossroad. You feel the double negative there? We are at a crossroad, and the answers that we once found maybe from our own dreams or from local input, the priest, the minister, the rabbi, the Imam, simply aren't working anymore. And that's when the call comes out, as in the hero's journey, as in the call of a poet. The call to the soul says, "We need to go to a place that may have the answer that we can't find at home."[4]

And while a pilgrimage is where you go when you can't find an answer at home, historically, pilgrimages have not been without danger. Anecdotally, it is surmised that up to half of pilgrims traveling before the nineteenth century were likely not to make it back home. Lack of food, disease, physical hardships, and banditry were a foregone conclusion. Anyone contemplating travel in those times knew for certain that there was risk involved. In fact, the word travel comes from the word "travail", which is a reference to a medieval implement of torture. To travel, one "stretches" oneself.

My hope was that I would finally find some peace in my life in the aftermath of so many years of my own "travail." I wanted to be able to forgive myself for my mistakes and cast off the shame attending them. I wanted to let go of the resentments and bitterness I harbored against my supervisors after 9/11, a poison pill that had been slowly killing me. I also wanted to get closer to Maria—hiking 100 km is a great way to get to know someone deeper, to find out if it really will work, and to foster a deep companionship on which we could build a future together. I wanted to reconnect to God, as well. Ever since I left church work, I had languished in attention to praying regularly and being spiritually accountable to any intentional fellowship. Hiking the epic spiritual journey of the Camino—during a year in which the great doors of the cathedrals would be opened as portals of penance, forgiveness, and mercy—culminating on the fifteenth anniversary of 9/11—seemed to be an opening, a portal to another dimension in my life.

On September 1, 2016, with joyful expectation and a bit of trepidation, on an exquisitely sun-kissed breezy day in Baiona, Spain, Maria and I set out to hike the Camino. We had followed our plans to fly into Santiago, then to take a bus to Baiona. We were a bundle of nerves when we arrived, but the butterflies all landed when we got to Baiona. Our hotel was across from a picturesque marina full of beautiful boats, where we easily found a delicious dinner and hiked around to take in the sights. Baiona dates back to the second century BCE, and, in 1493 CE, it was the first place to receive the news of Christopher Columbus's discovery of "the new world." A replica of the Pinta, Columbus' ship that had made its way back to share the tidings, still sits in the harbor. This was a surprise we weren't quite sure how to process. We continued our walk around the harbor, discovering the beautiful Fort Monterreal, dating back to the twelfth century, before finally returning to the hotel.

The next morning, with a satisfying breakfast in our bellies and packs on our backs, our pilgrimage officially began. We hadn't even crossed the street to pick up the trail before cars were honking and people were cheering, wishing us a "Buen Camino!" This goodwill never ceased. If there was ever a question as to which fork to take on the trail, an angel would suddenly appear—in the guise of a taxi driver, a man taking out his garbage, or a mother walking with her children—and direct us safely onward. It felt like there was a force field of love and peace surrounding us and guiding us onward. It was extraordinary. It was another unexpected community of love and safety.

Spain is generous and kind to its pilgrims, always offering an encouraging word, heartfelt wishes for a "Buen Camino," an occasional ripe red tomato left for pilgrim passersby and helpful recommendations posted on telephone poles along the way. Once, we were stopped by an older man on a bike—thin, sweaty, and with an urgent tone in his voice. He cried, "The fountain is this way, the fountain is this way." Not having any knowledge of a fountain, or a plan to get there, or much confidence in our broken Spanish, we thought, "Well, this must be important." I said to Maria, "The fountain is this way!" and we tacked in that direction. We did find a fountain, thanks to our wiry intrepid angel. And we were glad we did. Both the fountain and the ancient shade trees surrounding it were sublime. The gentle gurgling water, along with the pleasant breeze under the shade, made for one of our favorite Camino moments.

Each day, we set our faces to Santiago. Through rain, heat, and thirst, we made our way toward the "Portico de Gloria," the cathedral's great door. As an architectural masterpiece, carved by the hands of Maestro Mateo, this door is often considered one of the greatest works of Spanish Romanesque sculpture. It features stunning depictions of the crucified Christ in his twofold role as both Judge and Redeemer. In dramatic fashion, the crucified Christ is surrounded by the twenty-four elders of the Apocalypse as mentioned in John's Book of Revelation.[5] The otherworldly beauty of the portico is designed to create a sublime portal between Heaven and earth, past and future, disease and health, despair and hope. For me, it was a portal into a cathedral of forgiveness and an emotional new beginning for my life on the other side.

Day after day, Maria and I enjoyed a lovely hike, delicious food, and some of the best coffee and pastries in the world. We were enthralled by

Spain's exquisite beauty. With each drop of sweat outgoing and each ounce of water imbibed, my nervous system and my mind began to relax. The days spent under the Galician sun gave my mind permission to decenter. The heat of westernmost Spain induced a kind of meditative state as we walked. The present moment was all I needed—feeling good walking, companionship with my beloved, and beauty, breathtaking beauty all around us. Walking at the quiet, steady pace of the Camino, I allowed all thoughts of attachments to wash over me. My identity as a priest, my ego-centered need to resurrect my role as a Ground Zero worker, my desire to feel important. Past relationships that had nurtured me, the need to have my life together, the need to be "somebody." The false necessity to have my future mapped out and approved by others. All of these, whether conscious or not, began melting under the warm Iberian sun. In their place, somewhere deep beyond the comprehension of words, I could only say, "thank you."

In heartfelt gratitude for everything and everyone who had helped me in my life's journey to this point, I realized the best thing I could do for each person and experience—all of which were precious—was to choose life. To choose life was to be empowered and committed to becoming my best self, not my old self. To live in joy, not sorrow or depression. I often reflected on the words of the Psalmist: "Sorrow may spend the night, but joy comes in the morning." (Ps. 30:5). I have always embraced the divine understanding of Abraham's blessing in Genesis: the verb is reflexive—we have been blessed so that we may be blessings to others. Each and every person—friend, lover, challenger, or mentor—was and is precious. I would not be who I am without these relationships and experiences, and choosing to live on in joy would be the best way to pay forward my gratitude for the blessings I'd been given.

For much of my life after 9/11, I had secretly been a "dead man walking." But now, embraced by the extravagance of hiking the Camino with Maria, I wanted more than anything to live my life to the fullest. Although I hadn't yet arrived at Nietzsche's dictum, "Amor fati" ("love your fate"), I was getting close.[6] Whether conscious of it or not, I was practicing Fred Luskin's Breath of Thanks exercise: deep slow breathing in, with a slow exhale accompanied by "thank you." With each step on our quest "under a field of stars,"—the literal translation of the name, Compostella—I felt within my bones, within my spirit, a profound quickening born of what felt like a divine intervention. How could I have ever known that the young boy from Gaffney with stars in his eyes might someday be hiking under a field of stars in Spain? How could I have known that the wide-eyed young man searching for his corner of the sky might find part of it hiking an ancient sacred pilgrimage? Yes, there were many happy accidents and serendipitous moments bringing us here to hike the Camino, but it was more than luck. In my bones I felt it was God's providence.

Providence is such a strange word. Even saying it feels like invoking some grandiose interruption by a playful God. But my actual understanding is much humbler than that; I saw the providence of our Camino quest as an invitation to reconnect my soul with the Holy. Since leaving the priesthood, my sense of God had not substantially changed, but my spiritual practice had considerably languished. Seeing myself as a spiritual victim made it difficult to engage in any meaningful spiritual practice. After all, the incantation of "God smite my enemies" will only get you so far, and even then, it's going in the wrong direction. But now, finally, with an openness of heart to the unfolding miracle of this seventy-mile quest, I had the opportunity to let go of my burdens of the past, to release my anxieties about the future, and to live gratefully in the moment at hand. I saw myself joining Philippe Petit on the wire above the Twin Towers, feeling the freedom he felt: "Not looking behind you, or too far ahead; no past to regret, no future to dread."[7]

The assaults to my ego that often felt pervasive in the US didn't matter here. No one knew I had been a priest. No one cared that I wasn't anymore. When we had conversations with locals and fellow travelers, I was just Lyndon. No more, no less. Most importantly, I was a pilgrim, on a quest to learn something about myself, to make penance for my mistakes, and to let go of my grievances. And I was on an adventure to deepen my relationship with Maria, the one I hoped to spend my life with, if she would have me.

On our way, we fell into an easy pattern: hiking in hot sun, feeling mesmerized by the sights of the day, and resting our tired feet at the hike's end, and finding the "cevezzeria"—a welcome oasis of shade, comfort, and cold beer. Our next town, Vigo, was a charming hamlet with elegant architecture and beautiful beaches, so we took an afternoon to enjoy. On our way to the beach, we stopped by a market to gather supplies for a picnic: the recommended local and delicious Albariño wine, a hunk of cheese, some salamis, tomatoes, and a baguette. It was heavenly. The beach was pristine, and the water just the right amount of chilly. We were settling into our journey by the warmth of a friendly sun and with joy in our hearts.

Gratitude, as I have heard my friend Fred Luskin say it countless times, is the antidote to unforgiveness. Now, in the throes of one of the holiest events I had ever undertaken in my life, I believed him.

Our pilgrimage was not without challenge, nor was it without humor. The sixth day of hiking was scorching hot—"mucho calor" in Spanish. About five miles in, heat rash began to break out on Maria's legs in a frightening way. I wanted to help her but wasn't sure how. What caused it? How could we get her the care she needed? Who could we ask for help? We found a pharmacy along the way, which told us that a certain cream would help. But on a particularly scorching section of the hike, without shade, her rash and my worries continued to grow. Eventually, we made it to a shady park and settled in for a long afternoon siesta. We refilled our water bottles and drank deeply. Since the shade, rest, and rehydrating seemed to help, we decided to take advantage of the rest days we had built into our schedule in the middle of our trek. So, we found a beautiful hotel with an exquisite garden, including a pool shaded by thick, intertwined grapevines covered in bountiful bunches of green grapes. These comely vines not only provided cool comfort, but also the beauty of a European vision worthy of a Cezanne.

However, the hotel itself, like many in the region, was not air conditioned. Since we were staying there two nights, I asked the front desk what to do about the heat. The receptionist suggested I seek out the caretaker for our room to ask for a fan. I had a mission. I had a quest: to find our Dulcinea and procure a fan. It took a while searching, but finally, I found her in the supply room restocking her cleaning cart. Plaintively, I tried to describe the conditions of our room as I asked her for a solution to cool the room at night. I tried to convey how much we loved the hotel and the town and especially the people and the food. Not getting very far with my broken Spanish, I decided to cut to the chase and ask for a fan. I soon discovered that the Spanish word I should have used to describe our exceedingly warm room was the one mentioned above: "calor," which means *heat* in the context of temperature. Instead, I used a word that would bring shades of continued embarrassment to our blushing housekeeper: "caliente." Instead of asking for a fan because it was blazing hot in our room, I had inadvertently asked this guileless housekeeper for a fan because our room was so "Spicy"—and "spicy" not as a reference to food! Hot times on the ole Camino, indeed.

Another aspect of our trip actually was spicy—we discovered a delicious appetizer offered at every cervezzaria called "peppers Padron." Peppers Padron were spicy little shishito peppers coming to prominence from the township of Padron, one of our favorite stops along the way. We loved these peppers, but it was a bit like Spanish roulette—some were spicier than others, and you couldn't tell from their looks. Just take a bite, and *caliente*! The strenuous nature of hiking 100 kms meant we could eat what we wanted without (much) consequence. Each of the hotels and lodges we stayed in offered scrumptious breakfasts that included the expected eggs and muffins, but also a wide variety of cheeses, cured meats, and delicious breads. We ate our fill in the morning, and then I would make a delicious sandwich "to go" using cured meats, spicy mustard, and a variety of cheeses. It usually didn't make it to lunchtime. I think I might be the only person ever to hike the Camino and actually gain weight!

One of the questions suggested to us in framing our vision for our Camino was "What do you want cast off? How can you make your life's journey lighter?" For the Spanish equivalent of about five US dollars, we learned, we could have hired a service to collect our 40+ pound packs in the morning and deliver them to our lodging reservation for the night. But we didn't regret carrying them ourselves; our packs symbolized the weight we had each brought to the pilgrimage that soon we would be able to set down. With each glass of cerveza, each order of Padrón peppers, each blister on the foot, we made our way closer to Santiago. And before we knew it, we had arrived at the village of Padron—the one famous for its peppers—just 26 km from our destination.

I thought it would be best to break the last leg of our trek into two shorter hikes, so as to arrive in Santiago with enough energy to take it all in. So, on

September 11, we awoke in the village of Teo and enjoyed a relaxed breakfast, with lots of delicious Spanish espresso. I hoped the final 12 km march toward the "Portico de Gloria" could be more leisurely rather than the grueling pace that some of our hiking days had required. And, espresso notwithstanding, my nerves were jittery. What would it be like to walk through this portal of spiritual essence and promise? How would I change as I crossed to the other side? Would it be like a bolt of lightning—like Saul of Tarsus becoming the Apostle Paul? Or would I experience a still small voice whispering promises of new beginnings, healing for the past, penance for our mistakes? How might my experiences be integrated when all of it was over? Would my experience as a pilgrim allow me to return as something other than a pariah?

Pilgrims arriving at their destination often feel a profound sense of achievement and newfound belonging to a community so much bigger than the ones they left. There is a sense of spiritual fulfillment, a kind of "attaboy" from God that applauded me not just for hiking the Camino but for embracing a truth I knew deep down all along but didn't embrace: that I am loved beyond measure, that I am enough, and that my resentments, bitterness, mistakes, and trauma were not the last word for my life. We hoped for all this and more. Everything I believed I wanted in life was going to erupt in the next few hours. Would any of it be as I expected? Surely not; not even I am that naïve. But my expectations were high.

Nearing our date with destiny, we discovered a chapel designated for pilgrims to pray before making their final descent into Santiago. It was called the Capilla de Santa Maria Magdalena—and if anyone knew what it meant to be left out, I thought to myself, it was Mary Magdalene. We were glad to stop to pray, offering much thanksgiving for our health and safety after such a strenuous trek. I expressed deep gratitude for my Camino companion, who had captured my heart, and quietly added petitions that she might soon become my companion for life. I prayed for those whom I had wronged and offered penance for my mistakes and pledged amendment of life moving forward. I prayed for those I felt had wronged me, opening my heart in the spirit of Ram Dass: at the end of the day, we're all just walking each other home. On one grand universal Camino.

The gravity of the day intersected with our hiking reverie: it was the fifteenth anniversary of the terrorists' attacks on 9/11. So, I also prayed for the souls of the faithful departed and all who had died that day. I prayed fervently for those like me, whose lives had been radically disrupted by the events of that tragic day. And with the help of Mary Magdalene, the matron saint of pariahs, I prayed for the new life I was trying my best to claim and live into. Then we gave leave to her chapel, set our faces toward Santiago, beginning our descent.

It was a beautiful hike on a goldilocks kind of day—warm but not too hot, a bit of a challenge but not too strenuous, emotionally full but not overwhelming. The entrance from Teo felt like circumnavigating the cathedral, with the trail turning into a narrowing spiral, gently sloping toward our goal. We could see the cathedral from a distance, which made the walk all the sweeter and my expectations all the greater. Even though this leg of the hike was not demanding, my heartbeat increased and drops of sweat rolled down my back. On the outskirts of the city, the pilgrims were celebrating their arrivals, townsfolk were happy to welcome them, and the people we met glowed with jubilation and triumph. It was all I could do to keep from running toward the life that I felt the cathedral promised.

We entered the Praza de Quintana (Quintana Square), bordering the eastern side of the cathedral and the Portico de Gloria, then reached the cathedral, filled with hope and expectation. I was eagerly anticipating the spiritual juju that might happen when we walked through the famous door. But as we inched our way to the portal of glory, it was couched in shadows. Instead of the bright lights of a miracle, all we could see was the uncompromising reality of a blockade. As we got closer, we were flabbergasted to see that the door itself was closed. And, standing at about 14 feet tall, it's not a door that any normal visitor can open.

CLOSED?! How could it be closed? We had traveled thousands of miles to Spain and then hiked 100 km to get to this very door. Didn't they understand it was a Jubilee year? Pope Francis had said so himself! My disappointment came from a kind of supernatural fantasy that something magical might happen to me the minute I walked through the door, a kind of cosmic spiritual "fixing."

Aggrieved and anguished that my miracle was still out of reach, we went to the closest official-looking place to inquire: the visitor's bureau.

While others stood in line to get maps, I stood in line to give them the what-for. Disappointment and petulance were oozing from my eyes. How could the great door of the pilgrims' cathedral be closed to pilgrims? *In the year of Jubilee?* Finally making it to the front of the line, we asked about the door. The person working at the time assured us it was only temporary—it would be open after lunch. With a sigh of relief, and since it was siesta time, we decided to have an early lunch.

After lunch we trekked back to Mateo's masterpiece. Disappointingly, it was still closed. *CLOSED*. In fact, if I had paid attention earlier, I would have seen that it had scaffolding on each side of it. The portal of glory was ingloriously being refurbished and cleaned. All the spiritual capital I had built up while hiking the Camino seemed to fizzle in that moment. All of my good intentions seemed to end there, behind yet another church's closed doors.

In our forgiveness teachings, we refer to this challenge as "finding your positive intention." You might have made a mistake while pursuing one of your goals in life, or someone else's mistake might have prohibited your accomplishing a goal. But even though it didn't work out in that specific instance, you can still pursue the goal in different ways. I might have gotten a divorce, but I still wanted to make a life with someone—hopefully, Maria. I might not be a priest any longer, but I still wanted to make the world a better place through teaching.

Positive intentions are always bigger than our failures. On that day, the fifteenth anniversary of 9/11, my positive intention was to enter the cathedral, having hiked 100 km as a pilgrim, to pray for those who died on 9/11 and all those still affected, including me. I planned to pray for healing for myself and guidance for embarking on my future. I planned to offer gratitude to God for all the blessings of my life. I had prepared myself spiritually and emotionally to experience a rite of passage—passing from my old life of resentments, mistakes, shame, guilt, and remorse into a new beginning born of gratitude and forgiveness. It was to be a miracle, and I was counting on it.

After studying the Portal of Glory for a bit and seeing clearly that it would not be opening anytime soon, Maria and I walked around the outside of the cathedral, along with countless other pilgrims milling around. What we discovered is that—miraculously—other doors were open! Of course they were. This is perhaps one of the most fundamental spiritual and emotional truths I have learned to date: when one door is closed—even if it is a magnificent portal of glory—other doors into the same place might be open. In fact, there were more open doors than we could count. In the ultimate assessment of positive intention, the poet Rumi said, "Let the beauty of what you love be what you do. There are hundreds of ways to kneel and kiss the ground."[8](Figure 15.1)

We finally made it into the cathedral after the "pilgrims' mass" had begun. We joined in as we were able, delighting in the ritual of the gathering. We smiled at the movements of those commandeering the extremely large thurible, the container holding the burning incense, spreading its fragrant aromatics across the expanse so that it would overcome the sweat of pilgrims. We listened intently to the priest's sermon even though we didn't understand that much Spanish. His gestures were friendly and inviting, with kindness in his eyes and warmth exuding from his heart. We shared in the prayers of the people and offered our own, kneeling in that magnificent ancient cathedral. It was one of the most extraordinary experiences of my life—to swing from the depths of disappointment to the heights of spiritual nurture in such a short span. In the cathedral on that holy day, we made memories that will stay with us forever. In the safety of that sacred space, I was grateful for my life—for all its ups and downs, its failures and successes. I was grateful for the beautiful relationship I had with Maria that seemed to deepen with every step. And I was grateful to God who had welcomed this prodigal son home to community. I thought I had wandered far away from the circle of God's love, but years later I can see that it was right there all the time. It never left me. As John of the Cross, the fourteenth-century mystic would say when writing about the dark night of the soul, in our perception of God's absence, we just can't see that God is *most present* there. All of a sudden I had a flashback—a remembrance of the shocking assaults on 9/11 and the days following. Standing at the foot of the South Tower as it erupted into a fireball, running urgently away from the collapsing North Tower with a small child in tow, walking into the pile of

Figure 15.1 *Maria and I arrive at the Gate of the Cathedral in Santiago.*

twisted steel, detritus and death of the former towers laid waste, I remembered a passage of scripture that most of us growing up in the Baptist church would have memorized, Rom. 8:38:

> For I am convinced that neither death nor life, neither angels nor demons, neither the present nor the future, nor any powers, neither height nor depth, nor anything else in all creation, will be able to separate us from the love of God that is in Christ Jesus our Lord.

Lingering in the cathedral after the mass, I felt safe, seen, content, and excited. That day, we cried, we prayed, and we opened our hearts in celebration. Santiago was full of happy pilgrims, with no strangers to be found. Over a delicious seafood dinner that night, Maria and I toasted our achievement with a glass of Champagne and laughed about our disappointment—mostly mine—that the great door was closed. The next morning, feeling restored by a long sleep and the satisfaction of a goal achieved, we awoke and made plans to finish our journey to Finnes Terrae, 60 km away—this time, happily, by bus rather than foot.

For pilgrims, Finnes Terrae is the first test of life after pilgrimage. Tradition has it that the Pilgrim, having carried stones along the Camino that represent the parts of themselves that no longer serve them, must cast these representative stones over the rocky cliffs of Finisterre. Then, according to ritual and legend, the pilgrim must burn his boots as a symbol of new beginnings. We considered these traditions pragmatically. First, we liked our boots, so we decided not to burn them. Second, we hadn't been aware of the tradition of carrying stones along the Camino representing the things in our lives that we wanted to let go of. Thankfully, there were lots of available stones at Finisterre. Just like the doors of the cathedral, there are many ways to accomplish a goal.

Finisterre literally means "the end of the world" and is the traditional next stop after completing the Camino. Found on the westernmost point of the Iberian Peninsula, the so-called "jumping off point," for the ancients, it had been the edge of the known world. It was named by the ancient occupying Romans, who offered nightly sacrifices hoping to ensure that the sun would rise again the next day. Despite the advances of modern sonar technology, Finisterre is set as a tiny little conclave around a famous, still-operational lighthouse. There is a sense of foreboding at the top of the hill where the lighthouse stands sentry, dutifully emitting its light as a beacon to prevent ships from crashing into the treacherous coastline below. Sea spray rises from the waves crashing below, creating a kind of cloudy shadowland ensconced with mist.

In my mind's eye, I could easily conjure the image of Wagner's ship captain from the opera *The Flying Dutchman*, who put his sailors at risk in order to continue sailing in a terrible storm. For his arrogance, he was doomed by the gods to wander forever across the weary seas. The antidote for his arrogance was true love. Every 7 years, the Dutchman was granted leave of this fate to wander the land in search of someone who would return his love. Wagner's *Dutchman* is a tragedy in three acts. Approaching the precipice of the end of the world, I could imagine the dramatic overture for that opera from when I first heard it at the Met in NYC—brooding, foreboding, and dangerous.

Like the Dutchman, I too was on a quest to find love. I sailed aimlessly across the murky waters of the slough of despond in my post 9/11 years; I ran aground in an archipelago of anguish, trying to reclaim my life from trauma. And finally making it to the end of the world, I was given the promise of another chance at life and love.

Maria and I finally made it to the promontory of the Cape, our lumbering strides betraying our fatigue. We took a few moments to absorb the dramatic scene of the windswept cape and tumultuous ocean below. Maria was the first to gather up several available stones. She took each stone into her hand, whispering intentions, release, or gratitude into them before casting them to the gods of the fitful sea. I marveled as I witnessed this moment, so moved that this elegant, strong, accomplished woman had chosen to hike the Camino with me. To share this moment of her life with *me*. After tossing several stones into the abyss, she raised her hands in triumph, an emotion-filled, 1000-watt smile rippling across her face.

Then it was my turn. I gathered a handful of stones, some large and some small. I wanted to make sure I covered it all. I threw stones representing my shame and my mistakes, my disappointments in life and my resentments toward others. I could have gathered a whole collection of stones representing 9/11 and the years that followed. But while I threw stones of release over the cliff, I also improvised—I threw stones of intention. I wanted to live my life in the present—not poisoned by the past or worrying about the future. I wanted to live in this moment, right now. To be fully present to those I love, to be eternally grateful for all who have blessed me, and to give thanks for my abundant blessings from God. I have often wondered what I would do if today were the last day I had to live on this beautiful planet. My answer was in my intention, tossed into the stormy coastline, swearing an oath to the universe that I would show up for my new life.

I asked Maria to lead the way back from there. My heart was racing and my breathing challenged. Maria didn't have a clue as to what I was feeling, and I wanted to keep it that way for a little while longer. I couldn't contain the river of tears streaming down my face, given the life-changing proposition I was about to make. If I was walking behind her, she couldn't see. Eventually, we reached the chapel, the Iglesia de Santa Maria das Areas, and I remarked to Maria that it must be nice to have a chapel share your name. She chuckled. I nonchalantly suggested we take a minute to tour it, as though I hadn't researched this space in private for months leading up to this trip. Secretly, I had been planning a long time for this day.

In the garden on the other side of the chapel, we found a nice picnic table in the garden. I gestured toward it, and as soon as she sat down—before she could get a good look at my face—I knelt down in front of her. With a most unfortunate, however joyful, river of tears, I managed to say the words I'd held back throughout the Camino: "Maria, my beloved. I have followed you to the end of the world. Will you marry me?"

She was stunned. Her eyes flickered as she tried desperately to process what I had just asked. Her face turned several shades of pink and red, as joyful tears burst forth. Luckily for me, she said "Yes!" We held each other and wept for what seemed like hours. We laughed. We cried tears of joy. We drank the wine I'd insisted we bring. I was ecstatic—outside myself in a way that I have rarely felt. It was an experience of ineffable, indescribable joy—and relief. My heart fluttered like a kaleidoscope of butterflies, accompanied by an ocean of joyful tears. Something in me changed in that moment. In the act of asking Maria's hand in marriage, I was making a promise that I would be a worthy and life-giving partner, and that would require my best efforts. There was no more room in my life for my past resentments or my regrets. My heart felt stretched—in a good way. Spiritually I had traveled far. I was becoming the man I wanted to be.

The next day, we boarded our flight in Santiago and headed back to North Carolina, full of emotions—gratitude, joy, relief, hopefulness. Our glad tidings about getting engaged predictably eclipsed our stories of hiking the Camino.

We relished this victory lap of sorts as we made our rounds sharing our news with our circles of friends.

Looking back, I could see that my task at Finisterre was not at all like the Flying Dutchman's search for love. Rather, I was there to identify and release my impediments to love. The regrets I carried, and the guilt and shame they generated, had been a sort of perverse attempt to pursue perfection—a subtle, insidious manifestation of my unenforceable rule that I had to be perfect. But that isn't real; it's not even possible. To be fully present to Maria's love, I had to give my whole self to her.

16

It All Belongs

We began dreaming about our wedding, taking care to allow me the time necessary to follow through on the intentions I had made on the Camino. To begin marriage without the burdens of my past, I needed to take care of some things.

First, I needed to file for bankruptcy. Whether she agreed or not, I believed Maria deserved a Tiffany engagement ring, and I couldn't afford it. More than the ring itself, the shame I felt about my financial house falling into ruins had been an impediment to my ability to open my heart fully to Maria, and it was time to let that go. I had always been a hard worker. In NYC, I sometimes held three or four jobs to make ends meet and support my family. In college, I worked several part-time jobs to keep myself afloat. Now, everything was a struggle.

It took months of humiliating tedious work to get all the papers together that signified bills I hadn't been able to pay. But with the help of the kindest lawyer on the planet, Rod Kight and his terrific wife Ashley, and in spite of much fear and trepidation, I filed my papers that spring. After several hearings, the judge declared me free and clear of any past obligations. This in itself became a powerful lesson in forgiveness, and much deeper than finances alone. It was very emotional for me.

Second, I needed to get help for the grief work I knew I still needed to do. Being engaged to Maria had made me happy as a clam. But human beings are complex, and it's rarely possible to experience only one emotion at a time. I needed help, help beyond my circle of friends, beyond the therapists and spiritual directors I had seen. My friends Gareth and Brian—and the men's group that had been a constant source of encouragement and accountability for me—suggested I consider working with the West African shaman and grief alchemist Malidoma Somé. Malidoma was equally at home in the modern world of science and scholarship as he was standing regal in his tribal colorful dress. He would share therapeutic insights born of his research and, in the same breath, could cheer for his beloved Tampa Bay Buccaneers. I liked him immediately. Somé offered grief retreats in Florida, so I made sure to sign up for his next one in case it filled up before the wedding.

On Halloween, October 31, 2017, I began the 8-hour drive to the Deerhaven Retreat Center in Orlando, Florida, for the grief retreat. Deerhaven is a rustic oasis located in the Ocala National Forest about an hour north of Orlando, located on 64 acres of that largely undeveloped space. The drive down gave me lots of time to ponder what I hoped to accomplish there. To prepare myself on the drive, I listened to some of my favorite music, much of which had been imprinted with a measure of sadness. One was the Christopher Cross song, *Sailing*. While my pre-teen subscription to *Sailing Magazine* had long since terminated, I still held onto that dream. More significantly, I smiled whenever I heard the song, knowing that my friend Kiki Ebson—the owner of the Healing Equine Ranch in Agoura Hills, California, sang backup on the recording. *Sailing* is a beautiful example of multiple emotions existing at once, including a note of sadness, when it speaks of finding innocence again. I wondered if it were even possible to find innocence again. The idea seems aspirational at best. To me, this actually felt beyond reach, like trying to win a prize at a carnival: it always seems so close, so doable, until you realize your turn is over.

I listened to this song on repeat throughout my voyage to Orlando, my odyssey to pay grief a measure of what it was due. The canvas of lush, emotional strings plaintively summoned me forward, with Cross's smooth otherworldly baritone becoming the wind itself, while the repetitive notes of the guitar offered a sumptuous mantra of peace. And so, I set sail to open my heart to the work of grief, even if it meant I might never stop crying. My destination was set, but I was sailing uncharted waters.

Poetically, our retreat began the next day, on the feast day of All Saints—November 1, 2017—a special time to remember loved ones who have passed and to be inspired by the great saints of the church. I don't think he was inclined to follow the Christian liturgical calendar, but Malidoma's shamanistic methodology was centered upon grief work inspired by our ancestors. But, in my opinion, he couldn't have picked a better day. It was a day of remembering and acknowledging the "great cloud of witnesses" that surrounds us in our earthly pilgrimage: ancestors, departed loved ones, great saints of the church, and all whose memories and presences in our lives form a rich tapestry of love and experience.

We spent the week in dialogue with other participants and with Malidoma, who shared his shamanistic framework for grief. His approach was surprising for me as a westerner, but it helped me see my life as a continuation of those who have come before me, as he shared about the importance of connecting to our ancestors. All of us together are part of the great, unfolding human enterprise of community, connection, and hope. Expressing my grief in this community, I found support for letting go of the life I had planned—honoring the status, relationships, opportunities, and even whatever health I had lost—so that I could embrace the exquisite life waiting before me. I trusted the emotional container that Malidoma and his team created, and I cried for it all. I cried and cried. But after a while, my tears did stop. And I found I didn't have to fear befriending my grief. As I learned to do this, another impediment to love melted away.

On my way down to attend the retreat, I had listened to placid songs bordering on sorrow. On the way home, I couldn't stop practicing for my debut as a rap star, with spoken word riffs exploding from my now uninhibited consciousness. Luckily for Maria and all my friends at Tigg's Pond, I had 8 hours to work *that* out of my system.

Back in the kingdom of Zirconia, Maria welcomed me home and wrapped her arms of love around my tender heart. We dreamed about our wedding day. Our betrothal was such a sweet season, widening and merging our circles of friends, deepening our relationship and our love. My daughter Margaret and her husband Gavin enthusiastically welcomed Maria into our family, as did my sisters and brother, and about a million cousins. My grandchildren adored Maria from the start, and she was beyond smitten with them. While physically unable to have the children she longed for, Maria now not only had a daughter and a son-in-law, but also three extraordinary grandchildren. Our visits and travels together to be with them were the closest I had ever come to heaven.

Likewise, Maria's family enthusiastically welcomed me into their circle. I was both relieved and excited. While visiting Maria's sister Lisa and her husband James in Alexandria, Virginia, for Thanksgiving, we spent a day at the Torpedo Factory in Old Town Alexandria. Perusing the jewelry produced by local artisans, we discovered a ring style that Maria and I both loved—a beautiful golden band with a small, ever so delicate fern leaf attached. Because of Maria's deep love for the natural world, nature is where her heart finds peace and joy. While that ring was not the specific one for us, we couldn't stop thinking about it. Back home, we consulted with our neighbor, Molly Sharp. Molly and her husband David Voorhees are nationally renowned artists—she's a jeweler and he's a ceramicist—who offer workshops all over the world. Molly listened to us intently as we shared what we liked about the ring in Alexandria, how it had inspired us to think creatively about a bespoke ring that connected to the things Maria loved—simple understated elegance with an expression of nature. Just then, a wide beautiful smile spread across Molly's face like sunshine after a storm at sea: "Of course I can do that!" Elated, we commissioned Molly to design a beautiful silver band with a tender fern leaf and magnificent stone attached. It was better than Tiffany's. She also designed my ring to be a hammered silver band distinct in its own simplicity and elegance. I was relieved as I let go of my own unrealistic expectation for Maria's engagement ring—the one I had planned but could not have—and welcomed the one that showed up, which is the one she truly wanted and loved.

We agreed that we wanted the wedding to be small and unpretentious, casual but elegant, and decided that meant renting a house at Edisto Beach in South Carolina. Edisto had played a special role in my life, beginning when I met Laurel Weston and Freeman Smith in 1991. They were members of the Episcopal Church of the Advent, the church I served in Spartanburg, South Carolina. Both psychiatrists, they had bought a house on Edisto while they were in medical school in Charleston. It was a beautiful, modest house on a creek feeding into the North Edisto River, and they were always delighted and generous to share their home with me so that my family could spend time with our extended families, even after we moved to NYC. I will always treasure a memory of Margaret when she was just a little girl—in the dead of winter in frostbitten NYC, she exclaimed, "Dad, I can't wait to go down to Edisto and be bored." Our trips to Edisto and Charleston had meant so much to her that, when she was able to choose where to live, she moved with her family to Charleston. It was decided: Edisto would be the perfect place for our wedding.

It's hard to believe how much there is to plan for a humble, low-key wedding. Since we wanted to share in the important decisions, we looked at several wedding gowns together. By the third dress she tried on, I burst into surprising, involuntary tears. It was the most beautiful dress, and it adorned her perfectly—an elegant ivory gown, strapless and gathered sensually to the side, all accentuating her gorgeous figure, shimmering blond hair, transcendent blue eyes, and dazzling smile. I just couldn't believe this divine manifestation of a woman would marry *me*. Dante's Beatrice couldn't hold a candle. She startled me out of my reverie with a decisive comment: "Done!" This was the dress, and we laughed and celebrated another momentous step forward. A tan linen suit did nicely for me, with a white linen shirt, trimmed with a light blue-green tie. All this with a stylish straw fedora, of course. And there was no need to fuss about shoes; we'd go barefoot on the beach.

We found and reserved a no-frills, coral-toned, oceanfront beach house, humorously named "Conch Out." In the last week of July, we arrived at Edisto to lay claim to our coastal castle. My daughter Margaret had to work until the day before the wedding, but Gavin, my handsome and gifted son-in-law, brought the grands so they could practice their roles as ring bearer and flower girls. He's such a great father. And a self-taught chef who, at the young age of 19, worked in Gordon Ramsay's kitchen in NYC, and now, as an accomplished entrepreneur, owns his own restaurant on Folly Beach, South Carolina. Gavin can cook absolutely anything and have it turn out scrumptious. I could not be prouder of the man my son-in-law has become. We are still talking about even the guacamole he made that week.

Brother-in-law James, bon vivant, philosopher, standup comedian and the bartending hit at every party, pitched in too. James had served as chief of staff for Democratic Senator Howard Metzenbaum, the senator from Ohio, and is a brilliant conversationalist with amazing stories to tell. He honored us by creating a customized drink menu for one and all.

My sisters, Libby, Cheryl, and her daughter Karla, with her son Graham, arrived midweek. My niece Karla is a gifted young woman—an excellent writer, publicist, web designer, and all-around lovely human being. Karla also has an adventurous spirit and has traveled the world with me, most notably to Mumbai, India. Karla often came to NYC to volunteer at Saint Paul's, willing and able to do pretty much anything we needed done.

Cheryl and Libby arrived with their usual flair, unpacking a carload of "deals" they found at yard sales or thrift stores on the way down. Our older sister Cheryl brought her beautiful maternal energy, and Libby was in rare form, full of laughs, funny stories, and mischief. Libby is always the life of the party. Libby and I were the closest in age growing up and sympatico in practical jokes and mischievous pursuits.

Maria's two nephews, Rivers and Chase, whom she loves as if they were her own, arrived ready to celebrate our wedding and to honor their beloved aunt Maria. Affable and incredibly bright, these young men can converse about anything—especially sports, food, and culture. (What else is there?) Maria's high esteem and deep love for them meant she insisted that both walk her down the aisle, or across the sand, as it were. Maria's sister Lisa, mother of Rivers and Chase, was excited to play her part not only as Maria's cherished big sister, but also as matron of honor. Maria and Lisa were several years apart growing up but now are best friends as well as sisters. Lisa is an excellent manager of anything, especially life, and spent her career in high-level management for the Environmental Protection Agency (EPA). She got along with Libby like a house afire.

The night before our wedding, our officiants arrived. I had requested Posy, and Maria chose her friend and long-time co-worker Lucy Henry, who I am happy to claim as my friend too. Lucy and Posy came from different traditions—Posy, Episcopal and Lucy, Baptist—but had a similar approach to liturgy. They shared a laid-back flexibility that might have made some of the more uptight religious folks nervous. Happily, we didn't have any of those with us that week.

We planned to have the ceremony around 4 p.m., give or take a tide change or two. Before the ceremony that afternoon, Posy and Lucy recruited some from our crew to do modest cleanup and preparation on the section of beach where we would exchange our vows. Lightly brushing the sand, removing the washed-up seaweed, and generally orienting themselves to the position of the sun, they conferred with each other about how it would unfold. Then, at Maria's request, they invited our beach neighbors who were out enjoying the sun to join us if they liked. Posy and Lucy served a church that was open to all.

Finally, with an arrangement of flowers, we honored our family members now deceased: Maria's mother and father, Barrie and Roy; her two brothers, Robert and Peter; my mother Annie Laura, and my father, Wallace, would all be acknowledged and cherished. I couldn't help but think of her extraordinary family and the generations of her ancestors leading to this point in time. Her father, an immigrant from Norway, had enlisted in the Army to serve this country he loved. Not much more than a teenager himself, he had been part of the courageous forces liberating tortured souls from a concentration camp during World War II. Her mother, a world traveler, force of nature, and strong and devout in her Episcopal faith, had always hoped Maria might marry a priest. Maria and I had shared many chuckles thinking that her mother Barrie and my mother Annie Laura had been strategizing up in Heaven, pulling the necessary strings to bring us together. And with the bouquet, I also offered a prayer for my father, a man I didn't really know, but someone who had his own challenges and successes, and who had helped bring me into the world. He had served in the Navy. By holding space in our memories for those who had passed with an elegant floral bouquet, we honored them, bringing their presence and memory into our celebration.

At the appointed time, Posy and Lucy called us forth in a relaxed procession from the back porch of Conch Out. Posy, Lucy, family, and newfound beach friends in their bathing suits all formed a circle on the beach. I walked forward, arm in arm with my beloved daughter Margaret—who was stunning in her tan linen dress to complement my suit. I beamed with pride, admiring what she had made of her life's journey, her hard work, her courageous motherhood, and her kindness. I felt equally vulnerable, because Margaret knew me too—better than anyone—and yet her love for me was uncompromising. Even at her young age, Margaret's wisdom and generosity have helped me make my way in the world. I had lost so many things in my life, but thank God, I didn't lose her. This precious moment with her, after she'd offered an enthusiastic "Yes!" to our marriage, was yet another example of the many emotions we can hold in any given moment.

Then, expertly directed by Gavin, our granddaughters Lucy and Violet made their sensational debut as flower girls, tossing rose petals into the ocean breeze. These adorable innocent princesses in their dresses stole our hearts. Lochlan followed, our precocious and handsome grandson, carrying our rings that Lisa had tied to a pillow. And then, time stood still.

Maria, wrapped in the strong arms of her beloved nephews, stepped off the porch and onto the beach. With a radiant smile intermingled with tears of joy and her beautiful blonde locks kissed by the gentle ocean breeze, Maria was a vision of transcendent beauty. She wore a white rose in her hair and carried an elegant bouquet of roses—white, pink, and coral—along with blue hydrangea blossoms, which are Margaret's favorite flower, intertwined with baby's breath and greenery. She took my breath away.

She was a vision, yes, and she was walking right toward me. I had been waiting, longing, hoping for love for so long. And now, after heartbreak and disappointments, mistakes and challenges, and through the infinite mysteries of life and love—here she was. As a person who overcame the worry that if I started crying, I may never stop, I began to wonder. But these were tears of elation, not depression or sadness. And we all shared them. Arriving front center, Maria looked deeply into my eyes in a moment that will live in my memory forever. She took my hand as I took hers, and we could see through our tears of joy that we had been truly blessed.

We almost had to call an official time-out at "Dearly beloved . . ." to stop the ceremony and replenish everyone's Kleenex. After the initial prayers, Lucy had planned to say a few words and bless the rings. Sensing the importance of all the people gathered around us—including our newfound beach friends—Lucy decided that *everyone* should bless the rings. To be perfectly honest, this surprise unsettled me at first. One of the best ways to crash this wedding would be for someone to run away with the rings. . . It's silly to think that now, because her idea became clear just as soon as the procession of the rings began. They made their way from person to person, as each cherished attendee added a thought, a wish, a prayer, or a kind comment. Even our grandchildren participated. And our onlooking friends, in various degrees of undress depending on their bathing suits, became part of our community that day as they offered their blessings as well. This was a fantastic idea—it created a beautiful bond among all of us there that day. It was itself a tactile manifestation and expression of the ever-widening, ever-deepening sphere of God's love.

Then it was Posy's turn. Posy had a free-flowing, unconventional approach to life, and it was surely embodied in her sermon that day. She started by congratulating us and adding her warm wishes. Then, in great detail, she recounted for us and for family and friends gathered how Maria and I had hiked the Camino in Spain, and how we had gotten engaged at the end of it. She shared that, after completing the Camino, we followed the time-honored tradition of trekking out to Finisterre, the place ancient Romans referred to as the "end of the world," where pilgrims would burn their boots and cast a stone (or two or three, or a few dozen!) into the sea to represent the burdens we have carried, attitudes that no longer serve, and regrets we want to release.

After relating this part of our story, she acknowledged how important this experience was for us, and especially for me, as she knew the burdens I had carried. With a touching degree of eloquence, she explained that the things we may toss off are, nevertheless, still a part of us on some deep level. She said that even the painful things we've experienced are still important parts of our history, our psyche, our soul. And, more importantly, she said, *they all belong*. Every part of us belongs. Good, bad, happy, sad—it all belongs.

Just as I was assessing her comments, she upped the proverbial ante with an unanticipated tale that rang more true than literal truth. She continued by saying that those stones we had tossed over the windswept cliffs at Finisterre had, in fact, not disappeared at all. I was flabbergasted as she testified that they had gotten caught up in the tidal currents of the North Atlantic, along the coast of Spain. From there, magically, they had traveled down the coasts of Western Africa, tumbling by the seaboards of Morocco, Senegal, and Liberia. They were picked up in the dangerous rip currents and tossed to and fro as they were propelled toward South Africa, kissing the Cape of Good Hope. From there, the stones were pulled by the tides toward the continent of South America, drawn by an undertow toward Buenos Aires. Then traveling along by the coast of Rio de Janeiro, where they were drawn into the watchful gaze of (the Statue of) Christ the Redeemer. From there they were jettisoned up into the Caribbean, traversing Caracas, the Bahamas, Haiti, and Cuba, before the northward currents of the Gulf Stream laid claim to them. From there they were flung up the coast of Florida, Georgia, arriving finally at the coast of South Carolina.

Posy surmised that the rocks had been tossed by the ocean tides onto rock, sand, and coral, and contact with the forces of the ocean had polished down their rough edges. Then she paused, looked sternly, but with a mischievous twinkle, into our eyes, and said in barely more than a whisper and with unshakable confidence that the very same stones had washed up on the shores at Edisto, just a few yards from our conch-themed coral-colored abode. And, what's more, *this very morning*, she had *found* them. Pow! She had our attention!

With a quick retrieval, bordering on sleight of hand, she broke our collective bewilderment by producing two stunningly beautiful marble stones, each one fashioned into the shape of a heart. And on this most important day of our lives, she gave them back to us, with a big smile and a gentle loving reminder that it all belongs.

It *all* belongs.

The ups and the downs. The happiness and the heartaches. Triumphs and tragedies. Suffering and betrayal. Joy and delight. Our mistakes and our kindnesses. Our jealousies, our acts of cruelty, our expressions of love. Nights when we think we might not make it through, and days filled with endless joy.

It all belongs.

* * *

"I wondered if that was how forgiveness budded; not with the fanfare of epiphany, but with pain gathering its things, packing up, and slipping away unannounced in the middle of the night."

— Khaled Hosseini's, *The Kite Runner*[1]

Epilogue
Re-membering

So, dear reader, we've been on quite a journey together through this book. It may feel like you've been riding tumultuous currents through dangerous places as the river makes its meandering way to the sea. We've been through the desert, across oceans, and back and forth through time. I have opened my soul to you—the things I'm proud of and the things that make me shiver from raw vulnerability when I think of sharing them. I have done this not just to tell the story of my 9/11 experience, but to share with you my journey from trauma and tragedy, resentments, despair, and anger, to new beginnings through forgiveness and love. To enable you to see, if you are in any way struggling with resentments or bitterness, that there are more options than just shutting down or stewing in desires for revenge. I share my story as a cautionary tale of what can happen to you if you are not able to forgive. My hope is that I have transformed my woundedness into a medicine story that might, in some small way, offer a glimpse of healing to you.

For me to do this is to fulfill my mission in life, to meet at the place where my life finds meaning and purpose. To share insights, wisdom, mistakes, and lessons learned that, I hope, you might find helpful.

Whatever your suffering, whatever your joy—they all belong. That's not to say that any one of us should be abused or betrayed. It's not to say that any one of us should be humbled or humiliated. Far from it. But what I am saying is that every one of us will have some small share (or large) in these experiences. And they all belong. Every heartbreak endured; every act of abuse survived becomes a vital part of our life's journey. Every single one of us will get a no from life. May you find the courage, the wisdom, and the support you need to make peace with your no when it comes.

What I have discovered is that forgiveness is an essential ingredient in life that helps us make peace with the full range of human experience, the inevitable yeses and noes of life's exquisite and precious journey. Forgiveness helps us soften the edges to see the subtle beauty in even the most challenging experiences. This is the true journey of life (thank you Posy!): It all belongs. Through forgiveness even the roughest edges can find smoothness. All of you and all of me are welcome into the circle of healing, ever widening, ever deepening.

On the twentieth anniversary of 9/11, I was invited back to Saint Paul's Chapel to participate in the Calling of the Names Ceremony, an annual commemoration of those who died on 9/11/01 and who have died since. This is a day of sobering solemnity, with an unfortunate growing list of names. At the end of the year in 2018, Dr. Michael Crane, the director of the World Trade Center Health Program at the Mount Sinai Hospital in NYC, estimated that those who died from toxic exposure to the former World Trade Center site would outnumber those who died on the fateful day itself. He also declared that the rate of cancer diagnoses is thirty percent higher for 9/11 first responders than it is for the general population.[1] Each year at the Calling of the Names, many of us who served wonder if our names might someday be added to the list. In 2019, Fred Burnham's was. His death came by way of esophageal cancer, one of the more common cancers afflicting volunteers and first responders.

It was an honor to be asked back to Saint Paul's Chapel for this event, and I expressed my deep gratitude to Barbara Horn, who founded the ceremony along with her leadership team, including my dear friend Ralph Ferris and the poet Chester Johnson, who wrote "The Little Church that Stood." Simply reading the invitation brought tears to my eyes. Even so, I wondered what it would be like to return. How would it feel? Would I be overwhelmed?

Stepping through the doors that day, I was flooded with memories of the plan for the jazz mass that should have filled the halls in the fall of 2001 and the Ash Tuesday of 9/11 that changed our trajectory forever. I could hear the echoes of the upbeat music that soared from the rafters in that lost, sacred time. I remembered how the pews looked during the relief mission, pews made sacred by the scars and scuffs of turnout gear and helmets and guns and vests—the equipment necessary to firefighters and police officers. In my memory, I saw the faces of the men and women curled up asleep in those pews, many with teddy bears under their arms. Those pews are now gone.

This sacred chapel had witnessed some of the most traumatic events in the history of our country, and it certainly witnessed the traumatic events of my own life. But instead of remembering these moments with pain and resentment, I felt a deep-seated sense of joy, peace, gratitude, and freedom. Two decades of sorrow, pain, and anger had kept me from seeing the comfort and joy that had always lived in this place, waiting for me to reconnect, to *re-member* it in its fullness.

Anamnesis, the Greek verb in Jesus' words of institution in the Eucharistic liturgy—"This is my body, do this in remembrance ("anamnisi") of me," literally means "re-member-ing," as in reconnecting and seeing with new eyes the never-broken connection that we have merely lost sight of. My return to Saint Paul's for the twentieth anniversary was an important moment of reconnection—*anamnesis*—a remembering of the connection that had never been broken. I remembered my calling to serve as a priest and to care for those serving after 9/11. In this remembering, I was able to connect to my life's overarching purpose and mission to serve. While there, I was able to glimpse how my journey had prepared me to share what I've learned about the life-changing work of forgiveness to widen and deepen our connections to others and to ourselves through a love born of compassion, kind understanding, and humble service. Perhaps this has been my calling all along. The poet T. S. Eliot in "Burnt Norton" invites us all to ponder this work of healing and integration:

> What might have been and what has been
> Point to one end, which is always present.[2]

Forgiveness gave me the power to set down the heavy burden of resentments and bitterness that had kept me loyal to my suffering. I no longer needed to get even with those who had opposed me, or to worry about them getting even with me. I was able to confirm in my heart that all of us on staff at Trinity/

Saint Paul's aspired to do our best in the aftermath of 9/11, and that some days were better than others—for all of us. We were in an unprecedented crisis with no road map to guide us. In the words of my singer-songwriter friend Dave Wilcox, we had to "make the way by walking."[3] Surely forgiveness is such a pilgrimage—one in which we make our way by walking into the troubled places of our lives, discovering along the way the healing of forgiveness, compassion, and mercy. When we give up our need to be right, we are on our way to that blessed place of belonging, beyond right and wrong, where joy comes in the morning, and where there are a thousand ways to kneel and kiss the ground.

Since leaving Saint Paul's Chapel, my life's journey has taken me around the world. Every last part of our planet has a great need for forgiveness, a need to reject the destructive cycle of violence and revenge, to find peace for both present and historical traumas. Yet forgiveness remains a mystery. My life's mission is to meet that need: to share what I have learned about forgiveness—through training with Dr. Frederic Luskin, the Stanford Forgiveness Project, and through my own research, experiences, and offerings. To deliver a real-world understanding of the benefits of forgiveness that is both evidence-based and practical. That forgiveness does not mean forgetting. At its deepest level, forgiveness is remembering *differently*. The physical and mental health benefits of forgiveness are significant.[4]

More than 20 years ago, I set out to tell my story of 9/11, but it now has become clear that I am actually telling a story of fragile humanity. I have shared my resentments, my mistakes, my successes, and my shame. It's all laid out before you, naked and exposed, with the hope that my story will resonate with yours. I have shared my story as a cautionary tale, an example of the years you might lose if you are not able to grieve and forgive in the face of those grievances. I have also shared it as a hopeful vignette, a set of guideposts for anyone who has already lost those years. Through forgiveness even the roughest edges of life's circumstances can be softened into subtle beauty.

Two years after my return to Saint Paul's, I was presented with another opportunity for growth. This time, to prepare and deliver a talk at TEDx Asheville, specifically about forgiveness at Ground Zero. I knew it would be a difficult writing process and an emotional delivery, but I could not have prepared for the intensity of that challenge. Afterward, my body ached with physical pain, and I couldn't even enjoy what was to be a celebration dinner. But the biggest surprise I had was, a few days later, the great joy I felt on the other side of sharing. My ability to write this memoir is directly related to that positive experience of vulnerability. Perhaps most surprising of all was the comfort in my answer to what had previously been a painful question:

"How do we refer to you? Reverend or Reverend Dr.?"

"No. Just Lyndon."

Just Lyndon. This is not a consolation prize, but a celebration. Something I've earned through hard inner work, as I've sought to navigate the tumultuous seas of tragedy in my life. It took most of my life's journey to see that the validation from others that I had sought from childhood, the validation from spiritual fathers to make up for what I didn't get from my biological father—while it was nice when it happened—could never be a suitable substitute for my own self-validation. Or my own innate sense of worth that I believe comes from being a child of God. The validation from others, for someone of my personality type—an achiever—can be seductive. While attaboys from others are not necessarily bad, when they become our motivation, we can find ourselves doing the right things, but sometimes, for the wrong reason.

It has taken me the better part of my life to see and understand that my dignity and worth are not something conferred on me by others, but something I find within. I've traveled the world to discover this. I'm learning. Again, the wisdom of T.S. Eliot rings true:

We shall not cease from exploration
And the end of all our exploring
Will be to arrive where we started
And know the place for the first time.[5]

I have come a long way to say my name, with a sense of pride— pride in who I am, not in what I did or didn't do. It's not a pride that insinuates that I'm "better than" anyone else, but a sense of pride that celebrates my own unique dignity and worth—just like everyone else's in their own way.

So, dear reader, may this narrative of my journey back to myself inspire for you in your own pilgrimage a sense of hope, forgiveness, courage, healing, and joy. And may you never forget that you—and every re-membered part of you—truly belong.

Lyndon Fitzgerald Harris

Acknowledgments

The antidote to unforgiveness is gratitude. As you see, I have so much to be grateful for.

This book represents more than 20 years of learning and growth, struggle and healing. For all the friends and loved ones who have helped me on my journey, I am beyond grateful for your love and support. Thank you for believing in me.

First, I wish to thank my editors and my agent:

Sheryl Fullerton, who started a version of this book with me over 20 years ago and who believed in it enough to dive back in again and get it back on track.

Brannan Sirratt of Bee Seen Books, whose keen editorial insights were matched only by her gift of encouragement, allowing me not only to express it, but to love my story and my journey.

Tori Shi for her skillful editorial assistance in bringing this book to fruition.

Richard Brown, who saw the merit in such a book and brought the expertise of Bloomsbury Academic to bear in its production.

Rita Rosenkranz of the Rita Rosenkranz Literary Agency, who was kind enough to take a risk on this new writer.

Bloomsbury Academic Division, for accepting this work.

For our staff and leaders at Saint Paul's Chapel, the "little church that stood" after the terrorists' attacks on September 11, 2001:

Amy Boldosser-Boesch, whose courage and quiet strength guided me in service both before and after 9/11, and all our friends at Grace Church in New York City for your unwavering support. And especially Dana Newman whose hospitality and kindness gave me peace.

Courtney Cowart and Fred Burnham—your leadership and comradery made one of the darkest times not only manageable, but joyful.

Regan Burnham Roos—always stalwart, ever encouraging—I am so grateful for your kindnesses and your sense of humor.

For the most amazing staff who helped create the "Season of Love" at Saint Paul's Chapel after 9/11:

Katherine M. Anthony, Martin Cowart, Diane Reiners, Carter Booth, Dennis Fisin, and the inimitable Sister (Sargeant) Grace.

Bethany Putnam—your stay with us was short but your impact profound. Your contribution will not be forgotten.

For all the extraordinary volunteers (15,000 shifts served!), including Jessica Ives, Isaac Everitt, Peter Moffitt, Ralph Ferris, Pamela Wells, Susan Weinman, Barbara Horn, and Kathryn Hardesty, and so many others.

For Krystyna Sanderson whose photographic eye captured a glimpse of the extraordinary experience that was Saint Paul's Chapel's mission after 9/11.

With deep gratitude for the men and women of the Red and the Blue, and all the Ground Zero crisis workers deployed in that formidable task to bring even a small sense of order to the chaos of Ground Zero, and especially those who paid the ultimate price in courageous service, losing their lives on 9/11. And for all who, because of their sacrificial service following 9/11, have died since. May you rest in peace; you will not be forgotten.

For family members who lost loved ones on that fateful day—may their memory be a blessing to you and a reminder that in community we find healing and support.

For those along the way who have supported me more than I can say:

For Dr. David Grand and Dr. Sheryl Monaghan, therapists and friends who helped me focus on the light, even as I sat in darkness. You have had a life-changing impact on my healing.

For Hollis Bart, whose kindness and generosity in offering legal services was extraordinary.

For Mary Tufts, whose loving friendship has been one of the great blessings to have come to me from 9/11.

For Elissa Kleeman who kindness to my family will never be forgotten.

For Monica Willard for your tireless efforts to create a more compassionate caring world and for your kindness in including me in your many pursuits. I have learned so much from you.

For Dr. Hartmut Hanauske-Abel for the honor and kindness of always remembering.

For Sharon Benson, friend, muse and gifted musician. You sang the song of my soul's healing—I *finally* was able to hear it.

For Carly Ritter, Susan Crowson, Tim Skehan, and Linda Usher and friends at Saint John's Lutheran—your love, friendship, kindness, and joy inspired and sustained me more than you can ever know.

For the board and leadership of the non-profit, The Gardens of Forgiveness: The (late) Fred Burnham, Mary Tufts, Claire Silberman, Monica Willard, and for Fred Luskin, co-chair. Also for friends and colleagues who gave generously for this work: Alexandra Asseily, Rod Beckstrom, Robert Lawrence, Michael Kutzin, Carly Ritter, Angela Coyle, Daniel Neiden and Jessica Caron. And for Lynn McGuin, Rose Foti, and Diane Horning, 9/11 family members who courageously consented to participate in the Gardens of Forgiveness' mission to Beirut in 2006.

For Kathy Eldon and the entire team at the Creative Visions Foundation in Malibu. Kathy, creative activist extraordinaire—you always saw the best in me and inspired me to dream, hope, and work for the better world we know is possible. Your creative activism is needed now more than ever.

For Kiki Ebsen and the Healing Equine Ranch family, horses included—you gave me a place to land when I needed it and an opportunity to fulfill a dream. And especially Stacy Schneider Madden and her mare, "Miss Bonni," who gave me horse kisses to remind me that life is full of all kinds of love.

For the (late) Reverend Posy Jackson and the Tigg's Pond family, including Thea Everitt, Roy and Jimmie Harris, and all who were a part of that community who held on to me in love. Posy, your generosity, maverick spirit, and passionate embrace for helping the poor inspire me to this day. Your gifts to me were extravagant, especially the gift of space and time to battle the demons of my despair and push through to the light of a new day. Without a doubt, you are the most generous person I have ever met, and I am eternally grateful and will always remember you for your kindnesses.

For Clay and Jane Turner, beloved friends. Clay, you have been so much more than a mentor and friend to me—you instilled in me a vision of what it means to be a noble human being and a priest, one who acts from the heart with love and courage for the healing of the world.

For Tom and Cindy Rickenbaker, friends who were always encouraging to me and always ready to help.

For the kind folks at the Unitarian Universalist Fellowship of the Carolina Foothills meeting at the Whimsical World Art Gallery in Landrum, SC, friends who reminded me not to take myself too seriously—and especially Don Greeson, whose humor always brings a smile.

For Lucy Henry and Beth Kelly, dear friends of ours on life's journey.

For Fe Anam Avis and James Minshew—father confessors, counselors, and friends. Your love, insights, and encouragement have both challenged and sustained me, and especially Fe, for your reminder that *healing begins with being seen*.

For Pat Conroy—although we never met, your extraordinary work inspires me to be honest and courageous in my writing.

For the "Boss"—Bruce Springsteen, who read with devotion the "Portraits of Grief" section in the *NY Times* and honored the stories of those who died with *The Rising*. You gave voice to our collective grief and offered admiration for those who willingly gave their lives in service to others.

For Alexandra Asseily, visionary psychotherapist and peace activist who founded the Garden of Forgiveness in Beirut, Lebanon, who taught me that forgiveness is when you can have the memory, but not feel the sting.

For Fred Luskin—more than a friend, more than a mentor—you have taught me how to make peace with my life after failure and to find meaning and purpose by following the heroic path of forgiveness that your research has given the world. I count my lucky stars for the day we met.

For Jed Rosen and Loren Toussaint—friends, mentors, and co-travelers on the journey of forgiveness.

For Rod Beckstrom for all the myriad ways you supported my coming to see the light of forgiveness and for connecting me to Alexandra and Fred.

For Gareth and Brian, Dave and Nance, and Bill who not only spoke to me about the seventh story of healing and connection, you invited me in to experience it.

For my family:

Libby, Bo, Cheryl—siblings on an adventure from day one, whose love has sustained me from birth and reminded me not only who but whose I am and also from where I came.

My mother Annie Laura Harris—your love gave me birth and life and mission. Yours was always the crowded table where everyone was welcome, and you taught me the healing gift of hospitality, kindness, and community. In your loving memory, I thrive and am eternally grateful.

For my father Wallace—who knows how we might have gotten along, had we but time.

Kirsten, who gave to me and to the world our amazing daughter, Margaret.

Margaret, you fill my life with laughter and joy, and even on my darkest days you gave me reason to live, reminding me that despair is not our lot, and that hallelujah is our song. I treasure and celebrate the extraordinary woman you have become, and I cherish you.

Gavin (Margaret's husband), and their children—Lochlan, Lucy, and Violet. Each one of you fills my life with joy. What an immense privilege it is to share life with you.

And for Maria Lund, my life, my love, my soulmate. I met you on a hike and followed you to the end of the earth, intoxicated by your love every step of the way. More than anyone, your love has spoken comfort to me in my challenging times, encouragement in the face of adversity, and sheer joy in the beautiful life we share. You have inspired me to live to the fullest, and our life together is a pilgrimage of ever-widening, ever-deepening joy. You call forth the best in me, always, and I can never adequately express my love and my gratitude for you.

Appendix
Saint Paul's Chapel

Saint Paul's Chapel, a Georgian Classic Revival edifice, was designed by Scottish architect Thomas McBean,[1] with master craftsman Andrew Gautier in charge of construction. It was completed in 1766. It was modeled after Saint Martin's in the Fields in Trafalgar Square, London (James Gibbs, architect), and built on land gifted by Queen Anne of Great Britain. In 1796, the chapel's spire was completed after 2 years of additional work. The chapel's elegant symmetrical rectangular design, with balanced proportions of windows and doors and classic details, clearly manifest its Georgian architectural intentions. Small, rough-hewn field stones were quarried on the site, while window and door openings and corners were appointed in a more refined brownstone. The beauty of Saint Paul's was described at its opening in 1766:

> Thursday last the new Episcopal Chapel, in this City, called Saint Paul's, and esteemed one of the most elegant Edifices on the Continent, was opened, and dedicated to Almighty God. The Concourse of People of all Ranks and Denominations, (who attended on the Occasion) was very great.[2]

The entrance of the church faces west, with what was a pleasing view of the Hudson River, before the density of buildings emerged. Saint Paul's Chapel was a "chapel of ease" for Trinity Church parishioners, who at times preferred not to traverse the terrain of a country field in proper Sunday attire to attend church five blocks south.

Saint Paul's Chapel could reasonably seat about 200 worshippers with its pews intact, not including the gallery seating upstairs. The pews, however, were removed from the nave of Saint Paul's Chapel in 2010 and replaced with cathedral chairs to give more flexibility for worship and other events. When Saint Paul's Chapel was dedicated in 1766, there were two canopied box pews that came to be the domain of New York's first governor, Governor George Clinton (southside) and, later, President George Washington (northside).

On its exterior, a statue of Saint Paul the Apostle stands above the portico on the eastern (Broadway) side of the church. The current version is a replica of the original, a 7'10" 500-pound masterwork carved by an unknown artist from Tulip Poplar, which is now on display inside the church.[3] Underneath the niche hosting the statue of Saint Paul is an impressive monument to General Richard Montgomery, a highly venerated Revolutionary War general who died in 1775. This monument was the first memorial commissioned by the newly formed Continental Congress, and Montgomery's remains are now buried underneath it, having been brought from a battle site in Quebec and reinterred in July 1818. Because of the dearth of American sculptors, it fell to Benjamin Franklin to commission an artist in France for the work. He chose a distinguished member of the French Academy of Painting and Sculpture, Jean-Jacques Caffieri, to create the memorial and then he shipped it to the colonies. Its installation at Saint Paul's Chapel was supervised by Pierre L'Enfant in 1787. L'Enfant was himself a young French artist of distinction who volunteered to fight in the cause of the American Revolution, serving at Valley Forge under General Washington's command, and later severely wounded in the Siege of Savannah in 1779.[4,5,6]

But the installation of the Montgomery memorial under the portico of Saint Paul's presented another problem: its shadow in the window behind the altar created an unappealing sight from the inside of the chapel. L'Enfant worked quickly to come up with a plan, which he presented to the Trinity Vestry. L'Enfant was subsequently asked to resolve the issue, to "ornament that part of the great Window of the Parish Chapel which will be obscured by the Monument of General Montgomery."[7]

In response, L'Enfant produced an exquisite artwork entitled "The Glory" (Hebrew: "Shekinah"), representing the divine presence handing down the twin tablets of laws to Moses on mystical Mount Sinai. The Ten Commandments are inscribed on two tablets in the foreground of the Glory.

Atop the artwork, inside a triangle, is the "divine tetragrammaton," the four Hebrew consonants that represent the name of God, surrounded by golden beams of light and clouds of majesty. A crucifix is staged in the foreground of the Glory representing Jesus' internalization of the Law.

Behind the Glory and the altar are arched Palladian windows with mostly clear panes, although an odd pane of pale green or taupe can be found. While the windows are translucent, they are far from transparent, allowing the flickering light of Broadway's traffic to make its way inside. Fourteen cut-glass chandeliers adorn the nave of Saint Paul's, creating a sense of beauty and elegance. The glow of the chandeliers, illuminating the chapel, is warm and comforting, accentuating the clear clean lines of the Georgian-style architecture of Saint Paul's. Outside, its distinctive steeple, designed by James Crommelin Lawrence, was added in 1794, making Saint Paul's the tallest building in New York City at the time.

The pulpit in Saint Paul's Chapel is a towering lectern with coronet, from which many historic sermons and speeches have been given—from bishops and clergy to presidents to other notable public figures. On July 4, 1789, Alexander Hamilton gave a memorial speech in honor of General Nathanael Greene from that very pulpit. Months before, on April 30, 1789, immediately after being sworn in as our country's first president at Federal Hall in New York City, George Washington stepped into Saint Paul's Chapel to pray. Washington offered prayers of gratitude for the freedom and promise of this new country, as well as the honor of serving it. He also offered prayers of petition, asking divine guidance and mercy for this vulnerable new experiment in its infancy, a fledgling chick that would someday soar as a mighty eagle.

To honor this solemn occasion, Washington was attended by both houses of government, family members, and dignitaries. He was saluted and cheered along the quarter-mile procession to Saint Paul's from Federal Hall. Saint Paul's Chapel remained the principal place of worship for members of Washington's government, including Washington himself, Hamilton, and Jefferson, during the 2 years the Capital resided in New York before moving to Philadelphia and ultimately to the newly developed federal city, Washington, DC.

Hanging on the north wall of the nave, alongside where the Washington box pew used to be, is an impressive oil painting, commissioned by the Vestry of Trinity Church in 1785, to display the seal of the newly formed United States. The painting depicts Benjamin Franklin's preferred national bird: a turkey. In its right talon, it holds an olive branch, and in the left, a cluster of arrows. The gaze of the bird is cast to the right, with its focus on the olive branch, emphasizing strength guided by peace. Above the turkey's head is a field of thirteen stars, representing the original colonies, surrounded by beams of golden light. The bird's breastplate is an embodiment of the new republic—an azure blue header with thirteen vertical stripes, representing the thirteen colonies, alternating between white and red. In its mouth, there is a banner which advances the national ideal and motto, *E Pluribus Unum*—"out of many, one."

Saint Paul's Chapel is diminutive when compared to the great cathedrals of the world, but it is large in spirit, rich in history, and much beloved. It was saved from the Great Fire of New York (1776) through the heroic efforts of locals in the community led by Trinity's assistant minister, the Reverend Charles Inglis. Inglis was a British loyalist priest who would ultimately be banished from the colonies for his British sympathies. President Washington's ceremony of solemn prayers on the day of his inauguration made Saint Paul's Chapel the spiritual birthplace of the new republic. Today Saint Paul's is the only remaining colonial era building in New York City and its oldest public building in continuous use.

Saint Paul's Chapel is a sanctuary, a sacred edifice that has stood the test of both time and catastrophe, offering its peaceful interior for the gathering of good and noble souls. When the Great Fire of 1776 destroyed much of its surroundings (almost 500 buildings), Saint Paul's Chapel remained—just as it would survive the great fires from the terrorist attacks on September 11, 2001, 225 years later. On that fateful day in 2001, while multiple modern buildings nearby and across Church Street were destroyed, Saint Paul's Chapel stood, not in defiance, but, in this author's opinion, as a beacon of hope and a useful hub for services to support the men and women of the rescue services. At first, they sought survivors and, eventually, the remains of the dead at the former

World Trade Center. Much conversation has been given to the "miracle of Saint Paul's," whereby the chapel is considered to have been spared by divine protection. The miracle of Saint Paul's, to this author at least, is that Saint Paul's was spared—not because it is holier than anyone who died, but because there was a big job to do.

In the days and months following the attacks on September 11, 2001, the Saint Paul's community set about doing that important work, led by the minister assigned to Saint Paul's at that time. During the next eight and one-half months, the food services at Saint Paul's Chapel served over half a million meals. These efforts were born of the labors of many participating faith communities, neighborhood volunteers, and human services professionals who came from all over the US to serve. For almost nine months, the chapel was a haven of support. Even George Washington's box pew was enlisted, becoming a staging area for podiatrists working on the blistered and burning feet of the men and women serving at the former World Trade Center site. This was the longest burning fire in our country's history, and their boots literally were melting off their feet. Given the grave challenges of Washington's Valley Forge campaign, surely, he would support this new use of the space once set aside for his honor.

In closing, in continual prayer for our republic, let us invoke the prayer George Washington included in his *Circular Letter to the States*, sent on June 8, 1783,[8] a prayer preserved on brass, residing on the wall near the Great Seal of the United States.

George Washington's Prayer for His Country:

Almighty God: We make our earnest prayer that Thou wilt keep the United States in Thy holy protection; that thou wilt incline the hearts of the citizens to cultivate a spirit of subordination and obedience to government and entertain a brotherly affection and love for one another and for their fellow-citizens of the United States at large. And finally that Thou wilt most graciously be pleased to dispose us all to do justice, to love mercy and to demean ourselves with that charity, humility and pacific temper of mind which were the characteristics of the Divine Author of our blessed religion without a humble imitation of whose example in these things we can never hope to be a happy nation. Grant our supplication, we beseech Thee, through Jesus Christ, our Lord. Amen.

Respectfully offered by Lyndon F. Harris, Priest Associate for Ministries at Saint Paul's Chapel, April 2001 – October 2002.

Notes

Author's Note

1 John Bunyan, *The Pilgrim's Progress*, Oxford World's Classics (Oxford: Oxford University Press, 2003). The "slough of despond" refers to a state of deep despair or hopelessness, represented by a swamp in John Bunyan's allegory *The Pilgrim's Progress.* The slough of despond is a literal swamp encountered by the protagonist, Christian, on his journey from the City of Destruction to the Celestial City.

2 Carl Jung, *The Secret of the Golden Flower: A Chinese Book of Life* (New York: Harcourt, Brace and Company, 1932).

3 Courtney Cowart, *An American Awakening: From Ground Zero to Katrina: The People We Are Free to Be* (New York: Seabury Books, 2008).

4 Fred Luskin has published several books on forgiveness: *Forgive for Good: A PROVEN Prescription for Health and Healing* (2002), *Forgive for Love: The Missing Ingredient for a Healthy and Lasting Relationship* (2009), both from HarperOne. And a workbook on forgiveness for people in recovery, that he and I co-authored: *Forgive for Good Recovery Workbook Overcome Addiction, Heal Your Past, and Find Peace in Sobriety* (New Harbinger Press, 2025).

5 Steven Pressfield, *The Virtues of War: A Novel of Alexander the Great* (New York: Random House, 2004).

6 Ram Dass and Mirabai Bush, *Walking Each Other Home Walking Each Other Home: Conversations on Loving and Dying* (Boulder: Sounds True Publishing, 2018).

7 John Knox, "The Identifiability of the Church," published in *Theological Freedom and Social Responsibility*, ed. Stephen Bayne (New York: Seabury Press, 1967).

8 Brian Andreas, "About StoryPeople," StoryPeople, last modified March 10, 2023. https://www.storypeople.com/pages/our-story.

9 Jonathon Larson, "Seasons of Love," track one on *Rent (Original Broadway Cast Recording)* (Dreamworks Records, 1996), compact disc.

Prologue

1 Roger O. Hirson and Stephen Schwartz, *Pippin: Original Broadway Cast Recording*, performed by the Original Broadway Cast (Motown Records, 1972), LP.

2 This was inspired by Robert Schreiter's *Constructing Local Theologies* (New York: Orbis Books, 1985).

3 For this I have been inspired by Urban T. Holmes III, *The Priest in Community: Exploring the Roots of Ministry* (New York: Seabury Press, 1978).

4 Center for Inquiry. "UFO Abductions: A Skeptical Assessment." (Amherst: Center for Inquiry, 1993). https://cdn.centerforinquiry.org/wp-content/uploads/sites/29/1993/01/22165151/p34.pdf.

5 Joseph Campbell, *Reflections on the Art of Living: A Joseph Campbell Companion*, ed. Diane K. Osbon (New York: HarperPerennial, 1991).

Chapter 1

1 Trinity's governing board, which serves as the legal representative of the parish for all matters pertaining to its ministries.

2 See the appendix for a history of Saint Paul's Chapel.

Chapter 2

1 John Allen wrote a poignant reflection of this day in his article, "American Ubuntu: Springsteen, South Africa and 9/11," *JohnAllen.org.za*, accessed June 2025. https://www.johnallen.org.za/2014/01/25/american-ubuntu-springsteen-south-africa-and-911/.

2 Shannon Earl, "Chapel of Love," *The Washington Post*, March 31, 2002.

3 Cowart, *An American Awakening*.

4 *Village Voice*, September 25, 2001, cover, titled "Wish You Were Here."

Chapter 3

1 In Trinity's management chart, the Vicar reported to the rector and had as his ministry portfolio the day-to-day responsibilities for overseeing the spiritual life of Trinity Church and Saint Paul's Chapel. Throughout this memoir I will use names and titles

interchangeably, but in each instance, rector equals Dan Matthews, vicar equals John Howard.

2 There's a term for it: "ultra vires." Ultra vires is a Latin term that means "beyond the powers." Merriam-Webster, s.v. "ultra vires," accessed August 6, 2025, ULTRA VIRES Definition & Meaning.

Chapter 4

1 Cowart, *An American Awakening*, 38. Courtney adds helpful background for this uncomfortable question: "The rector of Trinity enters the chapel and surveys the scene: the recent $100,000 paint job defaced by thousands of pieces of tape and tacks hammered into the walls; the deep gouges on all the pews left by the workers' gun belts; the hundreds of loaded guns lying in their discarded holsters on the floor while their owners sleep; the thousands of votive candles sputtering under the cards and letters, and, of course, the thousand or so people he has never seen before eating, talking, getting body rubs, and playing Trinity's grand piano. My stomach instantly twists in knots when I see the shock on his face. His gasp may be one of wonder, but it is definitely not one of delight."

2 Fred Burnham, "Cops and Burgers," *Spirituality and Health*, Winter 2002.

3 Cowart, *An American Awakening*, 33.

4 Ibid., 38.

5 Anne Lamott, *Traveling Mercies: Some Thoughts on Faith* (New York: Anchor Books, 1999).

6 Gustav Niebuhr, "In Devastation's Shadow, A Landmark's Renewal," *New York Times*, November 3, 2001.

7 Eric Gibson, "Filling a Vacancy: Simple Symbols, Grand Designs," *Wall Street Journal*, September 28, 2001.

8 In November 2003, Ground Zero workers planted a Norway spruce replacing the sycamore tree that was struck down during the collapse of the World Trade Center. It was called a "Tree of Hope." Ultimately, the roots of the tree were bronzed by notable sculptor, Steve Tubin. See Randy Kennedy, "Uprooted in the Attacks, Now Planted in Bronze," *New York Times*, July 6, 2005.

Chapter 5

1 Cowart, *American Awakening*, 49–51.

2 Ibid., 48–9.

3 J. Everett Worthington Jr., interview in *The Power of Forgiveness*, dir. Martin Doblmeier (Journey Films, 2006).

4 Brene Brown, *Atlas of the Heart: Mapping Meaningful Connection and the Language of Human Experience* (New York: Random House, 2021).

Chapter 6

1 Rudyard Kipling, "If," in *Rewards and Fairies* (London: Macmillan, 1910).

2 Emil Brunner, *The Word and the World* (London: World Student Movement, 1931), 108.

3 As referenced in chapter 4, "Radical Hospitality."

4 Richard Rohr and Andreas Ebert, *The Enneagram: A Christian Perspective* (New York: The Crossroad Publishing Company, 2016), 46, 81–2, 85–6, 88. Richard Rohr is a Franciscan priest and writer who uses the Enneagram, a nine-fold spiritual framework for understanding personality, motivation, and meaning. Rohr characterizes Type 3 as "the Achiever"—one who is driven by a need to succeed. Success, for the type 3, provides validation and worth. The problem with this is that the drive to have others proclaim them worthy is self-defeating. According to Rohr, for their soul's sake, the type 3 must fail so that they can see that their worth is innate, God-given; and not because of Type 3's gift for intelligence, cleverness, or charm. This, in a nutshell, is my story: to realize that my worth as a human being is not dependent upon me being good or clever or successful in the eyes of others (e.g., my superiors), but finding and accepting my innate worth as a human being and as a child of God, to understand and to feel that in myself I am enough.

5 Niebuhr, "In Devastation's Shadow, A Landmark's Renewal."

6 Hartmut Hanauske-Abel, "Das Martyrium des Lyndon Harris, oder: Die Schändung von Saint Paul," *Die Zeit*, August 8, 2011.

7 Stephen Karpman, *A Game Free Life. The Definitive Book on the Drama Triangle and Compassion Triangle by the Originator and Author. The New Transactional Analysis of Intimacy, Openness, and Happiness* (San Francisco: Drama Triangle Publications, 2014).

8 Sanjiv Chopra and Gina Vild, "How to Forgive Like Nelson Mandela," *Psychology Today*, July 15, 2020.

9 David Emerald, *The Power of TED* (*The Empowerment Dynamic)* (Chicago: Polaris Publishing, 2015).

10 Mandela established the Truth and Reconciliation Commission (TRC) that granted amnesty to perpetrators who confessed their crimes and reparations to victims of the crimes. TRC was a restorative justice process seeking to promote forgiveness,

repentance, and reconciliation for the future good of South Africa. The TRC was chaired by Archbishop Desmond Tutu, the Anglican archbishop of Cape Town, whose moral authority was undeniable. His account of this process and its aims can be understood by the very title of his book, *No Future without Forgiveness* (New York: Doubleday, 1999).

11 Carl Greer, *Change Your Story, Change Your Life: Using Shamanic and Jungian Tools to Achieve Personal Transformation* (Moray, Scotland: The Findhorn Press, 2014).

12 Michael Lapsley, *Redeeming the Past: My Journey From Freedom Fighter to Healer* (New York: Orbis Books, 2012).

Chapter 7

1 In an uncomfortable twist of irony, this landfill happened to be called "Fresh Kills," which understandably upset many of the family members. This is depicted in an excruciating scene in the documentary *The Power of Forgiveness* as family members walked through the landfill finding bone fragments, credit cards, and other items. *The Power of Forgiveness*, dir. Doblmeier.

2 Lyndon Harris, "We're Not Leaving," unpublished song, 2012. This song is inspired by a collection of interviews with 9/11 workers, by Benjamin Luft, *We're Not Leaving: 9/11 Responders Tell Their Stories of Courage, Sacrifice, and Renewal* (New York: Greenpoint Press, 2011). The final chapter, "A Community of Faith," was an interview with me.

3 Tina Kelley, "Saint Paul's Chapel Is Closing for Cleanup of Debris," *New York Times*, March 16, 2002.

4 Dante Alighieri, *Inferno*, trans. Henry Francis Cary (London: Burk Publishing Company, 2013), Canto III.

5 Tina Kelley, "Chapel Delays Its Closing at Towers Site," *New York Times*, March 26, 2002.

6 Ibid.

7 Ibid.

8 Cowart, *An American Awakening*, 72.

9 Marilyn Jones, "People Making a Difference: Lyndon Harris," *The Christian Science Monitor*, July 27, 2009.

10 Peter Ostroushko, "A Meditation on the Thin Space at Saint Paul's Chapel," performed on *A Prairie Home Companion*, June 22, 2002.

11 *Newsletter of the Cathedral of Saint John the Divine* 12, no. 20 (Spring 2003).

12 Philostratus and Eunapius, *Lives of the Sophists*, trans. Wilmer C. Wright, Loeb Classical Library 134 (Cambridge, MA: Harvard University Press, 1921).

13 "Ground Zero Chapel Hosts Exhibit," *The Associated Press*, May 3, 2004.

14 Tara L. Gruenewald and Margaret E. Kemeny, "Acute Threat to the Social Self: Shame, Social Self-esteem, and Cortisol Activity," *Journal of Psychosomatic Medicine* (November 2004), pp. 915–6.

15 Lewis B. Smede, *Forgive and Forget: Healing the Hurts We Don't Deserve* (San Francisco: HarperOne, 2007).

16 Everett Worthington, interview for documentary *The Power of Forgiveness*, dir. Doblmeier.

17 Limor Goldner, Rachel Lev-Wiesel, and Guy Simon, "Revenge Fantasies After Experiencing Traumatic Events: Sex Differences," *Frontiers in Psychology* 10 (May 9, 2019), paras 1–5.

18 Smedes, *Forgive and Forget.*

19 Ibid., 170.

20 John Wesley, *A Plain Account of Christian Perfection* (Peabody: Hendrickson Publishers, 2007).

Chapter 8

1 Yehuda Amichai, "From the Place Where We Are Right," in *The Collected Poems of Yehuda Amichai*, edited by Stephen Mitchell. (Berkeley: University of California Press, 1988).

Chapter 9

1 Don Miguel Ruiz, *The Four Agreements: A Practical Guide to Personal Freedom* (New York: Random House, 1997). Ruiz's second agreement is not to take things too personally, stating: "Whatever happens around you, do not take it personally . . . Nothing other people do is because of you. It is because of themselves. . ." p. 47.

2 It's important to state clearly here that I am not equivocating on cases of abuse. Abuse, especially in cases such as domestic violence, is always wrong. There is a clear difference between perpetrator and victim.

3 James C. McKinley, "Crackdown Bleeds Kenya's Democracy Movement, Killing 7," *New York Times*, July 8, 1997.

4 After 9/11, Danny came to NYC frequently to volunteer at Saint Paul's Chapel on the night shift, serving alongside his mother, Deener Matthews. We were always glad to have them there. They were a part of our Saint Paul's family.

5 Burnham, "Cops and Burgers," *Spirituality & Health*, Fall 2002.

6 Ibid.

Chapter 10

1 Dan Wakin, "Chapel and Refuge Struggles to Define Role," *New York Times*, November 28, 2002.

2 This cultural exchange is one of the principal vignettes in the documentary, *The Power of Forgiveness*, dir. Doblmeier.

3 Pluff mud is the dark quicksand-like mud full of decaying matter found in the marshes in South Carolina and other coastal states.

4 Pope John Paul II, "Sunday Angelus address (in Adelaide, Australia, November 30, 1986)," *National Catholic Reporter*, April 2024.

5 I didn't know it at the time, but Ashley Tuttle is also from South Carolina, and, in 2011, she received an honorary doctorate from Wofford College in Spartanburg, SC, my alma mater.

6 Luna Kaufman, *Luna's Life: A Journey of Forgiveness and Triumph* (Margate: ComteQ Publishing, 2009).

7 Benjamin Luft, executive producer, *9/11: An American Requiem* (Stony Brook: World Trade Center Medical Monitoring and Treatment Program at Stony Brook University Medical Center, 2011).

8 Stewart Henderson and Martyn Joseph, "Brothers in Exile," on *Under Lemonade Skies* (Pipe Records, 2010), CD. Lyrics by Stewart Henderson, Copyright © Stewart Henderson, used with permission of the lyricist.

Chapter 11

1 Margery Williams, *The Velveteen Rabbit* (New York: George H. Doran Company, 1922).

2 Bill McKibbin, *Eaarth: Making a Life on a Tough New Planet* (New York: Henry Holt and Company, 2010).

3 T. S. Eliot's poem "Burnt Norton" from his collection *The Four Quartets* (New York: Houghton, Mifflin, Harcourt, 1943).

4 Eric Berne, *Games People Play: The Psychology of Human Relationships* (1964) (New York: Penguin, 2016).

Chapter 12

1 Krystyna Sanderson, *Light at Ground Zero: Saint Paul's Chapel after 9/11* (Baltimore: Square Halo Books, 2003).

Chapter 13

1 Babette Rothschild, *8 Keys to Safe Trauma Recovery: Take-Charge Strategies to Empower Your Healing* (New York: Norton and Norton, 2010).

2 Ron White, *I Had the Right to Remain Silent . . . But I Didn't Have the Ability* (New York: Penguin Books, 2006).

3 Mary Jo Bolton, "Phases of Trauma Recovery," *The Manitoba Trauma Information and Education Centre (MTIEC)*, accessed June 2025. https://trauma-informed.ca/recovery/phases-of-trauma-recovery/#:~:text=Recovery%20is%20the%20primary%20goal,time%20and%20in%20intentional%20stages.

4 *The Power of Forgiveness*, dir. Doblmeier.

5 Lyndon Harris, "The Future of Our Past: Some Thoughts on 9/11 Moving Forward," in *On the Ground After September 11: Mental Health Responses and Practical Knowledge Gained*, ed. Yael Danieli and Robert L. Dingman (New York: The Haworth Press, Inc., 2005), pp. 36–41.

6 Lyndon Harris, "Radical Hospitality: Houses of Worship Responding to Disaster," in *Spiritual Care and Mental Health for Disaster Response and Recovery*, ed. Stephen Harding (New York: New York Disaster Interfaith Services, 2007), pp. 41–53.

7 John O'Donohue, "Fluent," in *Conomara Blues* (New York: HarperCollins, 2001), p. 30.

Chapter 14

1 Dylan Stableford, "Families of Charleston Shooting Victims to Dylann Roof: We Forgive You," *Yahoo! News*, June 19, 2015, archived June 24, 2023. https://www.yahoo.com/news/familes-of-charleston-church-shooting-victims-to-dylann-roof--we--forgive-you-185833509.html?guccounter=1.

2 In 2010, at the invitation of Charleston's Mayor Riley, I was invited to dedicate a Garden of Forgiveness at the Phillips Simmons Park, at 64 Columbus Street, less than a mile away from Mother Emanuel Church. An article, "Lyndon Harris joins Mayor Riley to dedicate Charleston Garden of Forgiveness," appeared in the *Charleston Post and Courier*, January 19, 2010.

3 I want to honor the memory of the Emanuel Nine victims: Myra Quarles-Singleton Thompson, Sharonda Coleman-Singleton, Cynthia Graham Hurd, Susie Jackson, Ethel Lance, Depayne Middleton Doctor, Clementa Carlos Pinckney, Tywanza Sanders, and Daniel L. Simmons Sr.

4 Psychologists have begun to assess the traumas experienced during the crisis of 9/11 through the lens of moral injury. See Michele DeMarco, "The Enduring Moral Injury of September 11," *Psychology Today*, September 12, 2022.

5 PTSD has also been referred to by some clinicians as PTSI: Post Traumatic Stress Injury. While the term "disorder" in PTSD implies an individual's emotional inability to cope, PTSI's emphasis on "injury" acknowledges that there are physiological markers that can be measured in tests such as brain scans. While not yet a diagnosis accepted by the *Diagnostic and Statistical Manual of Mental Disorders* (DSM), shifting language from PTSD to PTSI is intended to reduce the stigma of a life-long condition, making the case that it's an injury that can be treated, instead of a permanent disorder. According to the group, First Responders First, PTSI refers to biological trauma, citing the physical changes that happen in the nervous system.

6 "PTSI VS. PTSD: What's the Difference?" *First Responders First*, October 1, 2020. https://www.firstrespondersfirst.com/post/ptsi-vs-ptsd-whats-the-difference.

7 "PTSD vs PTSI," *SoCal Mental Health*, accessed June 2025. https://socalmentalhealth.com/ptsd-vs-ptsi/.

8 Ibid.

9 Brene Brown, "Own Our History. Change the Story," *Brene Brown*, June 16, 2015. https://brenebrown.com/articles/2015/06/18/own-our-history-change-the-story/.

10 Ellie Violet Bramley, "The Trauma Doctor: Gabor Maté on Happiness, Hope and How to Heal Our Deepest Wounds," *The Guardian*, April 12, 2023.

Chapter 15

1 "Misericordiae Vultus: Bull of Indiction of the Extraordinary Jubilee of Mercy," *TheVatican*, April 11, 2015, accessed June 2025. https://www.vatican.va/content/francesco/en/bulls/documents/papa-francesco_bolla_20150411_misericordiae-vultus.html.

2 Ibid.

3 Johann Wolfgang Von Goethe, "The Holy Longing," in *Blessed Longing: Selected Poems of J. W. Goethe* (Victoria: Trafford Publishing, 2009).

4 Phil Cousineau, "The Art of Pilgrimage," *Praying at the Speed of Love*, May 14, 2020, accessed June 2025. https://mainbucketdgandco.s3.amazonaws.com/PSL+2020/PSL+Podcast+-+Episode+28+Transcript-+Phil+Cousineau.pdf.

5 Rev. 4:4.

6 Nietzsche made the love of fate central to his philosophy. In Ecce Homo he writes: "My formula for greatness in a human being is amor fati: that one wants nothing to be different, not forward, not backward, not in all eternity. Not merely bear what is necessary . . . but love it." Friedrich Nietzsche, *Basic Writings of Nietzsche*, trans. Walter Kaufmann (New York: Random House, 1967), 714.

7 Lyndon Harris, lyric from unpublished song, "Man on a Wire," 2014.

8 Jalāl al-Dīn Rūmī, *The Essential Rumi*, trans. Coleman Barks with John Moyne (San Francisco: HarperSanFrancisco, 1995).

Chapter 16

1 Khaled Housseini, *The Kite Runner* (New York: The Penguin Group, 2003), 313.

Epilogue

1 Nancy Cutler, "Deaths From 9/11 Diseases Will Soon Outnumber Those Lost On That Fateful Day," Mount Sinai, October 1, 2020, accessed June 2025. https://www.mountsinai.org/about/newsroom/2018/deaths-from-911-diseases-will-soon-outnumber-those-lost-on-that-fateful-day

2 Eliot, "Burnt Norton."

3 David Wilcox, "We Make the Way by Walking," on *The View from the Edge* (Freshly Baked Records, 2018), LP.

4 "Forgiveness: Letting Go of Grudges and Bitterness," *Mayo Clinic*, accessed June 2025. https://www.mayoclinic.org/healthy-lifestyle/adult-health/in-depth/forgiveness/art-20047692."Forgiveness: Your Health Depends on It," *Johns Hopkins*, accessed June 2025. https://www.hopkinsmedicine.org/health/wellness-and-prevention/forgiveness-your-health-depends-on-it.

5 T. S. Eliot, "Little Gidding," in *Four Quartets* (Gardners Books; Main edition, April 30, 2001), originally published 1943.

Appendix

1 Morgan Dix, *A History of the Parish of Trinity Church in the City of New York* (New York: G.P. Putnam's Sons, 1898), 315.

2 Ibid. 316.

3 James Melchiorre, "The Two Pauls at Saint Paul's Chapel Trinity Church NYC," *Trinity Church*, October 13, 2022. https://trinitychurchnyc.org/visit-history/places/st-pauls-chapel.

4 For a fascinating exploration of L'Enfant's unlikely rise in the Continental Army, see Michael Driskel's "By the Light of Providence: The Glory Altarpiece at Saint Paul's Chapel, New York City," *The Art Bulletin* 89, no. 4 (December 2007): 715–737.

5 Sally Webster, "Pierre-Charles L'Enfant and the Iconography of Independence," *Nineteenth-Century Art Worldwide: a Journal of Nineteenth-Century Visual Culture*. 7, Issue 1 (Spring 2008), accessed July 5, 2025. https://www.19thc-artworldwide.org/spring08/pierre-charles-lenfant-and-the-iconography-of-independence.

6 Charles Mobley, "Siege of Savannah Celebration to be a French Royal Affair," *Savannah Morning News*, October 8, 2015. Mobley asserts that L'Enfant was so severely wounded on October 7, 1779, that he was left for dead in the field, only to be hospitalized for several months following.

7 Sally Webster, *Nineteenth-Century Art Worldwide*. In the fall of 1779, L'Enfant was wounded in the Siege of Savannah, and the following year was captured and held as a prisoner of war in Charleston, SC.

8 "George Washington's Prayer for the States," *Mount Vernon*, accessed July 2025. https://www.mountvernon.org/the-estate-gardens/the-tombs/george-washingtons-prayer-for-his-country.

Index

www.ingramcontent.com/pod-product-compliance
Ingram Content Group UK Ltd.
Pitfield, Milton Keynes, MK11 3LW, UK
UKHW020145300726
473814UK00003BA/11

9 798216 279006